World Englishes

Volume II: North America

Also available from Bloomsbury:

Corpus Linguistics and World Englishes, Vivian de Klerk

World Englishes
Volume II: North America

Edited by
Tometro Hopkins

Series: *World Englishes*
Edited by Tometro Hopkins

Volume I: The British Isles
Volume II: North America
Volume III: Central America

B L O O M S B U R Y
LONDON • NEW DELHI • NEW YORK • SYDNEY

Bloomsbury Academic
An imprint of Bloomsbury Publishing Plc

50 Bedford Square	175 Fifth Avenue
London	New York
WC1B 3DP	NY 10010
UK	USA

www.bloomsbury.com

First published 2013

British Library Cataloguing-in-Publication Data
A catalogue record for this book is available from the British Library.

ISBN: HB: 978-0-8264-7848-1
ePDF: 978-1-4411-5718-8

Library of Congress Cataloging-in-Publication Data
A catalog record for this book is available from the Library of Congress.

Typeset by Deanta Global Publishing Services, Chennai, India
Printed and bound in Great Britain

Contents

Acknowledgements

The *World Englishes* series could not have gone forth without the help of many who tirelessly contributed in various ways. First, I am indebted to Loreto Todd for imparting this project to me and for giving me advice, support and encouragement along the way. In the early stages of the project, I consulted with Braj Kachru, who provided invaluable guidance for the development of the series.

The editors are grateful to all those who have identified contributors and provided advice or research materials for various chapters. For Volume I, John McKenny and I express our gratitude to Dave Britain, Graeme Davis, Christina Lee, Richard Marsden, Esther Asprey, Gerald Kelly, Kim Willcocks, Bill Griffiths, Lifang Wang, William Lancaster, Peter Sercombe, Gus John, Peter Craumer, Lynn Berk, Marian Demos, Joan Baker, Heather Blatt; for Volume II, I am grateful to Michael Montgomery, Barbara Burnaby and William Kretzschmar; and I am grateful to John Holm for his comments on Volume III.

I am especially thankful for the encouragement and support of my colleagues in the Linguistics Program and the English Department at Florida International University: Ellen Thompson, Mehmet Yavas, Feryal Yavas, Virginia Mueller Gathercole, Asher Milbauer, Kemp Williams, Meri-Jane Rochelson, Kathleen Mccormack and Donna Weir-Soley. During the course of the project, the students in my World Englishes seminars always kept me upbeat and motivated.

Both John McKenny and I are thankful to the University of Nottingham Ningbo China and Florida International University respectively for the faculty development grants we received for the production of the maps.

Also, I would like to acknowledge the staff at Bloomsbury: Jennifer Lovel, formerly of Continuum, made helpful suggestions in the early design of the series; and Colleen Coalter and Gurdeep Mattu provided unwavering support, guidance and patience throughout this publication. The editors owe an enormous debt to Subitha Nair for her painstaking work in the final editing and typesetting of the volumes.

These acknowledgements would be incomplete without an expression of gratitude to my friend, Robert Kohn; he is always a source of advice and inspiration.

As one would expect in a project of this size, there were many others who contributed in multiple ways. I have benefitted from them all and to them I give my heartfelt thanks. Any omission of their names is unintentional.

Text

Permission has been granted to Ramish, H. 2008. Channel Island English: Phonology. in B. Kortmann and C. Upton (eds), Varieties of English. *The British Isles.* Vol. 1. Berlin: Mouton de Gruyter. 223–236.

We are pleased to grant permission for the non-exclusive use of your article.

Decker, K. 'Belize Kriol', in Vol. III: *Central America,* 'Portions of this chapter were published previously in Decker, Ken. 2005. The Song of Kriol: A Grammar of the Kriol Language of Belize. Belize Kriol Project: Belize City'.

Permission has been granted by the Belize Kriol Project for this chapter to be published as an abridgement of a book previously published as: Decker, Ken. 2005. The Song of Kriol: A Grammar of the Kriol Language of Belize. Belize Kriol Project: Belize City.

Maps/Illustrations

Regional maps, Vol. I–III, prepared by Himadri Biswas, GIS-RS Center, Florida International University.

Map of South east Englishes produced by the author.

Map language data adapted from 2009 *Ethnologue: Languages of the World, Sixteenth Edition,* (C) SIL International, Inc. Used by permission.

'Indigenous Peoples and Languages of Alaska, compiled by Michael E. Krauss. Copyright 2011 Alaska Native Language Center and Institute of Social and Economic Research. Used with permission'.

'Canada population centres' compiled by J.K. Chambers. Copyright 1999. Used with permission.

'Route of the African Seminoles', compiled by Ian Hancock.

Simon, Beth Lee, 'Midwest American English', Vol. II, **North America.**

All map figures were generated by Erica Wyss to whom I am grateful.

Figure 1. Murrray, T. E., Frazer, T. C., and Simon, B. (1996), 'Need + Past Participle in American English'. *American Speech,* 71, 259.

Figure 2. Lavov, W., Ash S., and Boberg, C. (2003), Atlas of North American English, www.ling.upenn.edu/phono_atlas/.

Figures 3, 14. Ash, S. (2006), 'The North American Midland as a dialect area', in Murray, T. and Simon, B., *Language Variation and Change in the Midland; a new look at 'Heartland' English,* pp. 41, 47.

Figure 4, 5, 6, 10, 11, 12, 13. Responses to *Dictionary of American Regional English (DARE) Questionnaire* prompts and material from DARE files compiled from data provided by Joan Hall and Luanne von Schneidermesser.

Figure 7. Murray, T. E., Frazer, T. C., and Simon, B. (1996), 'Need + Past Participle in American English', *American Speech,* 71, 159.

Figure 8. Murray, T. E. and Simon, B. (1999), 'Want + Past Participle in American English', *American Speech,* 74.
Figure 9. Benson, E. J., (2009), 'Everyone Wants In: Want + Prepositional Adverb in the Midland and Beyond', *Journal of English Linguistics.* 37, 33.

Every effort has been made to trace copyright holders and to obtain their permission for the use of copyright material. The publisher apologizes for any errors or omissions in the above list and would be grateful if notified of any corrections that should be incorporated in future reprints or editions of this book.

Contributors

Lamont D. Antieau
139 Longspur Ln
Commerce Township, MI 48382
Email: lamont@antieau.org

J. K. Chambers
Department of Linguistics
University of Toronto
Sidney Smith Hall 4073
Toronto M5S 3G3
www.chass.utoronto.ca/~chambers

Charles E. DeBose
Professor Emeritus
Department of English
California State University, East Bay
Hayward, California
Email: charles.debose@csueastbay.edu

Carmen Fought
Pitzer College
Linguistics
Scott 225
1050 North Mills Avenue
Claremont, CA 91711
Email: cfought@pitzer.edu

Ian F. Hancock
University of Texas, Austin
Linguistics Department
Austin, Texas
Email: xulaj@mail.utexas.edu

Ellen Johnson
Dept. of English, Rhetoric, and Writing
Berry College
P.O. Box 490350
Mt. Berry, GA 30149
Email: ejohnson@berry.edu

Patricia Kwachka
Professor Emeritus
University of Alaska, Fairbanks
312 Main Campus
P.O. Box 757720
Fairbanks, Alaska 99775-7720
Email: pbkwachka@alaska.edu

Beth Lee Simon
Department of English
Indiana University/Purdue University,
Fort Wayne
Fort Wayne, Indiana 46805-1499
Email: simon@ipfw.edu

List of Maps

List of Figures

List of Abbreviations

AA	African American
AAE	African American English
AAVE	African American Vernacular English
AE	American English
AN	Alaskan Native
ANAE	Atlas of North American English
ASC	Afro-Seminole Creole
AWN	Access World News
CE	Canadian English
DARE	Dictionary of American Regional English
EAA	Early African American
EB	Ebonics
ESL	English as a Second Language
LAMSAS	Linguistic Atlas of the Middle and South Atlantic States
LE	Local Englishes
LEP	Limited English Proficient
NCS	Northern Cities Shift
SE	Standard English
SIC	Sea Islands Creole
SME	Samana English

Series Preface

World Englishes surveys the huge richness and varieties of the English language and its diffusion worldwide, looking beyond the documented popular English varieties to include lesser known varieties and emerging English varieties, especially in geographical regions where English has not been previously documented.

Given that we are surrounded by the global presence of English written and spoken – from its proliferation in the mass media, the translation of works from other languages into English to the internet, online communication and its use as the main language in medical, diplomatic, scientific and international discourses – it would not be practical in a series of this kind to focus only on the structural features of an English variety. The globalization of English is a topical issue in geography, international relations, anthropology, sociology, political science and other related fields. Consequently, chapters have been structured in such a way to give liberty to those contributors with expertise in various disciplines, or who could co-author with contributors who have, to include chapter sections that would reflect the needs of the other social sciences.

While the primary aim of *World Englishes* is to appeal to linguists and English language specialists, the series focuses more on the geographical region and the variety of English spoken there than on the type of English variety involved. For instance, English as a first language, a second language, a third language, an International language and English pidgin and creole varieties.

Each chapter follows a general template that reflects the linguistic, social and historical needs of the English variety. The chapters consist of a linguistic description, as applicable to that particular English variety, of the components of the grammar: phonetics/phonology, morphology, syntax and semantics. Chapters also include demographic data, a brief description of the historical and sociocultural background of the English variety, the present and (if possible) future social, political and economic implications of English language use within the region, its use in literary works and in the social media, and wherever the use of English is applicable and of its importance in the region.

In Volumes I, II and III, the contributors are considered to be well informed of the particular English variety in the region, The chapters are illustrated with maps outlining the region or location of the particular English variety. Each volume will describe several varieties of English within the specified territory.

Some descriptions will be more detailed than others, depending on the variety described and its use of English.

World Englishes serves to function as a reference book, an educational tool and a work of history, geography and anthropology. The series aims not only to appeal to linguistic and English language scholars and students but also to scholars and students in other of the social sciences: geographers, anthropologists, sociologists and economists. The volumes are accessible to undergraduates, as well as graduate and postdoctoral students: any student or scholar who is interested in a comprehensive guide that encompasses all aspect of a particular English variety as a new line of research or expanding existing knowledge of a particular English variety.

The *World Englishes* series is intended to be the first series of volumes to offer comparable, accurate descriptions of English varieties within a given territory and to provide a systematic model for linguistic description and comparison. We hope that as the volumes become available our efforts will complement previous works on world Englishes, contribute to the growing knowledge of English as a global language, and support the development of research in this area.

Bibliography

Crystal, D. (2003), *English as a Global Language*, 2nd edn, Cambridge: Cambridge University Press.

Kachru, B. B., Kachru, Y. and Nelson, C. L. (eds) (2006), *The Handbook of World Englishes*, Malden, MA: Blackwell Publishing.

Kachru, Y. and Smith, L. E. (2008), *Cultures, Contexts, and World Englishes*, New York and London: Routledge.

Kortman, B. and Schneider, E. W. (eds) (2006), *A Handbook of Varieties of English: A Multimedia Research Tool*, Berlin: Mouton de Gruyter. (Edited together with Kate Burridge, Rajend Mesthrie, and Clive Upton.)

McArthur, T. (ed.) (2002), *The Oxford Guide to World Englishes*, Oxford: Oxford University Press.

Svartvik, J. and Leech, G. (2006), *English: One Tongue, Many Voices*, London: Palgrave MacMillan.

Introduction

English Spreads to North America

Tometro Hopkins

In the sixteenth and seventeenth centuries, the English language took the first steps toward becoming a world language by acquiring a large group of nonnative speakers. Almost imperceptibly at first, it began spreading beyond the British Isles, along the oceanways of the world. At about the same time it came to be spoken on the North American continent.

J. L. Dillard, *All American English*

Following Christopher Columbus's exploration of the Americas in 1492, word travelled back to Europe telling of the vast lands, the natural resources, gold and the legendary youth-restoring waters, opened the way for further European explorations and settlement of the region, later called by Europeans the *New World*. Thus began the transatlantic journey of Europeans from most parts of The British Isles, as well as from Spain, France and other parts of Europe in search of wealth and a new home. They left their homelands because of over crowdedness, the poor economy and the desire for freedom from religious persecution. The Europeans and their languages – English, Spanish and French, among others – came in contact with one another and with the languages of the indigenous population, with English emerging as the most widely used language in the United States and most of Canada. Volume II reflects on the rich tapestry of historical, social and cultural factors that gave us the many varieties of English currently being spoken in North America. The chapters in this volume are structured in a way as to provide an overview of the historical, linguistic, social and cultural descriptions of the English varieties across the United States and Canada.

The 'First Americans' migrated from Siberia to Alaska over 20,000 years ago, later spreading throughout North America. Patricia Kwachka in Chapter 8, on *Alaskan Englishes*, provides observations of this first language contact in North America.

In Chapter 1, J. K. Chambers outlines the development of Canadian English which became one of the oldest surviving varieties of colonial English. This survival was the outcome of the contact situation that developed between the newly arrived English and the already established French. According to Chambers, the English aptitude for warfare was the catalyst that ensured the survival of Canadian English.

Ellen Johnson, in Chapter 2, approaches Southern English by providing a description of *White Varieties of English in the American South*. The South has always been a complex region to describe linguistically, historically and geographically. The region embodies a number of ethnic groups, each with its unique variety. Johnson reduces the complexity of her description of Southern English by focusing on the white varieties in the region.

In Chapter 3, Ian Hancock, shares with us the rich sociocultural history that led to the development of Texas Afro-Seminole Creole, spoken today in south Texas, central Oklahoma and Mexico. According to Hancock, Afro-Seminole Creole and Sea Islands Creole are genetically linked. The parent creole, Gullah, is still spoken today in the Sea Islands off the coast of South Carolina and Georgia, and adjacent mainland areas, extending to Northern Florida.

In Chapter 4, on *Midwest American English*, Beth Lee Simon provides historical evidence and linguistic data that defines the Midwest as an identifiable region with its own variety of English.

The Spanish language arriving with Columbus preceded English in the New World, and the two languages have remained in contact ever since. In Chapter 5, Carmen Fought provides a description of Chicano English, a contact variety that is spoken by people of Mexican American origin in the Southwestern part of the United States. Today, Spanish is the second most widely spoken language in the United States.

In Chapter 6, Charles De Bose provides a social and linguistic description of the distinctiveness that defines African American English or African American, his preferred term of this English variety. De Bose discusses African American English in a way that informs us of some of the issues that have engaged scholars in the description of this variety since the sixties.

There have been varying opinions on what constitutes the American West and the English varieties that are characteristic of the region. Lamont Antieau clears up this confusion in Chapter 7, providing a historical background of the region and the contact situation which gave rise to the English in this region.

These chapters taken together show how the American language was forged from contact among English speakers from regions of the British Isles with and a whole range of indigenous and immigrant peoples converged together in North America. This consolidation of the English language on the continent of North America co-occurred with the rise of the United States as a political, economic and technological leader in the global sphere. Thus the conditions were set in place early on for English to become the first truly international language or *lingua franca* (for business, science, technology and travel). The volumes that are to follow will show the trajectory of English expansion and linguistic variation throughout the world.

Bibliography

Dillard, J. L. (1975), *All-American English.* New York: Random House.

—. (1992), *A History of American English.* London, New York: Longman.

Jenkins, J. (2003), *World Englishes: A Resource Book for Students.* London, New York: Routledge.

McCrum, R., Cran, W. and MacNeil, R. (1986), *The Story of English.* New York: Viking.

Svartvik, J. and Leech, G. (2006), *English: One Tongue, Many Voices.* New York: Palgrave.

North America Sub Region

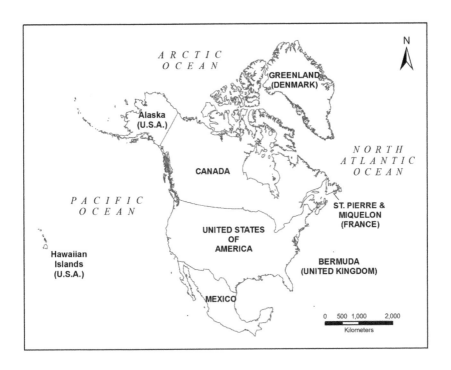

Chapter 1

English in Canada

J. K. Chambers

Background, Including Demographic and Geographical Information

Geographical information

Canada is the second largest nation in the world, after Russia, occupying almost ten million square kilometres. It encompasses six time zones, spanning four-and-a-half hours from the Atlantic coast to the Pacific coast. Climate, topography, local networks, geographical orientation and other factors vary regionally so that the physical experiences of Canadians in the far north, for instance, bear little resemblance to those in the southernmost regions.

Culturally, Canada is complicated by the existence within the Canadian boundaries of two long-standing national consciousnesses that simultaneously share Canadian nationality and maintain their own. Quebec is the power base for the francophone minority, equal partners in Confederation since its inception in 1867. Newfoundland (now officially Newfoundland and Labrador) joined Confederation only in 1949 after centuries of colonial ties to Britain and self-government.

Linguistically, their presence affects Canadian English (hereafter CE) in interesting and very different ways (Chambers 1991). Quebec's location interrupts the continuity of the English-language majority, splitting the Atlantic provinces from the central and western provinces and perpetuates bilingual buffer zones in the adjacent provinces of New Brunswick on the east and Ontario on the west (see Map 1.) Newfoundland, though overwhelmingly anglophone, did not share mainland Canadian settlement history, and her political autonomy gave rise to an indigenous standard accent, though that accent is beginning to reflect the influence of mainland CE (Clarke 1991). Any generalizations that might be hazarded about CE must necessarily be qualified – implicitly or explicitly – by their presence.

Demographically, the population of 30 million (29,639,035 in the 2001 Census) is often called 'sparse', but it is hardly that in world terms. Canada's population is twice Australia's, and three and a half times greater than Sweden's. It is almost the same as South Africa's and only slightly less than Spain's. The sparseness of Canada's population is noticeable mainly when one considers the thousands of square kilometres available for settlement. By comparison, the United Kingdom, which would fit handily into even the smallest of Canada's seven inland provinces, has about twice the population, and the United States, more comparable in size as the fourth largest nation in the world, has eight times the population.

One of the sources of Canadian national unity is the fact that the population is geographically concentrated along the southern border. Most Canadians live within two hundred kilometres of the US–Canadian border. Map 1 shows the major urban areas, which house nearly two-thirds of the Canadian population; the remaining third live mainly in smaller cities and towns in the catchment area of the larger cities. The border is enormous, stretching more than 4,000 kilometres, but the population concentration in that long, thin ribbon belies the popular stereotype of Canada as a country of isolated homesteads.

Canadians are not only highly urbanized but also overwhelmingly middle-class, to an extent that can scarcely be comprehended by outsiders. As in the New-World societies of the United States and Australia, two factors conspired to determine the relatively homogeneous class structure (Chambers 1998c). On the one hand, Canada's earliest settlements offered virtually no amenities to settlers with aristocratic predilections, with the result that they were excluded from most mainstream society. On the other, the earliest political initiatives

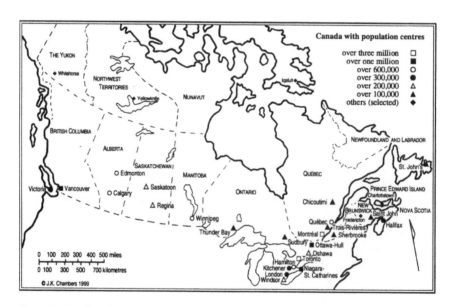

Canada, showing the ten provinces and three territories, with the largest metropolitan areas and cities.

fostered geographical mobility as a means of uniting the enormous expanses that needed to be governed. The combination of social egalitarianism and freedom of movement led to occupational and social mobility on a scale unknown in the colonizing nations.

Social trends in the first half of the twentieth century further increased the class homogenization. Urbanization shrank the agricultural class to less than 10 per cent of the population, and occupational mobility keeps the unskilled labour group at less than 5 per cent (Camu, Weeks and Sametz 1971). More than 85 per cent of the population is thus middleclass, sharing to a greater or lesser degree their values, aspirations, living standards and (outside of Quebec and Newfoundland) speech standards.

Brief history

Canadian English is one of the oldest varieties of colonial English. Because Canada is due west of England, it was one of the first discoveries in the European quest for a sea route to the Orient. The English first laid claim to Newfoundland, Canada's easternmost province and thus the nearest land on the Atlantic Ocean to Europe, in 1497, just five years after Columbus made his historic landing to the south. Newfoundland's discoverer was a Venetian, John Cabot, but he sailed from Bristol in England under the authority of the English king, Henry VII (Chadwick 1967).

The English claim to the rest of Canada was not as direct. In the Atlantic region of the present-day Maritime Provinces (Nova Scotia, New Brunswick and Prince Edward Island on Map 1), the French arrived before the English and established colonies in what they called Acadia. Samuel de Champlain, the first French governor, founded a settlement called Port Royal at the inlet to the St. Lawrence River in 1605. Three years later, in 1608, he established *Nouvelle France* inland on the St. Lawrence River in the vicinity of present-day Quebec City and Montreal.

However, France seemed uninterested in its imperialist role in North America. By the middle of the eighteenth century, the population of the entire St. Lawrence colony numbered only about 70,000 (Chambers and Heisler 1999). The colonists were the descendants of some 10,000 individuals sent out to the New World from the mother country in a period of 150 years. Even though the birthrate in Nouvelle France was among the highest in the world, this trickle of settlers was hardly enough to establish critical mass (Joy 1972: 51–54; on birthrate and immigration, see section on *Immigration and insularity* below). By contrast, England, with only one-third the population of France, sent many more settlers to its North American colonies, usually with incentives of free sea passage and freehold farmland to encourage them. This disparity had important consequences not only for Canadian history but for world history. They were described eloquently by the demographer Alfred Sauvy (translated by Lachapelle and Henripin 1982: 10):

> It sufficed that one of the two countries competing for a vast continent sent a few thousand settlers each year, while the other sent a few hundred, and the course of history was radically changed. This is both tragic and symbolic, since, just when the French language had reached international predominance in Europe, through its great demographic superiority, it was sealing its fate in the world at large because a few boats more, filled with illiterates, left England every year.

Partly as a result of this disparity, France was forced to cede both colonies to England after suffering defeats in two wars.

- In 1716, the Treaty of Utrecht resolved Queen Anne's War, and one of its terms made Acadia a British possession. The English divided the colony into the provinces of Nova Scotia, New Brunswick and St. John (since 1798, Prince Edward Island).
- In 1763, England's victory on the Plains of Abraham in Quebec City ended the French and Indian War, and by the terms of the Treaty of Paris, France was forced to surrender its hold on the inland colony.

So, the English language came to be spoken in Canada because of the English aptitude for warfare. In the Middle Ages, the English people themselves had narrowly escaped becoming colonials dominated by the Normans and, in extricating themselves they inadvertently developed the political and military strengths that would eventually lead to the global spread of their language. Protracted wars against Normandy in particular and France in general, especially the Hundred Years War (1337–1453), developed military prowess and a readiness for aggression. Defending the surrounding seas required the English to develop navigational skills and sea-faring prowess. As a result, when the era of New World exploration dawned in 1492, the English were well equipped to compete with their rivals from France, Spain, Portugal and Holland.

In inland Canada, as in most parts of the New World, British explorers discovered vast land masses sparsely populated by native hunters or subsistence farmers. Exactly the same discoveries were made by the Spanish in Argentina, the Portuguese in Brazil, the French in Vietnam and the Dutch in Indonesia. In all instances, the European imperialists subdued the native peoples either by conquests or treaties. In North America, the native peoples often became allies of their British overlords, joining them in battles against their European rivals, especially the French. For more than two centuries, European foreign policies were dominated by these imperialist struggles. Although the historical record shows the English as world-beaters, fending off the Dutch in South Africa, the Spanish in the southern United States and the French in Canada, in all these countries conflicts still arise among groups divided along linguistic lines. The descendants are now united not by fealty to their imperial founders but by fealty to their distinctive regional cultures.

The British turned out to be relatively benevolent governors in Canada. They immediately issued proclamations safeguarding certain rights of the native peoples, including the requirement that ancestral lands could be surrendered only upon execution of legal treaties (Chambers 1990). Their relations with their French-speaking subjects proved equally benevolent with one notable exception that took place in the first years of their government. In 1755, when England and France engaged one another in the French and Indian War, many Acadians chose to remain neutral. The British governors, fearing they might side with France and thus provide a hostile element behind their lines, evicted some 10,000 of them. Most Acadians went southward into the United States, and many of them made their way to the former French colony of Louisiana, at the mouth of the Mississippi River, where they adapted their Acadian culture to local conditions. They are known today as 'Cajuns', the southern US pronunciation of the word Acadian.

That incident remains vivid in Canada's francophone history. It was a mistake that the British seemed determined to avoid in the newly acquired Nouvelle France. They instituted the Quebec Act in 1774 in order to establish the legal boundaries of their French-speaking colony. In 1791, when hundreds of English-speaking immigrants arrived as refugees from the American Revolution (discussed in **The Loyalist base** below), the governors passed the Constitution Act dividing 'Quebec' into two separate colonies called Lower Canada (present-day Quebec) and Upper Canada (present-day Ontario). As a result, the boundaries of the French-language colony remained distinct even as the French-speaking population became a minority. In effect, these administrative divisions guaranteed that the cultural and linguistic heritage of the French colonials would be perpetuated in the new land.

In 1867, the four provinces of Nova Scotia, New Brunswick, Quebec and Ontario joined in the Canadian Confederation. The other Maritime province, Prince Edward Island, where the Confederation Act was drafted and signed, was admitted in 1873. Expansion into the vast western territory known as Prince Rupert's Land came later: Manitoba (1870), Saskatchewan (1905), Alberta (1905) and British Columbia (1871) followed the development of the transcontinental rail link. In 1949, Newfoundland joined as the tenth province. The vast sub-arctic regions, the Northwest Territories and the Yukon, were incorporated as territories, not provinces, the former in 1870 and the latter in 1898. In 1999, a new territory, Nunavut, was created by partitioning the Northwest Territories to establish an Inuit-majority region (see Map 1.)

Demographic information

Canada's population statistics as they relate to language use – Canada's 'demolinguistics', to use Lachapelle and Henripin's (1982) uncomely but functional word – are somewhat complicated by the fact that Canada has two official languages, English and French. But they become much more complicated by the fact that Canada has an astounding number of 'non-official' languages as well. The aboriginal peoples of Canada spoke at least a hundred different languages at the time of European discovery, and a few dozen survive to this day, though many are threatened with extinction. More significant demographically, throughout the twentieth century, Canada provided a land of opportunity for immigrants and a haven for refugees. The newcomers have brought with them the languages of the world. I discuss the two great immigrations of the last century in **The peopling of Canada** below.

As a result of these immigrations, Canada is perhaps the most multilingual nation in the world not only in the obvious sense that countless languages are spoken there but also in the sense that those language groups tend to sustain themselves beyond the second generation.

Canadian mother tongues

Statistics Canada, the government office responsible for the census, incorporated a useful distinction starting in 1991 in response to Canada's flourishing multilingualism. They asked respondents to distinguish between their 'mother tongue', defined as the first language learnt at home in childhood and still understood by the individual, and their 'home language', defined as the language used daily in family situations. In this section, I will describe the Canadian population in terms of their mother tongues (from Statistics Canada 2001; for comparative analysis of both mother tongue and home language, see Chambers 1998c: 264–68).

Table 1.1 provides a finely detailed snapshot of Canada's linguistic diversity at the beginning of the millennium. It lists the Canadian demolinguistics in terms of the major language groups, starting with the official languages, including true bilinguals, that is, people who have more than one mother tongue, and then continues with specific listings for 15 non-official languages. In addition to the figures for the country as a whole, Table 1.1 lists the figures for the two largest provinces, Ontario and Quebec, in order to underscore some points I want to make about the distribution of the official languages. Readers who might feel overwhelmed by the amount of detail can look at the summary lines indicated by the 'Totals' following each sub-category.

The aboriginal languages

The non-official languages listed in Table 1.1 include only those with more than 100,000 speakers with two exceptions. Cree and Inuktitut are aboriginal

Table 1.1   Demolinguistic statistics for Canada as a whole, and for the provinces of Quebec and Ontario (based on Statistics Canada http://www.statcan.ca, last modified 20 January 2003)

Mother Tongue	Canada	Quebec	Ontario
English	17,352,315	557,040	7,965,225
English and non-official language	219,860	15,045	114,275
Totals (English)	17,572,175	572,085	8,079,500
French	6,703,325	5,761,765	485,630
French and non-official language	38,630	26,890	8,000
Total (French)	6,741,955	5,788,655	493,630
English, French	112,575	50,060	37,135
English, French and non-official	10,085	5,355	3,200
Total (French–English bilingual)	122,660	55,415	40,335
Chinese	853,745	43,745	404,250
Italian	469,485	124,695	295,205
German	438,080	17,690	156,080
Punjabi	271,220	9,900	110,540
Spanish	245,495	70,095	118,690
Portuguese	213,815	33,355	152,115
Polish	208,375	17,155	138,940
Arabic	199,940	76,285	94,640
Tagalog (Pilipino)	174,060	9,550	88,870
Ukrainian	148,085	5,125	48,620
Dutch	128,670	3,220	69,655
Vietnamese	122,055	21,640	55,240
Greek	120,360	41,980	65,285
Cree	72,885	11,810	4,405
Inuktitut	29,010	8,620	160
Others	1,506,965	214,550	869,400
Total (non-official languages)	5,202,245	709,415	2,672,095
Total (all mother tongues)	29,639,035	7,125,570	11,285,560

languages of the most populous Algonquian nation and of the Inuit peoples (formerly called, respectively, Indians and Eskimos). These are non-official languages, of course, but unlike the other non-official languages on the list, they are native (non-immigrant) languages. The Inuit are exhaustively represented by these numbers, but there are 20 other native (Indian) languages besides Cree listed in the census tables, accounting for a few thousand speakers in the 'Others' category. The reason for the large difference in the Inuit populations in Quebec and Ontario is geographical: Quebec occupies much more territory above the boreal tree line, where Inuit settlements are located. Greatest Inuit concentration (18,605 of the 26,670 total) is in Nunavut, which was created in 1999 to provide territorial autonomy for them. Inuit thus constitute about 70 per cent of the population. Almost all the rest, 26 per cent, have English as their mother tongue, making Nunavut the least linguistically diverse administrative region in the country.

The immigrant languages

Among the non-official languages, Chinese is the largest mother-tongue group. Although some Chinese in Canada arrived in the 1870s to work as 'coolies' on the construction of the trans-Canada railroad, the Canadian Pacific, most arrived much more recently, since the 1960s, in the diaspora from south mainland China and Hong Kong. The great majority of Chinese–Canadians are speakers of the Cantonese 'dialect'. Because many Chinese arrived in a relatively recent influx, few of them have completely assimilated and become monolingual English speakers and, as a result, the proportion of Chinese–Canadians whose mother tongue is Chinese rather than English is large.

The 1996 census was the first in which Chinese topped the list of non-official languages. As recently as 1991, and for five decades before that, the largest non-official language group was Italian. (Toronto is said to be the second largest Italian city in the world after Rome.) Many third- and fourth-generation Italo–Canadians speak 'kitchen Italian' with their grandparents and parents but their mother tongue is English. For the first time in 60 years, the Italo–Canadian community shows signs of linguistic assimilation to the English majority. In the 1990s, though their rank order fell to second among immigrant groups after the Chinese, it was not the result of attrition of people whose mother tongue is Italian: in 1991, they numbered 449,660, and in 1996 they numbered 484,500, an increase of almost 35,000. However, in 2001, as Table 1.1 shows, they numbered 469,485, a decrease of about 15,00 – not many (in fact, only 3 per cent) but significant as a counter-trend to the pattern of the last half-century. The change in rank order is the direct result of growth in the Chinese–Canadian community: in 1991, the Chinese mother-tongue respondents numbered 444,940; that number grew by 270,700 in the next five years, and, as Table 1.1 shows, by another 138,100 in 2001, over 400,000 in a decade.

Immigration and insularity

One point of contrast in Table 1.1 that has significant sociolinguistic implications is the difference between Quebec and Ontario with respect to non-official languages. In Ontario, 23.6 per cent of the population (2,672,095 of 11,285,560) has a mother tongue other than French or English, whereas, in Quebec, only 9.9 per cent (709,415 of 7,125,570) do. This difference reflects a sharp distinction between the two provinces. Ontario, and indeed all of anglophone Canada, chose immigration as the principal means of expanding its population base, as will become evident in the next section where I discuss the peopling of the nation that has taken place over slightly more than two centuries. Like other New World countries, Canada adopted immigration naturally, as a critically under-populated nation with an abundance of uncultivated land, unmined natural resources and developing industry. In Quebec, only the city of Montreal receives immigrants at a rate comparable to the major anglophone cities. Elsewhere in the province of Quebec, immigration is negligible.

This contrast has distinguished the francophone and anglophone regions from the beginning of Canadian history. After the French and Indian War, Quebec's population growth from about 10,000 citizens in 1760 to over seven million today included about 20,000 anglophones at the end of the eighteenth century, mostly refugees from the American Revolution as described in the next section, but otherwise the growth has been almost entirely due to Quebec's birthrate (Lachapelle and Henripin, 1982: 97–117). Throughout the nineteenth century and the first half of the twentieth century, Quebec's birthrate was around 65 per 1,000, one of the highest in the world. It is now around 13 per 1,000, one of the lowest in Canada. With a declining birthrate and relatively little immigration, Quebec's population is decreasing proportionately in Canada. Faced with this dilemma, the Quebec government in 1988 inaugurated a cash incentive to mothers who bore three or more children (Joy 1992: 34–38). This 'natalist' policy, unfashionable and unworldly as it seems in an era that extols zero population growth and women's rights, indicates the deep-seated isolationism in Quebec culture.

Though Quebec nationalism appears to be based on linguistic differences, its basis goes much deeper (Chambers 2004: 107–11). The sociocultural contrasts between societies with significant and continuous immigration and those with stable populations, that is, without significant influxes from outside, are sharp. Belief systems in immigrant societies like anglophone Canada tend to be diffuse because of the importation of diverse creeds, rites and customs. Ethnicities are more diverse and racial mixing more common. Language is more varied and unstable across generations, with second-language varieties as well as native varieties, different mother tongues in the same household, and loanwords, code-switching and inter-language. Patriotism is likely to be more diffuse (less focused) and less fervent.

One of the more extreme branches of Quebec culture is called *pure laine* nationalism, where *pure laine* (literally 'pure wool', a term used on garment labels) stands for ethnic purity in the sense of direct descent from the original *Nouvelle France* settlers. In the rest of Canada and in much of Quebec, this kind of nationalism is viewed as narrow-minded at best and racist at worst. It is a strain of political thought at odds with Canadian openness and tolerance. It has little to do with the official languages themselves, which coexist by virtue of that general openness and tolerance, as manifested by the extraordinary measures taken by the federal government to protect and elevate the minority language, as discussed in the next section.

The official languages

All regions of Canada are institutionally bilingual. Every citizen has the right to be served in either French or English by government agencies, tried in either language in federal courts, informed in either language in public announcements on radio and television, and advised in both languages on product labels, tax forms and all other official documents. Only two provinces have linguistic provisions in their constitutions: New Brunswick is constitutionally bilingual, and Quebec is officially monolingual French (Joy 1992: 79–80). Quebec provincial laws forbid employers to require any language but French of prospective employees (Joy 1992: 9) and forbid merchants from displaying English-language signs. Ironically, federal provisions on bilingualism ensure a nation-wide presence for French from the Atlantic to the Pacific, even in regions where the francophone population is non-existent, but the nation-wide presence of English is interrupted officially, though not actually, by Quebec monolingualism.

Table 1.1 shows that there is a considerable discrepancy in sheer numbers between the French-speaking and the English-speaking populations. In percentages, the mother-tongue groups are proportioned as follows: 59.2 per cent speak English, 22.7 per cent speak French, 0.4 per cent are English–French bilinguals and 17.5 per cent have a mother tongue that is neither English nor French. It is important to point out, as a cautionary note, that these mother-tongue figures grossly under-represent bilingualism in all guises. The French–English bilinguals in these figures count only 'true bilinguals', rare individuals who learnt both languages from birth (Weinreich 1967: Chap. 3). There are, of course, millions of other bilinguals in Canada whose competence in the two languages is asymmetrical or unequal. In fact, French–English bilingualism has been increasing by leaps in the Ontario region bordering Quebec under the stimulus of educational immersion and equity policies (Cartwright 1988).

Bilingualism aside, the French mother-tongue population is heavily concentrated in the province of Quebec. The concentration shows up dramatically when Quebec's numbers are left out of the demolinguistic calculations as in Table 1.2. Outside of Quebec, English is the mother tongue of 75.5 per cent (about 17.5 million of 22.5), French of 4.2 per cent (953,300), bilingual French–English (true bilinguals) make up 0.2 per cent (67,245) and non-official languages are mother tongues of 19.9 per cent (almost 4.5 million).

Table 1.2 also provides quantitative evidence for the observation made above that Quebec accounts for a relatively small percentage of immigrant

Table 1.2   Demolinguistics of Canada including Quebec and excluding Quebec (based on Statistics Canada, last modified 20 January 2003)

Mother tongue	Canada		Excluding Quebec	
	%	Total	%	Total
English	59.2	17,572,175	75.5	17,000,090
French	22.7	6,741,955	4.2	953,300
English–French bilingual	0.4	122,660	0.2	67,245
Non-official	17.5	5,202,245	19.9	4,492,830

languages: the percentages of non-official mother-tongue speakers are very similar across Canada whether or not Quebec is counted. However, other proportions on the table change dramatically.

When we compare the percentages for English and French mother-tongue speakers in Table 1.2, the concentration of French speakers in Quebec stands out clearly. Not only is French the mother tongue of fewer than 4.5 per cent of the population outside Quebec, but a glance back at Table 1.1 will reveal that more than half of those French speakers outside Quebec live in adjoining Ontario. The proportion of French speakers in Canada has been increasing in Quebec and decreasing in the rest of Canada at least since 1931, the first year the census recorded mother-tongue statistics (Lachapelle and Henripin 1982: 39). The relative isolation of francophones within the provincial boundaries is one obvious source of Quebecois anxiety about the survival of its language and culture. The effect is a spiral. Legislation of protective measures such as French-only language laws in Quebec leads to disaffection among the English-language minority and emigration to other provinces, which further isolates the French speakers in the province.

Because Table 1.2 tabulates mother-tongue statistics rather than functional language use, it inadvertently obscures the extent to which Canada is an English-speaking country. The figure for the English-speaking population outside Quebec is large at 75.5 per cent, but in addition, Canadians whose mother tongue is a non-official language, almost 20 per cent of the population, are almost unanimously speakers of English, not French, as a second language. That brings the actual proportion of anglophones outside Quebec to 95 per cent. The next section outlines the various routes by which these English-speaking peoples came to the country.

Linguistic Background and Contacts

The distinctiveness of Newfoundland

Newfoundland, the tenth province, did not participate in the events that shaped mainland Canada until 1949, when it joined the Confederation. It had a very different settlement pattern and colonial history (Shorrocks 1997), and consequently it is the most linguistically distinctive region of English-speaking Canada.

Newfoundland was first discovered by Norse adventurers around 1000, but they appear to have settled there only temporarily, perhaps seasonally. At the time of Newfoundland's rediscovery by Europeans 500 years later, the Norse contact had left so few traces that it took archaeologists until the 1960s to unearth them (Ingstad 1969). Newfoundland's waters teemed with codfish, and fishermen from Portugal as well as England rushed to harvest them. Permanent settlers arrived soon after, mostly from south-western England, especially from the seafaring regions of Devon, Dorset, Somerset and Hampshire. Then, in the eighteenth century, Irish immigrants began arriving in such great numbers as to dominate many areas, including the capital, St. John's.

Because of its years of autonomy, there are many features that distinguish Newfoundland speech from mainland Canada in sound and in vocabulary (Story 1977, Clarke 2004, 2008). Sociolinguistic studies show, however, that the successive post-confederation generations are adopting some mainland features, especially the urban middle class (Clarke 1991). As geographical and occupational mobility further increases, the differentness of Newfoundland English will undoubtedly diminish.

The peopling of Canada

While Newfoundland was being settled by West Country fisherfolk and Irish workers, the rest of Canada was being wrested from the French on the Atlantic seaboard and then receiving settlers progressively westward. It took two centuries for the settlers to cover the vast expanse, and they arrived in four significant waves of immigration. Each wave had linguistic implications – that is, the immigrants influenced the way in which English is spoken in Canada to some extent. But, predictably, the first two waves were much more important linguistically than the subsequent ones because they took place when the character of CE was not yet formed, and thus they had a formative influence.

The four major waves of immigration were these

- Beginning in 1776 and reaching its peak in 1793, hundreds of refugees from the Thirteen Colonies (soon to become the United States of America) entered Canada; these were the people known in Canadian history as Loyalists, the citizens of the southern colonies who chose to maintain their allegiance to the imperial mother-country, England, and fled rather than participating in the American Revolution.
- Beginning around 1815 and reaching its peak around 1850, thousands of immigrants from England, Scotland and latterly Ireland (because of the Potato Famine of 1845–7) arrived in Canada as a result of systematic, large-scale recruitment by the British governors of the colony in order to counteract pro-American sentiments among the settlers, especially in the face of American border invasions in the War of 1812.
- Beginning in the 1890s and reaching a peak around 1910, thousands of immigrants not only from Scotland and Ireland but also from more diverse European homelands such as Germany, Italy, Scandinavia and Ukraine were recruited as farmers for the vast wheatlands of the newly opened Prairie Provinces and as workers for the industrializing cities in Ontario and Montreal in Quebec.

- Beginning in 1946 and reaching a peak around 1960, a highly diverse immigrant population arrived first as a result of the post-War diaspora in Europe, with thousands of Italians, Portuguese, Dutch, Belgians, Greeks, Ukrainians, Poles, Finns and Yugoslavians among others, and later, even more diversely, from Hungary, Czechoslovakia, Korea, China, Vietnam and the United States, as a result of political unrest in those countries.

In the last 25 years, Canada has received another significant wave of immigrants, often as political refugees from such countries as Pakistan, Chile, Brazil, Cambodia, Somali and El Salvador, but also from English-speaking countries in the Caribbean and from Hong Kong. The linguistic diversity evident in Table 1.1 above is largely the result of this wave combined with the previous one.

By the time of the latter two immigrations – the ones that peaked in 1910 and 1960 – the linguistic character of Canada was firmly established. The immigrants could thus have only a mild, and minor, immediate influence. Their long-term influence, however, may be more significant. The preponderance of ESL accents in Canada's major cities is truly remarkable. In Toronto, for instance, four of every 10 people (40 per cent) speak an immigrant language natively, and so do 27 per cent in Vancouver, 21 per cent in Winnipeg and 17 per cent in Montreal. As a result, in the most densely populated parts of Canada, people encounter ESL accents daily, and they have done so for two generations or more. If some features of those ESL varieties persist in the native varieties of the immigrants' offspring, they will enter CE as markers of urban or ethnic accents. Though no one has yet documented such persistent features, they clearly exist. Because of them, listeners can often identify speakers as having, say, Yiddish ancestry or an Italian background, even in the speech of native Canadians far removed from their immigrant roots. From a sociolinguistic perspective, it seems inevitable that some of the diversity currently heard as inter-language will ultimately be recognized as markers of urban CE accents (Chambers 2004: 105–107).

The Loyalist base

The first immigrants to arrive in Canada were the refugees from the American Revolution, the Loyalists, in the last decades of the eighteenth century.

There were two main paths of immigration for the Loyalists. One was from the coastal New England States – especially Connecticut and Massachusetts, where the first skirmishes of the Revolution took place in 1776, but also Maine and Rhode Island – into the Canadian province of Nova Scotia. Many of these refugees, perhaps most, bided their time in Halifax or Lunenburg, the main seaports of the province, until they could arrange passage to England. Some others stayed in Nova Scotia or in nearby New Brunswick and Prince Edward Island, finding work on the land or in towns. Still others took advantage of government offers of generous land grants further inland, along the banks of the St. Lawrence River and the north shore of Lake Ontario, and made the trek into the regions of Lower and Upper Canada.

These refugees from New England brought with them a distinctive home dialect. New England speech was then, as it is now, r-less and also had several readily identifiable vowel sounds. Wherever the New England refugees became the founding population of a community, the local speech came to sound like New England English. But this happened only in a very small, highly localized region. The town of Lunenburg (about 40km south of Halifax on Map 1) and some rural areas in Lunenburg County and the Annapolis Valley were marked linguistically as descendants of the New England dialect region (Trudgill 2000). In this century, with accelerated mobility and urbanization, the distinctive sound of that New England ancestry has receded in these regions.

In the inland regions, no trace of the New England accent persevered or survived. By the time the New England Loyalists reached their inland destinations, they were greeted by other Loyalists – refugees who had taken the second route into Canada. And though they too were native Americans, they brought with them a very different accent.

These other Loyalists set out principally from the states of Pennsylvania, New Jersey, New York and Vermont, and they moved by inland routes to entry points at the narrows of the lower Great Lakes, mainly crossing the border at the upper St. Lawrence River from Montreal westward, along the Detroit River in the region of present-day Windsor, and especially at the Niagara frontier in Upper Canada. There, they were met by Canadian government officials and sent, with a modest allotment of provisions and tools, to homesteads in the richly forested parklands of the Great Lakes basin. In every district where they landed, they formed the first settled population. Native peoples – the Iroquois (Hurons, Tobacco, Oneidas and others) and Algonquians (mainly Delawares, Odawas, Ojibwas) – circulated through the regions harvesting roots or grains and hunting game, and white or mixed-blood trappers (*coureurs de bois*) cut across the regions chasing pelts and hides. But the Loyalists were the first people to fence in parcels of land, clear them of roots and rocks and raise houses and outbuildings on them. Where their numbers were concentrated, some of them quit farming to provide goods and services for the others: mills for lumber and mills for flour, blacksmithing, slaughterhouses, tanning, spinning and weaving, rooms and meals for travellers, arithmetic and spelling lessons and Sunday sermons. Towns grew up as central places for distributing goods and services, with churches, schools, markets and stores.

These people became the founding population of inland Canada. Socially, they brought with them the manners and mores of the middle American states where they originated, as distinct from the Yankees north of them in New England and the planters south of them in Virginia and Georgia. Linguistically, they brought with them the sounds and syntax of those same middle states on the Atlantic coast.

The founding population of any place exerts many subtle and largely unintentional dictates on those who succeed them. They set the pattern for roads in the country and streets in the town, establish local practices (land-clearing, crop selection, house construction, religious observance, educational practices and much more), determine norms of communal cooperation (midwifery, health care, sewing bees, barn raising) and set the moral tone of the community.

One of the subtlest dictates – and one seldom considered because it is beneath consciousness – is linguistic. The people who come after the founding population, the second or third generation of settlers, may come from far and wide, but their children will speak, under ordinary circumstances, just like the children whose parents arrived before them. So it came to pass in inland Canada–Lower Canada and especially Upper Canada, destined to become the economic and political wheel horse of the nation for the next century – that the sound of the speech was directly descended from these Loyalists.

As a result, it is a common experience of young Canadians today, whether their ancestry is Scottish, German or Bangladeshi, to be mistaken for Americans when they go travelling across the globe. To foreigners, unless they have a good ear for subtle differences, Canadians sound American. That is the heritage of the Loyalist founders.

The British and Irish arrivals after 1812

The Americans began looking covetously northward soon after they gained their independence. In June 1812, the United States declared war on Britain and launched a series of raids on the Canadian borders. The event is known as the War of 1812 but it actually lasted until 1814, when the Treaty of Ghent ended the conflict with neither side gaining any advantage over the other. Militarily, the war was a draw, but from the Canadian viewpoint it seemed a victory. The aggressor had been repelled, after all, and the Canadian border remained intact.

The American invasions took place at the very sites where the Loyalists had entered the country. The British were embroiled at the same time in the Napoleonic Wars in Europe and could spare very few troops for defending their North American colony, but the outnumbered defenders eventually beat back the American insurgents. The Canadian victories aroused the first significant show of national pride, and, today, virtually all the battle sites are marked by monuments.

British intelligence later discovered that the Americans relied on finding widespread sympathy for their cause in Canada. They had expected their invading armies to be swelled by anti-English sympathizers as they marched through the colony. Instead, they met with stout resistance at every step. Though the Canadians proved their loyalty, the governors felt uneasy about the broad base of American ancestry in Canada, and they set about diluting that base by recruiting British settlers with promises of transport and generous gifts of land.

Between 1830 and 1860, thousands of British and Irish emigrants settled in Canada, especially along the north shores of the two Great Lakes, Ontario and Erie, but also inland in regions where the Loyalist presence was sparse. Their numbers more than doubled the population of Upper Canada, which at that time comprised the second- and third-generation Loyalists. Economically, the immigrants broadened the consumer base and brought new initiatives. Politically, they brought debating skills and imperialist power lust. It is an astounding fact that three of Canada's first five Prime Ministers arrived in Canada as immigrant children – the first, John A. Macdonald (in office 1867–73 and 1878–91), and the second, Alexander Mackenzie (1873–78), were native Scots, and the fifth, Mackenzie Bowell (1894–96), was born in England.

Linguistic influence of British and Irish immigrants

Linguistically, the long-term influence of the British immigrants was highly restricted. Most of the immigrants settled, naturally, in the towns and villages founded by the Loyalists, and, predictably, their Canadian-born children grew up speaking not like their parents but like the children who became their schoolmates and playmates. The essential Loyalist character of CE persisted.

In two accidental senses, the British accents and dialects of the nineteenth-century immigrants made a direct and indisputable impression on Canadian speech. First, in relatively isolated regions where the immigrants became the founding population, their speech formed the basis of the local accent. To this day, one can discern the Scots roots of rural speech in Cape Breton, Pictou and Antigonish counties in Nova Scotia, the Ottawa Valley, Peterborough county, the West Lorne district on the north shore of Lake Erie and other places. Since Newfoundland joined the Confederation, Canada has come to encompass a large and influential enclave where the speech descends from Irish ancestors.

The second impression was made at the opposite pole, so to speak. Though the English immigrants could not impose their speech sounds on their offspring, they often did succeed in imposing norms of propriety and correctness on them and on the community in general. Many English immigrants frankly promulgated their linguistic superiority to the benighted natives. Thus Susanna Moodie, whose snide and snobbish account of her immigrant experience, *Roughing It in the Bush* (1852), greatly amused the Victorian gentlefolk she left behind in England, described the first Canadian dialect she ever heard, that of the immigration recruiter, by saying he 'had a shocking delivery, a drawling vulgar voice; and he spoke with such a twang that I could not bear to look at him or listen to him. He made such grammatical blunders that my sides ached laughing at him'.

English immigrants took it upon themselves to try and change linguistic practices that differed from their own. In almost all cases, these practices differed because they were based on American rather than British models. The first schoolteachers in inland Canada were Loyalists or descendants of them, and they used the pedagogical tools they were familiar with. Noah Webster's spelling book, for instance, was almost universally used in Upper Canada schools. It included spellings like *color, neighbor, center, meter* and *connection* instead of *colour, neighbour, centre, metre* and *connexion*, and it included pronunciations like *secretARY, reNAIssance, lootenant* (for *lieutenant*), *eether* (for *either*) and *zee*, instead of *SECret'ry, renaissANCE, leftenant, eyether* and *zed*.

One result of the belated intervention on language standards by the English immigrants is the Canadian double standard in many matters of spelling and pronunciation. Wherever British and American practices differ from one another, Canadians usually tolerate both. For instance, many Canadians freely vary their pronunciation of *either* and *neither* without noticing any discrepancy or raising any controversy, and different regions sometimes maintain different norms, as when, for instance, Ontarians prefer the spellings *colour* and *neighbour* but Albertans prefer *color* and *neighbor* (Ireland 1979: 178–179). These double standards are the linguistic legacy of the first two immigrations in Canadian history.

Another result, much less obvious but no less real, was attitudinal. In the second half of the nineteenth century, Canadians came to regard British standards as superior, whether or not they were the ones in common use. This attitude insinuated itself into the Canadian ethos politically as well as linguistically. At many points in Canadian history, being patriotically Canadian has defined itself as being anti-American, either mildly or vituperatively, and in decades past – though probably not since the 1940s – it often also entailed being pro-British.

Many genteel Canadians affected British speech and manners. Linguistically, they adopted Briticisms such as initial /hw/ in *which, whale* and similar words, /tj/ in *tune* and *student*, and pronunciations such as tomAHto for *tomato*, rather for *rather* and SHedule for *schedule*. The accent, called Canadian Dainty, carried prestige until the final decades of the twentieth century (Chambers 2004). At its most extreme, many Canadian-born military officers, diplomats, professors, CBC newscasters, actors and other members of the self-styled cultural élite made themselves 'Anglo–Canadian'. The poet, Irving Layton, took that as the title of his satirical poem describing a professor of English at Queen's University (Scott and Smith 1967: 75).

Anglo-Canadian
A native of Kingston, Ont.
—two grandparents Canadian
and still living

His complexion florid
as a maple leaf in late autumn,
for three years he attended
Oxford

Now his accent
makes even Englishmen
wince, and feel
unspeakably colonial.

Nowadays, the Anglo–Canadian élite have become relics, along with the Union Jack, the British Commonwealth and 'God Save the Queen'. Britain's failure to impose itself on recent generations of Canadians coincides with the decline of Britain as a world power, but, more to the point, the ethnically diverse immigrations of the twentieth century have diluted the Anglo–Celtic hegemony. The image of Britain as Canada's mother country is a historical fact, but it is as far removed from Canada's daily affairs as is Victorianism.

Homogeneity of urban, middle-class Canadian English

As Canada settled its western region in the second half of the nineteenth century, the first settlers were mainly white Protestants from southern Ontario. Their prominence there was not accidental. In 1870, when the Canadian governors first attempted to carry out a land survey of the Red River Valley – the region around present-day Winnipeg, then (as now) the most populous part of Manitoba – they were opposed by the people who were already there. The strongest opposition came from the Métis, French-speaking Catholics of mixed Quebecois and Algonquian ancestry who comprised about half the population of 12,000. They were quelled forcibly by Canadian troops, and their leader Louis Riel fled to the United States. Riel returned in 1885 to lead a second rebellion against Canadian expansion in Saskatchewan. This time, when the rebels were defeated by Canadian troops at Batoche, the Métis capital, Riel was captured. He was imprisoned in Regina, tried for treason and hanged.

Following these rebellions, the governors ensured that the first significant wave of settlers in the prairies would be sympathetic to their plans for expansion by making generous land grants to the infantry volunteers who had quelled Riel and to other Ontarians. In so doing, they transplanted not only the central Canadian ethos but also, inevitably, the Ontario accent. As a result, CE is remarkably homogeneous across the vast expanse of the country. Except for Newfoundland, urban, middle-class anglophone Canadians speak with much the same accent in Vancouver and Ottawa, Edmonton and Windsor and Winnipeg and Fredericton. The greatest variety, as mentioned above, is found away from the cities, in those rural enclaves founded by settlers from different linguistic backgrounds. In the twentieth century, another source of variety arose in working-class neighbourhoods populated mainly by immigrants who are speakers of English as a second language. Their children and grandchildren normally speak like other Canadians of their age and social class, but there is some evidence for socially significant linguistic variation from this source, as described in **The peopling of Canada** above.

Phonology

Canadian English forms one branch of North American English, with historical affinities to the speech of Midland and Northern United States (Bloomfield 1948). The primary bough in the family tree for world Englishes splits the North American branch from the others, usually known as the British branch.

North America received its first permanent settlers more than a century before Britain's southern hemisphere colonies, with the result that the starting-point in the two regions was essentially different. The differences were maximized because in the eighteenth century, after the North American settlement, the English spoken in the motherland underwent several changes. For one thing, it became largely r-less, so that the *r* sound was no longer pronounced in words like *bark* [bɑːk], *bar* [bɑː] and *barber* ['bɑːbə]. For another thing, the vowel in words like *laugh, bath, chant* and *dance* came to be pronounced long and usually farther back as [ɑː]: thus [lɑːf], [bɑːθ], [tʃɑːnt] and [dɑːns]. Most Canadian and American varieties lack these features, and most Australian, New Zealand and South African varieties have them. The presence of these and other similar features in the southern hemisphere varieties link them more closely to the accents of England.

Other general features that occur in North American English accents but not in the varieties spoken in England and the southern-hemisphere countries include the following.

- the vowel contrast in words like *logger* and *lager* is generally lost, so that North American varieties have the same vowel in both words and also in *bother* and *father, bomb* and *balm* (Trudgill and Hannah 1982: 33). The North American vowel is usually unrounded /ɑ/ though it differs regionally, but the British varieties usually distinguish them as /ɒ/ in *logger* and /ɑː/ in *lager.*
- voicing of /t/ inter-vocalically when the preceding syllable is stressed: thus *city* is ['sɪdi], *little* is ['lɪdəl] and *hearty* and *hardy* are both pronounced ['hɑrdi].

Some US varieties have flap [ɾ] here, but Canadian varieties normally have voiced [d].

- nasal plosion in words like *mitten, button, fountain* and *Trenton*, where the final unstressed nasal syllable is pronounced by lowering the velum to allow the release of the stop /t/ through the nasal cavity (Chambers 1998a).

Within the North American branch, standard CE is distinguished from other varieties by two very distinctive phonological features. One is the merger of low back vowels, so that CE has only one low back vowel phoneme where most other standard varieties of English have two. Phonologically, this is the most structurally significant feature of CE. It has been a feature of standard CE from the earliest records, remarked upon as early as 1850 (Chambers 2008: 11–13). Because of it, sets of words which are distinct elsewhere are homophones in Canada. In most of the United States, for example, the words listed below are distinguished from one another in this way:

/ɑ/	/ɔ/
cot	caught
bobble	bauble
dotter	daughter
don	dawn
stocking	stalking

In these and dozens of other pairs of words, the phonological distinction does not exist in Canada, and the words in both lists have the same vowel. The vowel is usually (but not always) the unrounded [ɑ], so that *cot* and *caught* are both pronounced /kɑt/, *don* and *Dawn* both /dɑn/ and so on. For some Canadians, the vowel in both words is slightly rounded /ɒ/. What is distinctive is not the quality of the vowel but the fact that the vowel is the same in both words of the pairs.

It is noteworthy that this merger is spreading rapidly in the United States at the present time. Labov (1991a: 30–32) sketches the geographic distribution of the merger throughout Canada and the western States with a mid-western transition zone cutting across Wisconsin, Minnesota, Iowa, Kansas, Arkansas and the Texas panhandle and angling southward to California. If the rate of change continues for another generation or two, the merger will be established as a general North American feature rather than distinctively Canadian (Chambers 1999). Mergers are favoured over splits in language change, and the spread of this merger provides an instance in which a Canadian feature is disseminating southward into the large, domineering country.

The second distinctive phonological feature of CE is allophonic rather than phonemic and in that respect is structurally less significant, but it is nevertheless more salient as a marker of the Canadian accent. Many astute listeners distinguish Canadians from other North Americans by their pronunciations of words like *wife, mice, right* and, especially, *house, couch* and *about*. Canadians pronounce the diphthongs in these words in a singular way, so that outsiders sometimes claim that they are saying, for example, *aboot the hoose* for 'about the house'. That perception is not phonetically accurate, but what they are noticing is the higher vowel at the onset of the diphthong.

The process is called Canadian Raising (Chambers 1973, 2006). Phonetically, the onset vowel is mid, back and unrounded, the same vowel that occurs in simple form in words like *butt* and *rust*. Thus, in *wife, mice, right* and similar words, the diphthong is [ʌj], and in *house, couch, about* and similar words the diphthong is [ʌw]. The distinctive diphthong occurs before tautosyllabic voiceless consonants but not elsewhere: thus *wife* has [ʌj] but *wives* and *why* have [ɑj], and *house* has [ʌw] but *houses* and *how* have [ɑw], with low onsets rather than mid.

Exactly how this feature originated in CE is uncertain. One certainty is that a similar diphthong with raised onset occurs very generally in Scots English, not only in words like *wife* and *house* but also in words like *mine* and *foul* (where it never occurs in Canadian speech). The Scots have been a constant presence in Canada ever since the English language came to be spoken there. One plausible explanation is that Canadian Raising came about by adapting the Scots vowel into the Canadian sound system (Trudgill 1984, Chambers 2006).

Vocabulary

Even before Canada had a significant and widespread population, many distinctive features of the Canadian vocabulary came into being. Explorers and adventurers learnt the names of all the places they visited from the natives, and in many cases the native names stuck. Canadian place-names resound with words from the native language stocks: from east to west, Pugwash, Buctouche, Miscouche, Kejimkujik, Chicoutimi, Saguenay, Temagami, Napanee, Ottawa, Moosonee, Coboconk, Oshawa, Mississauga, Kakabecka, Wawa, Winnipeg, Saskatoon, Ponoka, Wetaskiwin, Squamish, Esquimault, Nanaimo, Tuktoyaktuk and Iqaliut, to cite just a few. Other place-names, scarcely less exotic, translate native names: Medicine Hat, Moose Jaw, Red Deer, Kicking Horse Pass, Yellowknife and Whitehorse, among them. Some places had more than one name because the indigenous name contended with an imperial one: Toronto was called York after the nondescript duke who was George III's second son, but in the end, since 1834, the Mohawk name, Toronto, meaning 'trees standing in water', prevailed.

Indigenous plants and animals usually kept their native names, such as tobacco, potato, tamarack, skunk, raccoon, beaver, grizzly (bear), moose and caribou. The European adventurers were novices in the wilds, and those who survived were the ones who availed themselves of native know-how and materials: they learnt to use foodstuffs such as pemmican, weapons such as tomahawks, watercraft such as kayaks and apparel such as anoraks, mukluks and moccasins. Because the first explorers were often Quebecois, a number of French terms attached themselves permanently to forest and plain: prairie, portage, bateau and snye (< *chenail* 'channel').

As the population of the country grew with the influxes described earlier, the distinctive vocabulary grew with it. When the land in Upper and Lower Canada was surveyed into lots for the first settlers, the main survey lines, usually a mile apart, were called *concessions*, the French term, and country roads along them are called *concession roads*. In Ontario, the secondary roads that intersect concessions are called *side roads*.

Some of the earliest political terms used in Canada were either obscure terms in England or became obsolete there, so their perpetuation in Canada and the meanings they took on make them unique. Among these are *reeve* as the political head of a county, a *riding* as an electoral district, *acclamation* as the election of a candidate without opposition and *shiretown* as the government seat in Nova Scotia counties.

One obvious area for vocabulary development comes from terms for technological innovations. Because the settlement of North America took place before the Industrial Revolution, the North American and the British branches of the language almost always developed different vocabularies for talking about machines. The automobile provides a well-known example: British English has *bonnet* for North American *hood, boot* for *trunk, estate car* for *station wagon, windscreen* for *windshield, hooter* for *horn* and so on. Similarly, British English has *lift* for North American *elevator, pavement* for *sidewalk, rates* for *taxes, lorry* for *truck, coach* for *bus* and numerous other differences in names for post-colonial developments.

Though the southern hemisphere colonies were also populated before the automobile and other technologies came into being, those colonies were still tied so closely to England that they adopted the British terms. Thus in the lexicon as well as in phonology, their closer link to the English of England is evident, and the distinctiveness of the North American branch from them is further defined.

Syntax

In matters of syntax, CE generally conforms to worldwide standards. Most regional variants are traceable to Old World sources. For example, the Hibernian completive construction *after* + present participle is heard in Newfoundland (Shorrocks 1997, Clarke 2004) and in rural areas around Port Hawkesbury, Ottawa, Peterborough, and no doubt other Canadian–Irish enclaves (Chambers

1986: 8–9). Sentences such as *Mary's after telling us about it*, meaning that Mary has recently finished telling us, are exotic to most Canadians, though not to all.

One construction that occurs in standard Canadian syntax and also in some parts of the United States, perhaps all, is the *ever* exclamation, in constructions like *Does John ever drive fast!* and *Is John ever stupid!* The meaning is highly emphatic, signifying, in these instances, that John drives incredibly fast and that he is astoundingly stupid. The *ever* in the exclamations has the meaning 'habitually, at all times' as it also does in *forever* 'for all time'. The syntax, oddly, is the same as for Yes/No questions, requiring auxiliary inversion or *do*-support, but the intonation is falling, not rising, and there is no sense of interrogation implied (Chambers 1986: 9–10).

One construction that has so far been reported only in CE is the *'cep'fer* complementizer (Chambers 1987). Syntactically, this construction has the form *'cep'fer* [ʃɛpfɛr] introducing a subordinate clause, as in *We could sit on the floor 'cep'fer the teacher would probably tell us not to.* The complementizer seems obviously to be a phonological reduction of *except for*, which has long been used as a preposition (*We're all here except for Tom*) but not heretofore as a complementizer. This usage is common in the speech of young Canadians, but there is anecdotal evidence that it is not peculiarly Canadian. Rather, it appears to be on the rise in the United States and perhaps elsewhere.

The most salient piece of dialect grammar found in CE is positive *any more*. This construction is fairly well studied in the United States (Eitner 1949, Labov 1991b, Murray 1993), though its provenance and exact distribution remain mysterious. In standard grammar the world over, the adverbial *any more* occurs freely in negative contexts, as in *Mary doesn't listen to rock any more.* In a relatively small region, *any more* can also occur in a positive context, as in *John listens to rock a lot any more.* Positive *any more* is linguistically interesting for many reasons. Perceptually, it causes extraordinary comprehension problems for people whose grammars do not include it; the sentence above simply means that John listens frequently to rock nowadays and it includes the necessary implication that he formerly did not and the incidental implication that the speaker probably does not fully approve. (Even some speakers who are users of positive *any more* fail to recognize it in citation forms and misconstrue its meaning.)

Geographically, users of positive *any more* are plentiful in the United States in the Atlantic seaboard region of Pennsylvania, and they are found in decreasing numbers in the inland regions settled from there. In Canada, positive *any more* occurs sporadically in Southern Ontario speech and then much more sporadically across western Canada (Chambers 2008: 9–11). In other words, it occurs in the region settled by Loyalists, as described in section, **The Loyalist base**, above, and it was carried westward with the Ontario homesteaders, as described in section, **Homogeneity of urban, middle-class Canadian English**, above. As such, it is a remarkable linguistic vestige of settlement history going back more than two centuries.

Semantics

Apart from the meanings associated with the grammatical constructions described above, CE offers little of linguistic interest in terms of indigenous semantics. In most respects, peculiar Canadian meanings share their peculiarities with America at large, thus underlining again the global split between North American and British varieties. Most such Americanisms are well known: words like *store, sick, fix* and *guess* have generalized their meanings to include what the British mean by *shop, ill, repair* and *suppose*. Regional meanings are abundant in Newfoundland, as might be expected, with *fish* for *cod, ballicatter* for the icy fringe on a shoreline, *fiddler* for someone who plays the accordion, *horse's fart* for a puffball, and dozens more, all beautifully documented in Story, Kirwin and Widdowson (1982; for other provincial vocabularies, see Pratt 1988, Dollinger and Brinton 2008).

In nation-wide use but peculiarly Canadian are hundreds of words and uses which arise from Canadian predilections, including *deke* 'to feint', *bang-bang* 'quick, successive actions', *house league* 'a group of teams housed in one arena' (all from hockey, or 'ice hockey' as it is called outside Canada), *skunky* for tainted beer, *salt* as a verb 'to apply ice-remover to' (as in *salt the steps*), and expressions such as *done like dinner* 'utterly defeated' and *pinch of coonshit* 'valueless'. These meanings and numerous others are recorded, many for the first time, in the *Canadian Oxford Dictionary* (Barber 1998).

Media Use of English

Canada has a federally funded national broadcasting arm called the Canadian Broadcasting Corporation (CBC), with both television and radio branches, including short-wave transmissions to Canadian military installations overseas. As a federal institution, the CBC is constitutionally bilingual. The form it takes is actually divided, with English-language and French-language (called Societé Radio-Canada) networks independent of one another under the aegis of the Ministry of Culture. Virtually all regions of the country can receive broadcasts in both languages. In addition, there are two private-enterprise national television networks, both English.

Newspapers use the language of their communities. For example, Toronto has three daily newspapers, all English, and Quebec City has two, both French. Of the major cities in the French–English bilingual belt, Ottawa has three dailies, two English and one French, and Montreal has four, one English and three French. All major cities publish newspapers and broadcast in various immigrant languages as well as the official languages.

Literature in English

Canadian literary tradition is long and distinguished. One of the great English-language literary hits of the first half of the nineteenth century – an international bestseller before such a concept existed – was the work of Thomas Chandler Haliburton (1796–1865), a third-generation Canadian from Halifax who wrote eleven volumes of stories about an itinerant clock salesman in Nova Scotia in 1835–1855. Haliburton's salesman, Sam Slick, was prized by readers in England, Scotland and the United States as well as Canada for his tall tales and worldly wisdom. Haliburton represented Slick's dialogue in a full-blown, authentic Yankee accent, and the novelty of this literary dialect helped to usher in the use of dialect in fiction that culminated a few decades later in the work of Thomas Hardy and Mark Twain.

Linguistically, Haliburton's writings provide the fullest record available of pre-Confederation accent, and have thus attracted the attention of dialectologists (Bailey 1981, Avis 1969). A few other literary works have also attracted linguistic attention. Robert Traill Spence Lowell, brother of James Russell Lowell, wrote a novel *The New Priest of Conception Bay*, set in Newfoundland in 1858; Hiscock (1977) separates features used to represent the five accents of the book, including Newfoundland English and Newfoundland Anglo–Irish. Ralph Connor's rambling novels (1901–1934) set in Glengarry County in eastern Ontario represent a mélange of accents in the Ottawa Valley setting; Pringle (1981) discusses Connor's method of representing dialect and puts the various accents in their historical places. Percy Janes's novel *House of Hate* represents the dialogue of four generations in non-standard Newfoundland English, which has been described linguistically by Shorrocks and Rodgers (1993).

Though Canadian literature was in thrall to British models in the nineteenth century, it grew progressively independent from then on. Canadian literary critics seem to believe that there is a distinctive Canadian voice in the country's mainstream literary tradition. Northrop Frye (1971: 132) said, 'No one who knows the country will deny that there is something, say an attitude of mind, distinctively Canadian, and while Canadian speech is American, there is a recognizable Canadian accent in the more highly organized speech of its poetry.' Such a claim is sociolinguistic if it has any meaning at all, and it could perhaps be elucidated or in some way concretized by linguistic evidence. That is not, however, a task that either linguists or literary critics seem inclined to take on. In Canada as elsewhere, applications of sociolinguistic methods to literature are largely untried.

The novel most readily cited as an emblem of Canada's French–English tensions is Hugh MacLennan's *Two Solitudes* (1945), which focuses on personal conflicts in Montreal, with battle lines clearly drawn on a linguistic plane. MacLennan's novel can be read as an attempt at dramatizing the ethnic and linguistic segregation within Montreal, which Lieberson (1965, 1970) charted sociologically about a quarter of a century later. But even the most sympathetic readers of *Two Solitudes* today are bound to notice that MacLennan's characters are dim stereotypes of a bygone era. They include Fr. Beaubien, a symbol of the reactionary Quebec clergy: 'The priest envisioned the whole of French Canada as a seed-bed for God, a seminary of French parishes speaking the plain old French of their Norman forefathers, continuing the battle of the Counter-Reformation.' Huntly McQueen, the shadowy financier, stands for the *maudits anglais*: 'Being an Ontario Presbyterian, he had been reared with the notion that French–Canadians were an inferior people, first because they were Roman Catholic, second because they were French. Eighteen years of living in Montreal had modified this view, but only slightly.'

The Beaubiens and the McQueens have long since disappeared if they ever existed. Even MacLennan renounced them in his last years. 'I found it the easiest book I ever wrote,' he said (Ross 1987), 'probably because I didn't know enough about the problems.' More abiding than the novel itself is the title's image of 'two solitudes', which resonates in Canadian consciousness more deeply than the amateurish novel that coined it. The continuing retrenchment of the francophone population in the province of Quebec (discussed in **The official languages**, above) brings with it the threat that the 'two solitudes' will become complete isolates unless the federal policy of bilingualism softens the provincial insularity.

Linguistic conflicts occupy modern Canadian novelists much more than class conflicts, which are the bedrock of fiction writing in the traditions of most other nations. Social class is scarcely noticed in novels set in anglophone Canada, except for the early novels of Robertson Davies, which are unconvincingly Canadian anyway because they are so freighted with late-Victorian British conventions and pretensions. More common are tensions between non-standard 'country' speakers and urban standard speakers. In *The Stone Angel* (1968), Margaret Laurence's first novel set in Manawaka, a fictitious region of Manitoba, both her main character Hagar Shipley and Hagar's husband Bram are native Manawakans but Bram is said to be 'common as dirt'. At one point (1968: 71), Bram says, 'Look, Hagar – this here one is half the price of that there one.' Hagar responds, 'This here. That there. Don't you know anything?' And Bram says, 'I talk the way I talk, and I ain't likely to change now.' In Ernest Buckler's *The Mountain and the Valley* (1952), set in the Annapolis Valley of Nova Scotia, half the continent away from Manawaka, the same conflict surfaces in dozens of incidents, as David Canaan, a young Werther in overalls, rails about the constraints imposed upon him by the backward Valley society though in the end he chooses to remain there. At one point, David attempts to run away by hitching a ride with some 'city folk' (1952: 169). Of his casual conversation during the ride, he muses, 'They were communicating with him. They were all talking as if they were all alike. He talked to them their way. There was nothing angular about their speech.' As David grows older, he notices the Valley changing around him (1952: 229): 'And the people lost their wholeness, the valid stamp of their indigenousness. . . . In their speech, (freckled with current phrases of jocularity copied from the radio), and finally in themselves, they became dilute.'

Both Laurence and Buckler were dramatizing the tensions that accompanied the urbanization of Canada in the first half of the twentieth century, including the spread of the standard dialect. MacLennan dramatized the insularity of an urban area split by, among other things, two languages. These authors are not alone by any means, and Canadian literature offers a largely unexplored lode of social lore that might elucidate and to some extent validate the social implications of linguistic research in a nation where vastness and regionality make generalizations difficult.

Current Trends

The two immigration waves of the twentieth century, as mentioned in **The peopling of Canada**, above, peaked around 1910 and 1960, but it is probably more realistic to think of them as one continuous immigration briefly interrupted by the two world wars. These immigrations effectively wiped out the Anglo–Celtic hegemony that was the heritage of the earlier immigrations. Nevertheless, the essential features of CE descend directly from the Loyalist base. The most obvious developments in the language in the last 30 or 40 years appear to augment it without altering its basic character.

As we have seen, the oldest vocabulary imported words from Inuits, Indians and *coureurs de bois*. Most of those words were necessary because the word-stock of European languages provided no equivalents for the actions and objects they named. But this importation of words is not an isolated or strictly historical event. Exactly the same thing is happening today, for exactly the same reasons, and it is happening at an unprecedented rate.

The broader base of Canadian ancestry as a result of recent immigrations influences daily affairs in many ways. One of the more pervasive is gustatory. New foodstuffs require names, and most of them retain their 'foreign' name not just for convenience but also for the sake of fashion: caffe latto, capuccino, vermicelli, linguini and countless other items of Italian cuisine, salsa from Mexico, sushi and teriyaki from Japan, dim sum from China, souvlaki, saganaki, gyros, teramasalata and other Greek items, shish kebab from Turkey, falafels and pita from the Middle East and samosa and nan from India. In a few cases, loanwords from two different languages mean the same thing, and CE ends up with synonyms: hence brochette (from French), shish kebab (from Turkish) and souvlaki (from Greek) are all names for meat roasted on a skewer, or smorgasborg (from Swedish) and buffet (from French) both name meals where diners serve themselves from a communal board. If the foreign names are considered too difficult to pronounce, descriptive terms are sometimes substituted: so sautéed *zhou dzi* (fried dumplings) are usually called 'pot-stickers' in Chinese restaurants. As loanwords come into common use, they occur with CE phonology (gyros, for instance, sounds like 'heroes') and grammar (teriyaki is an adjective preceding nouns like steak or chicken, capuccino is pluralized as capuccinos). From a historical viewpoint, by accommodating foreign words of all kinds, CE is simply perpetuating a venerable English tendency.

That ancient tendency has never been exercised more vigorously than now, when the Canadian vocabulary – indeed, the vocabulary of every modern nation – is swelling more rapidly than ever with words from technology, medicine, international politics and many other sources. Gigabyte, best-before dates, PMS, quark, glasnost, sexism, ageism, auto-immunity – these words and numerous others were coined recently, but they are already known and used in most parts of the world.

The adoption of words like these on an international scale is itself a recent linguistic phenomenon. Less than a century ago, technological and cultural innovations were much more likely to give rise to different (or partly differ-ent) vocabularies in widely separated places, as we saw in the distinctive British and American automobile vocabulary. The reason for the global spread of terms like these is the accessibility of formerly remote regions by modern communications.

Exactly the same kind of adoption is taking place at deeper structural levels as well, and for the same reason. Standard CE is undergoing changes in phonology and grammar so rapidly that there appears to be a headlong rush to re-form the language at the millennium. Using a method known as Dialect Topography for gathering sociolinguistic dialect data rapidly and efficiently (Chambers and Dollinger 2011), we have amassed enormously detailed information about CE in the 1990s (for instance, Chambers 1998b, Chambers and Heisler 1999, Chambers 2000, Boberg 2004, Burnett 2006, Chambers and Lapierre 2011). In all the changes in progress we have charted, there is a common pattern. A form with a long history as a minor variant in CE comes into increasing use by younger speakers to the point where, for the youngest group, the teenagers, it has become not only the major variant but sometimes virtually the only form they use. Lexically, this is happening with the replacement of the Canadianism *chesterfield* by *couch* (Chambers 1995) and of *serviette* by *napkin*; phonetically, with the replacement of *leisure* with [ɛ] in the stressed syllable by [ij]; phonemically, with the replacement of [hw] by unaspirated [w] in words like *where*, *when* and *whale* and the loss of yod [j] as an onset of the diphthongs in words like *duke*, *tune* and *news*; morphologically, with the replacement of past tense forms *dived* and *sneaked* by *dove* and *snuck* (all the above, and more, are discussed in detail in Chambers 1998b); and phonologically, with the fronting and non-raising of the onsets of diphthongs in words like *couch*, *scout* and *south* (Hung, Davison and Chambers 1993).

These and other changes have sometimes been attributed to the reshaping of CE based on the American model (for instance, Nylvek 1992, Woods 1993). Not surprisingly, American cultural and economic intrusion is a perpetual fear in Canada, and Canadians routinely attribute changes in Canadian culture and society to it, even in the absence of concrete evidence. Fuller information from the Dialect Topography project and other sources shows that attributing the CE changes to Americanization oversimplifies what is really happening. In coming to an understanding of the motivation for these considerable changes, the linguistic evidence leads us into a consideration of some of the cataclysmic social changes of our time.

The Future

The main historical thrust of the last fifty years, in the broadest perspective, has been the compression of space and time. Rail and sea travel are supplanted by air travel and jet propulsion, postal and telegraph communication by fax and e-mail, gas and electrical cooking by microwave, radio and phonography by television and laser disk, abacuses and adding machines by calculators and computerized spreadsheets, short wave antennae by satellites, scalpels by laser beams, carbon copies by photocopies, linotype by photo-plates and stroboscopic motion pictures by virtual reality. In 1964, when Marshall McLuhan said that the world was becoming 'a global village', his words had the ring of science fiction. Now, a few decades later, they seem very close to the literal truth.

Such global proximity will inevitably affect the way we speak. The consequences are not yet visible (or audible), but it is possible to project from discernible trends into the future. One likely result is that the various and different standard Englishes in Canada, the United States, England, Australia, Scotland and elsewhere will someday be superseded by an accent that is somehow neutral with respect to all of them. Sociolinguists are beginning to understand some of the necessary conditions that would give rise to an oceanic English.

On the one hand, we know for certain that accents are not transmitted by mass media. Listeners or viewers can be exposed to endless hours of speech on radio or television without significantly changing their own accents or grammars (Chambers 1998d). They may adopt some vocabulary items, and they may develop a tolerance for the media accent and even an admiration for the users of the accent, but they still sound like themselves. For that reason, Newfoundlanders in the outports, for instance, have retained their indigenous accents after more than fifty years of hearing mainland accents daily on the CBC.

On the other hand, we know for certain that accents are altered by face-to-face interactions between peers. People who move from one end of the country to the other come to sound – more or less – like their new work-mates or playmates. Their proficiency in the new accent is determined partly by age. For people over 14 years, the adopted accent will always be less than perfect, so that they will never sound exactly like natives even though they come to sound quite unlike the people they moved away from; for people under seven, their adopted accent will sound just like the natives; and for people between the age of 7 and 14, it is impossible to predict how fluent they will become. The inception of an oceanic English depends, therefore, upon close interaction among young people, and for that to happen the globe will have to become even smaller.

The global standard may be some years off, but one of its harbingers is already discernible. It appears that at the beginning of the twenty-first century, there is a new continental standard coming into being in North America. Some of the changes in CE noted in the preceding section appear to be motivated by the formation of the new standard. CE is participating along with every other region of the North American continent in the shaping of a superordinate standard dialect.

There are at least four clear indications that this is what is happening, all of them copiously supported by age-correlated data on specific variables from a large, representative population (Chambers 1998b: 31–33).

First, the variants that are on the rise in Canada are sometimes associated with American English but they have had some currency in CE as far back as the historical record goes. Three changes that incontrovertibly favour American variants are the lexical replacements *couch* and *napkin* and the /iː/-variant of *leisure*. Other variants on the rise are not endemically American by any definition. Though the international ascendancy of *snuck* is not documented, it is apparently gaining ground outside North America as well as inside. Yod-dropping and WH-loss, beyond any doubt, are on the increase virtually everywhere English is spoken and in all the standard accents except Scots. These changes in CE are no more American-based than are the same changes taking place right now in, say, New Zealand or England.

Second, some of the American variants that are increasing in Canada are also increasing in American regions as well. In the replacement of *dived* by *dove*, for instance, young Canadians are adopting the form that is used by Americans across the border from Canada in New York state. But on closer consideration it becomes clear that in doing so they are not choosing *the* American variant. Exactly the same change is taking place in Texas English and other southern American varieties (Bernstein 1994), where *dove* never occurred before. The younger Texans are replacing *dived* with *dove* as the past tense form of the verb exactly as the young Canadians are. So Texas English and Canadian English are both adopting a variant that was formerly a minor one. In doing so, Canada is no more 'Americanizing' than is Texas.

Third, other variables with long-standing status as American–Canadian shibboleths appear to be persisting without any change whatever. The stable and venerable American–Canadian distinctions include, for instance, pronunciation differences such as the past tense *shone* with /o/ in the United States and /ɑ/ in Canada and *vase* with /ɑ/ in Canada and /eː/ in the States, and lexical differences such as Canadian *running shoes* for *sneakers* in the United States and Canadian *tap* for American *faucet*. So far, we have identified eight pronunciation differences and five lexical differences that are persisting with no sign of change at the border. The Canadian–American border remains a dialect boundary.

Fourth, some of the changes spreading in North America are exactly contrary to Americanization. Instead, some endemically Canadian features are on the rise in American regions. The change called (aw)-Fronting, which we have been tracking in Canada for several years (Hung, Davison and Chambers 1993, Chambers 2006), is now occurring in the American mid-west (Dailey-O'Cain 1997). There, the onset of the /aw/ diphthong undergoes not only Fronting but also Canadian Raising. It is, as Dailey-O'Cain (1997: 117) says, 'a case of convergence'. Most notably, the merger of the low back vowels /ɑ/ and /ɔ/ is spreading rapidly in the United States, as discussed in §3 above. The spread of these features could lead someone to conclude that American English is Canadianizing, but we know better. In reality, they are converging.

As the North American standard language takes shape, the old regionalisms remain to some extent: varieties such as Southern, Northern, New England, Texas and Canadian remain identifiable by the presence and persistence of certain features. On top of those regional standards is a new variety or at least a developing variety in which a set of variants is shared or coming to be shared across a large region. That region apparently covers the continent, and it may spread much further. It appears that the new standard will be marked by a constellation of features from several North American varieties. Some of them will be Northern features like *dove* for *dived*, but not all of them will be. Because mergers are favoured in linguistic changes, the low back vowel merger – standard in Canada since the beginning of the historical record – will be one of them.

These features and others are regularizing across a large area in North America presumably under the influence of increased mobility that brings people from disparate regions into face-to-face contact with unprecedented frequency. The changes in CE appear to be adjustments similar to those that are reshaping many middle-class varieties in North America.

Now that Canada has become post-colonial both historically and spiritually, CE is likely to undergo a great many linguistic changes. They will come not only from global networking. Modern technology extends our reach around the globe, but in another sense the globe has come to Canada. The largest cities and towns are cosmopolitan; they make neighbours of people of diverse creeds and colours. The majority of the Canadian population no longer traces its ancestry to either the Loyalists or the British Isles. The integration of diverse peoples into the social fabric will have subtle effects just as the integration of the Scots and English did in the 1850s.

Bibliography

Avis, Walter S. (1969) 'A note on the speech of Sam Slick.' In *The Sam Slick Anthology*, ed. Reginald E. Watters and Walter S. Avis. Toronto: Clarke Irwin. xix–xxix.

Bailey, Richard W. (1981) 'Haliburton's eye and ear.' *Canadian Journal of Linguistics* 26: 90–101.

Barber, Katherine, ed. (1998) *The Canadian Oxford Dictionary*. Toronto, Oxford: Oxford University Press.

Bernstein, Cynthia (1994) '*Drug* usage among high school students in Silsbee, Texas.' In *Centennial Usage Studies*, ed. Greta D. Little & Michael Montgomery. PADS 78. Tuscaloosa: U of Alabama Press. 138–143.

Bloomfield, Morton W. (1948) 'Canadian English and its relation to eighteenth century American speech.' *Journal of English and Germanic Philology* 47: 59–66.

Boberg, Charles (2004) 'Dialect Topography of Montreal.' *English World-Wide* 25: 171–198.

Buckler, Ernest (1952) *The Mountain and the Valley*. New Canadian Library 23. Toronto: McClelland and Stewart.

Burnett, Wendy (2006) 'Linguistic resistance at the Maine-New Brunswick border.' In *Canadian English in a Global Context*, ed. Peter Avery, J. K. Chambers, Alexandra D'Arcy, Elaine Gold and Keren Rice. Special issue of Canadian Journal of Linguistics 51: 161–176.

Camu, Pierre, E. P. Weeks & Z. W. Sametz (1971) 'The People.' In *Canadian Society: Sociological Perspectives*, ed. B. R. Blishen, F. E. Jones, K. D. Naegele and J. Porter. Toronto: Macmillan of Canada. 21–50.

Cartwright, Don (1988) 'Language policy and internal geopolitics: the Canadian situation.' In *Language in Geographic Context*, ed. Colin H. Williams. Clevedon: Multilingual Matters. 238–266.

Chadwick, S. J. (1967) *Newfoundland: Island into Province*. Cambridge: Cambridge University Press.

Chambers, J. K. (1973) 'Canadian raising.' *Canadian Journal of Linguistics* 18: 113–135.

—. (1986) 'Three kinds of standard in Canadian English.' In *In Search of the Standard in Canadian English*, ed. W. C. Lougheed. Occasional Papers 1. Kingston: Strathy Language Unit. 1–15.

—. (1987) 'The complementizer '*cep'fer*.' *American Speech* 62: 378–380.

—. (1990) 'Forensic dialectology and the Bear Island land claim.' In *The Language Scientist as Expert in the Legal Setting*, ed. Robert Rieber and William Stewart. Annals of the New York Academy of Sciences, Vol. 606. 19–31.

—. (1991) 'Canada.' In *English Around the World: Sociolinguistic Perspectives*, ed. Jenny Cheshire. Cambridge: Cambridge University Press. 89–107.

—. (1993) '"Lawless and vulgar innovations": Victorian views of Canadian English.' In Sandra Clarke, ed., *Focus on Canada*. Amsterdam/Philadelphia: John Benjamins. 1–26.

—. (1995) The Canada–U.S. border as a vanishing isogloss: the evidence of 'chesterfield'. Harold B. Allen memorial issue, *Journal of English Linguistics* 23: 155–166.

—. (1998a) 'Nasal plosion and other mysteries.' In *American English and the International Phonetic Alphabet*, ed. Arthur J. Bronstein. Publication of the American Dialect Society 80. Tuscaloosa and London: University of Alabama Press. 69–77.

—. (1998b) 'Social embedding of changes in progress.' *Journal of English Linguistics* 26: 5-36.

—. (1998c) 'English: Canadian varieties.' In *Language in Canada*, ed. John Edwards. Cambridge: Cambridge University Press. 252–272.

—. (1998d) 'Myth 15: TV makes people sound the same.' In *Language Myths*, ed. Laurie Bauer and Peter Trudgill. Harmondsworth: Penguin. 123–131.

—. (1999) 'Converging features in the Englishes of North America.' In *Variation and Linguistic Change in English*, ed. Juan-Manuel Campoy-Hernández and Juan Camilo Conde-Silvestre. *Cuadernos de Filología Inglesa* 8: 117–127.

—. (2000) 'Region and language variation.' *English World-Wide* 21: 1–31.

—. (2003) 'Sociolinguistics of immigration.' In *Social Dialectology*, ed. David Britain and Jenny Cheshire. Amsterdam/Philadelphia: John Benjamins. 97–113.

—. (2004) 'Canadian Dainty: the rise and decline of Briticisms in Canada.' In *Legacies of Colonial English: Studies in Transported Dialects*, ed. Raymond Hickey. Cambridge, UK: Cambridge University Press. 224–241.

—. (2006) 'Canadian Raising retrospect and prospect.' In *Canadian English in a Global Context*, ed. Peter Avery, J. K. Chambers, Alexandra D'Arcy, Elaine Gold and Keren Rice. Special issue of Canadian Journal of Linguistics 51: 105–118.

—. (2008) 'The Tangled Garden: relics and vestiges in Canadian English'. *Focus on Canadian English*, ed. Matthias L. G. Meyer. Special issue of *Anglistik* 19: 7–21.

Chambers, J. K., and Troy Heisler (1999) 'Dialect topography of Quebec City English.' *Canadian Journal of Linguistics* 44: 23–48.

Chambers, J. K. and André Lapierre (2011) (with André Lapierre) 'Dialect variants in the bilingual belt'. *Homage à Raymond Mougeon*, red. France Martineau et Terry Nadasdi.

Chambers, J. K., and Stefan Dollinger (2011) *Dialect Topography: A Research Handbook*. IMPACT Studies in Language and Society. Amsterdam and Philadelphia: John Benjamins.

Clarke, Sandra (1991) 'Phonological variation and recent language change in St. John's English.' In *English Around the World: Sociolinguistic Perspectives*, ed. Jenny Cheshire. Cambridge: Cambridge University Press. 108–122.

—. (2004) 'The legacy of British and Irish English in Newfoundland.' In *Legacies of Colonial English: Studies in Transported Dialects*, ed. Raymond Hickey. Cambridge, UK: Cambridge University Press. 242–261.

—. (2006) '*Nooz* or *nyooz*? The complex construction of Canadian identity.' In *Canadian English in a Global Context*, ed. Peter Avery, J. K. Chambers, Alexandra D'Arcy, Elaine Gold and Keren Rice. Special issue of Canadian Journal of Linguistics 51: 225–246.

—. (2008) 'Newfoundland and Labrador English: phonology and phonetic variation.' In *Focus on Canadian English*, ed. Matthias L. G. Meyer. Special issue of Anglistik 19: 93–106.

Dailey-O'Cain, Jennifer (1997) 'Canadian raising in a midwestern U.S. city.' *Language Variation and Change* 9: 107–120.

Dollinger, Stefan, and Laurel J. Brinton (2008) 'Canadian English lexis: historical and variationist perspectives.' In *Focus on Canadian English*, ed. Matthias L. G. Meyer. Special issue of Anglistik 19: 43–64.

Eitner, Walter H. (1949) 'Affirmative *any more* in present-day American English.' Papers of the Michigan Academy of Science, Arts and Letters 35. Reprinted in *Dialects of English: Studies in Grammatical Variation*, ed. Peter Trudgill and J. K. Chambers. London: Longman. 267–272.

Frye, Northrop (1971) *The Bush Garden.*

Hiscock, Philip (1982) 'Dialect representation in R. T. S. Lowell's novel The New Priest of Conception Bay.' In *Languages of Newfoundland and Labrador*, ed. Harold Paddock. St. John's: Department of Linguistics, Memorial University of Newfoundland. 114–123.

Hung, Hernrietta, John Davison and J. K. Chambers (1993) 'Comparative sociolinguistics of (aw)-Fronting.' In *Focus on Canada*, ed. Sandra Clarke. Amsterdam/Philadelphia: John Benjamins. 247–267.

Ingstad, Helge (1969) *Westward to Vinland: The Discovery of Pre-Columbian Norse House-Sites in North America.* Trans. Erik J. Friis. Toronto: Macmillan.

Ireland, Robert (1979) *Canadian Spelling; An Empirical and Historical Survey of Selected Words.* Ph.D. thesis. York University.

Joy, Richard J. (1972) *Languages in Conflict: The Canadian Experience.* Ottawa: Carleton University Press.

—. (1992) *Canada's Official Languages: The Progress of Bilingualism.* Toronto: University of Toronto Press.

Labov, William (1991a) 'The three dialects of English.' In *New Ways of Analyzing Sound Change*, ed. Penelope Eckert. New York: Academic Press. 1–44.

—. (1991b) 'The boundaries of grammar: inter-dialectal reactions to positive *any more.*' In *Dialects of English: Studies in Grammatical Variation*, ed. Peter Trudgill and J. K. Chambers. London: Longman. 273–289.

Lachapelle, Réjean, and Jacques Henripin (1982) *The Demolinguistic Situation in Canada: Past Trends and Future Prospects.* Deirdre A. Mark, trans. Montreal: Institute for Research on Public Policy.

Laurence, Margaret (1968) *The Stone Angel.* New York: Knopf.

Lieberson, Stanley (1965) 'Bilingualism in Montreal: a demographic analysis.' *American Journal of Sociology* 71: 10–25. Reprinted in *Language Diversity and Language Contact*, ed. A. S. Dil. Stanford, Calif.: Stanford University Press. 1981. 131–57.

—. (1970) 'Linguistic and ethnic segregation in Montreal.' *International Days of Sociolinguistics.* Rome: Instituto Luigi Sturzo. 69–81. Reprinted in *Language Diversity and Language Contact*, ed. A. S. Dil. Stanford, Calif.: Stanford University Press. 1981. 218–248.

McLuhan, Marshall (1964) *Understanding Media: The Extensions of Man.*

Moodie, Susanna (1852) *Roughing It In The Bush.* Modern Canadian Library 31 [1962]. Toronto: McClelland and Stewart.

Murray, Thomas E. (1993) 'Positive *anymore* in the Midwest.' In *Heartland English: Variation and Transition in the American Midwest*, ed. Timothy C. Frazer. Tuscaloosa: University of Alabama Press. 173–186.

Nylvek, Judith (1992) 'Is Canadian English in Saskatchewan becoming more American?' *American Speech* 67: 268–278.

Pratt, T. K. (1988) *Dictionary of Prince Edward Island English.* Toronto: University of Toronto Press.

Pringle, Ian (1981) 'The Gaelic substratum in the English of Glengarry County and its reflection in the novels of Ralph Connor.' *Canadian Journal of Linguistics* 26: 126–140.

Ross, Oakland (1987) 'Suddenly you wake up and you're 80' [Interview with Hugh MacLennan]. *The Globe and Mail.* 18 April 1987. C1.

Scott, F. R., and A. J. M. Smith, eds. (1967) *The Blasted Pine.* Toronto: Macmillan.

Shorrocks, Graham (1997) 'Celtic influences on the English of Newfoundland and Labrador.' In *The Celtic Englishes*, ed. Hildegard L. C. Tristram. Heidelberg: Universitätsverlag C. Winter. 320–361.

Shorrocks, Graham, and Beverly Rodgers (1993) 'Non-standard dialect in Percy Janes' novel House of Hate.' *Regional Language Studies Newfoundland* 14. St. John's: Department of English, Memorial University of Newfoundland. 2–25.

Story, George (1977) 'The dialects of Newfoundland English.' In *Languages in Newfoundland and Labrador*, ed. Harold Paddock. St. John's: Department of Linguistics, Memorial University of Newfoundland. 74–80.

Story, G. M., W. J. Kirwin and J. D. A. Widdowson (1982) *Dictionary of Newfoundland English.* Toronto: University of Toronto Press.

Trudgill, Peter (1984) 'New-dialect formation and the analysis of colonial dialects: the case of Canadian Raising.' In *Papers from the Fifth International Conference on Methods in Dialectology*, ed. H. J. Warkentyne. Victoria, BC: U of Victoria. 35–46.

—. (2000) 'Sociohistorical linguistics and dialect survival: a note on another Nova Scotian enclave.' In *Language Structure and Variation*, ed. Magnus Leung. Stockholm: Almqvist & Wiksell International. 195–201.

Trudgill, Peter, and Jean Hannah (1982) *International English: A Guide to Varieties of Standard English.* London: Edward Arnold.

Weinreich, Uriel (1967) *Languages in Contact.* The Hague: Mouton.

Woods, Howard B. (1993) 'A synchronic study of English spoken in Ottawa: is Canadian English becoming more American?' In *Focus on Canada*, ed. Sandra Clarke. Amsterdam/Philadelphia: John Benjamins. 151–178.

Southeastern US

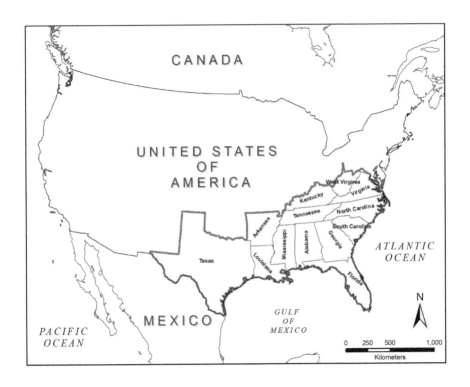

Chapter 2

White Varieties of English in the American South

Ellen Johnson

Introduction

The most widely recognized regional variety of American English in the United States is Southern English, a term that usually applies to the kinds of English spoken by whites who identify themselves as members of the cultural region known as the South. While these speakers share some language features, they differ in others. There is no single way of speaking across the whole region; several dialects can be identified as kinds of Southern English (Algeo 2003). White varieties of Southern English share most, but not all, of their features with African American Vernacular English (AAVE), which could be considered as yet another type of Southern English (Mufwene 2003). As AAVE is treated in its own chapter, however, the term Southern English will be restricted to Southern varieties spoken by whites in the region.

Background of the Region

The southeastern part of the United States does not form a single geographical region, but it does form a cultural region, loosely based upon shared interests from before the US Civil War of 1861–65. This war pitted 'The North' against 'The South', or 'the Confederacy', as the latter is sometimes called in reference to the war years. Today the cultural region of the South has as its core those states where slavery was still legal when the Civil War began, but its boundaries are not coterminous with the Confederacy, as it does not include all the states where slaves were owned, and it does include states that did not fight on the side of the South. In addition, some varieties of Southern English are spoken far from their geographic hearths by communities of people who migrated from the South, including Appalachian speakers who moved to the North Central States in search of work in the mid-twentieth century (Anderson 2003) and supporters of the 'Lost Cause' who founded settlements in Brazil after the Civil War (Montgomery and Melo 1990, Schneider 2003).

Map 1 shows the area that is most often considered to be Southern in character and language. It includes the core area of Tennessee, the Carolinas, Georgia, Alabama, Mississippi and Louisiana, along with Arkansas and Kentucky and, some would say, West Virginia. Two states that have historically been part of the South, Florida and Virginia, have lost much of their Southern culture and accents as newcomers from other regions of the United States have diluted their 'Southernness'. In Texas, the eastern part of the state was a slave-owning, cotton-growing area affiliated with other Southern states, but today Texans identify more with their own state than with either of the neighbouring South or Southwest regions. Thus I consider Virginia, Florida and Texas to be only marginally Southern. The most important division within the core area of the South is the distinction between Upper South and Lower South (Kurath 1949, Carver 1987), as exemplified in language differences between 'Up-Country' and 'Low Country' South Carolina (R. McDavid 1979 [1948]). This boundary is based on topography, with environmental factors leading to cultural differences. The Upper South includes the Southern Appalachian Mountains, whose hilly terrain was not suitable for the crops grown in the coastal plain bordering both the Atlantic Ocean and the Gulf of Mexico (Pederson, McDaniel, and Adams 1991). Upper and Lower South are now being merged linguistically with the movement of the economic centre of gravity in the South from the coast to the piedmont region, historically a transition zone between dialects. McNair (2005) writes of the two cultural groups confronting one another in Griffin, Georgia; the same scenario is played out in many piedmont area towns. Linguistic influence flows outward from economic and cultural centres like Atlanta, so the piedmont language zone where Upper and Lower South came together is now affecting the speech of both regions, while historical cultural distinctions between the two areas lessen as well (Johnson 1997).

Even in colonial times, areas of the South were culturally distinct from those of the North. Historian David Hackett Fischer (1989) traces cultural patterns based on social class, religion and region of origin in the British Isles, with the Lower South having more than its share of large landowners of aristocratic origin and belonging to the Church of England (i.e. today's Episcopalians) and the Upper South as a frontier populated by Presbyterian Scotch-Irish, Scots who had first migrated to Ulster and then to America seeking land and opportunity. The South had some sense of regional identity as a whole in antebellum times as an agriculture-based economy in contrast with the earlier industrialization of the northern United States. For agriculture to be profitable, low-cost labour was needed, hence the greater importation of slaves of African origin to the area. The presence of slaves and their descendants had a great impact on the language and culture of the whites, as well as their sense of themselves as different from other regions of the country, which were much more likely to bring in immigrants from the poorer countries of Europe (e.g. Ireland, Italy, Poland) to provide their cheap labour (Smith 2001). The Civil War (the 'War Between the

States') was the watershed event that solidified the identification of Southerners and intensified their linguistic distinctiveness as a region (Bailey 2001). Urbanization beginning in the 1880s led to dialect contact within the South, producing many shared language forms across the region (Tillery and Bailey 2003). Today some cultural and language differences remain between the Upper South and Lower South, but the southeastern United States as a whole (with the two exceptions noted previously) shares many language features as well as cultural traits, being for the most part conservative in politics and religion and having a strong sense of place and pride in its rural origins, though urban dwellers outnumber rural ones today.

Languages other than English have always been a part of the cultural landscape of the South (Wilson 2007). Indigenous languages spoken in the area at the time of settlement include Cherokee, Choctaw, Chickasaw, Mikasuki, Catawba, Creek, Seminole, Tuscarora, Koasati, Mobilian Jargon, Powhatan, Natchez, Yuchi, Caddo and others, though only Cherokee (an Iroquoian language), Creek/Seminole and Choctaw (Muskogean languages) have a substantial number of speakers today. Beside American Indian languages during colonial times, there were also the African languages spoken by newly imported slaves (Turner 2002 [1949]) and European languages, most notably French in Louisiana (Klingler 2003, Valdman 1997), but with a multilingual culture in most port cities. Charleston in 1790, for example, was a multi-ethnic mixture of English, Barbadians, French Huguenots, Scotch-Irish, Germans, Africans speaking many different languages, and Sephardic Jews from Spain and Portugal, making it a cosmopolitan centre of culture and commerce that for its time was comparable to New York City today (R. McDavid 1955, Joyner 1996), and New Orleans became a similar polyglot city over the next few decades (Eble 2003b).

By the nineteenth century, the number of immigrants to the South from outside the British Isles had dwindled (with the exception of European immigrants who came to work the coal fields of West Virginia, for example). The use of African languages died out quickly among slaves once importation of new slaves from Africa was made illegal (1808), and American Indians and their languages by and large either died out or were removed to Indian Territory (present-day Oklahoma). English had supplanted French in much of Louisiana (Picone 1997). This left the South a monolingual English-speaking region with only a few exceptions: Cuban Spanish near Tampa, as well as Seminoles in Florida, Creole and Cajun French in south central Louisiana (Eble 2003c), Cherokee in the mountains of western North Carolina and small groups of Creek speakers in Mississippi and Louisiana. The last decade of the twentieth century saw an expansive growth in the population of non-English-speaking immigrants in the region, mostly from Mexico and Central America, both in the number of speakers and in their distribution across both urban and rural areas throughout the Southeast.

English has, however, been the sole language in the South over most of its territory and history; the region includes a diversity of white dialects of English. These include Ozark and Appalachian varieties of English, the English of the Outer Banks and Chesapeake Bay, Lumbee English, Cajun English and the distinctive sounds of Charleston and New Orleans Englishes. Broad dialect areas are the Upper South and Lower South as described previously. Much of what we know about the details of Southern English phonology and lexicon comes from the large Linguistic Atlas Projects and scholarly research towards Southern English conducted by McMillan and Montgomery (1989). The Linguistic Atlas of the Middle and South Atlantic States (LAMSAS) covers the Southern states that border the Atlantic Ocean, including West Virgina but excluding Florida (Kretzschmar et al., 1994). LAMSAS was directed first by Hans Kurath, then by Raven McDavid, and for the past two decades, William Kretzschmar. The Linguistic Atlas of the Gulf States (LAGS) covers most of the rest of the South and was headed by Lee Pederson (Pederson 1986, 1993, Pederson et al. 1991). Following Kurath and McDavid's division of American English into three main dialect areas, North, Midland and South, the Upper South area is sometimes called South Midland (Kurath 1949).

The core of South Midland speech patterns is to be found in the Appalachian Mountain region of the South, discussed more fully in another chapter of this volume. This language is described in great detail in the recently published historical dictionary, ***Dictionary of Smoky Mountains English*** (Montgomery 2004a). A classic sociolinguistic study of the area is ***Appalachian English*** (Wolfram and Christian 1976). In the description of Southern English below, some Appalachian features are noted; those described as Upper South are quantitatively more common in the Southern Appalachians. The Ozark Mountains can be seen as an extension of the Appalachian English dialect, with few distinctive forms, but a similar intensification of Upper South characteristics.

Geographically part of the South, but with distinctive cultural and language traits developed in isolation from the mainland, are the barrier islands. These islands are found all the way down the Atlantic Coast, extending in the South from Virginia to Florida. The dialect of Chesapeake Bay (Shores 2000) is very much like the neighbouring Outer Banks English (Wolfram, Hazen, and Schilling-Estes 1999). The population is mostly white on these islands off the coast of Virginia and North Carolina, respectively. Residents are sometimes called 'Hoi Toiders' because of their obviously centralized version of the /ai/ diphthong (Wolfram and Schilling-Estes 1997). They have many unique vocabulary terms, and the combination of unknown words with pronounced phonological differences makes their vernacular almost unintelligible to most other Southerners (Wolfram 2003). On the islands off the coast of South Carolina and Georgia, on the other hand, most residents were black before the feverish construction of bridges, condominiums and luxury resorts began in the late twentieth century. The speech there is also quite distinct. Gullah, or 'Geechee' as it is sometimes called (Montgomery 1994: 14n), it is the only one of a very few English-based creoles in the United States, though its speakers consider it a type of English (Mufwene and Condon 1993, Mufwene 2001). (Afro-Seminole Creole was spoken in South Florida and in Texas, following the Indian Removal (Hancock 1986) and Hawaii Creole English is still in use in Hawaii.)

The parts of the South where the English language shows the most direct influence from contact with other languages are south and south-central Louisiana (from Acadian French), New Orleans (colonial French and later, working class immigrants from Europe [Coles 2001]) and Charleston (West African languages). This may change in the twenty-first century, as bilingual communities develop across the Southeast (Tillery, Bailey, and Wikle 2004). Spanish, in particular, is likely to make its mark on Southern English. Linguists are researching varieties of Hispanic English as spoken by immigrants and their descendants in several Southern locations (Wolfram, Carter, and Moriello 2004). Previously monolingual Southern English speakers are also learning Spanish in the new communicative contexts that continue to arise wherever recent immigrants arrive, though many of those learning Spanish are doing it reluctantly (Hamann 2002, Johnson and Boyle 2006). The long-term effects of Spanish on Southern English in general remain to be seen.

Phonology

The United States, unlike Britain and some other countries, does not have one single accent that is standard across all regions. The existence of these regional standards, well documented by Kurath and McDavid (1961), means that even the best educated and most influential Southerners are likely to speak with a Southern accent.

As with most dialects of American English, the features that distinguish Southern varieties are usually vowels. Crawford Feagin, following her 1979 landmark study of variation by social class in a small city in Alabama, tried to define what people meant when they referred to the 'Southern drawl'. She concluded that, despite popular belief, Southerners do not pronounce words more slowly than other speakers of American English. The phenomenon perceived as a drawl is a result of adding glides to vowels to create diphthongs and triphthongs. Words may seem slower because they contain more sounds. An example is the word bed: [be-i-ɪd]. Feagin (1997) has argued that the drawl is a result of the influence of West African speech patterns used by slaves.

Glides may not only be added, but also taken away. Perhaps the most salient variable in identifying a speaker as a Southerner by an outsider is the pronunciation of /ai/ as a monophthong rather than a diphthong. The resulting sound has been caricatured by dialect writers and imitators of Southern speech as an 'ah' sound. Unfortunately, some linguists also pronounce it this way when discussing monophthongization. The best IPA representation of the sound is [a], since it is a low front vowel, not a low central or back vowel; thus, the monophthongal variant of /ai/ is closer to the [æ] sound than it is to [ɑ]. One reason this feature has received so much attention is that it varies geographically, socially and phonologically.

While the [a] variant for /ai/ is found throughout the southeastern United States, it is sometimes a categorical shift and sometimes an allophone that alternates with [ai] depending upon the following environment. Speakers in the Upper South and peripheral areas like Texas and Arkansas historically tend to use [a] in all environments (Thomas 1997, Bailey et al. 1991), while Lower South speakers exhibit phonological variation, using [a] before voiced consonants and at the end of a word, but using [ai] before voiceless consonants. Thus the words *I, five* and *nine* would contain the monophthong, but *night* and *ice* would not. This geographical variation turns into social variation in the transition zone between Upper and Lower South, the economically important region called the Piedmont. Though the largest and most influential Southern cities were historically in the coastal region (e.g. Charleston, Savannah, Richmond, New Orleans), today the most economically important cities are in the Piedmont: Birmingham, Atlanta, Greenville/Spartanburg, Charlotte and the 'Research Triangle' Raleigh/Durham area (Johnson 1996). Thus for many English speakers in the South, the pronunciation of *nice white rice* with monophthongal [a] in each word is a shibboleth identifying the speaker as working class and/or rustic. This may change, however, since the monophthongal version of /ai/ seems to be spreading as part of the Southern Shift, a pattern of vowel change identified by researchers at the University of Pennsylvania led by William Labov. The

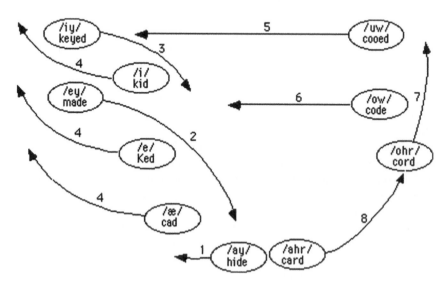

FIGURE 2.1   The Southern Shift.

Southern Shift is an important part of contemporary research on Southern English (Labov and Ash, 1997, Feagin 2003, Fridland 2001).

The Southern Shift is a pattern of chain-shifting in the pronunciation of phonemes where the vowels rotate in a different direction from the ones in the Northern Cities Shift (see figure 1). The most obvious effects of this vowel shift on Southern English pronunciation are a centring of the back vowels /u/ and /o/ and a raising and tensing of the lax front vowels /ɪ/ and /ɛ/. Thus the word *blue* sounds like [blɪu] and the word *go* sounds like [gɛu]; the word *kick* sounds like [kiyɪk] and the word *bed* sounds like [beyəd]. The /ai/ diphthong is monophthongized (see above), and the /au/ diphthong is raised to /ɛyu/. Interestingly, the raising of /au/, /ɪ/ and /ɛ/ is perceived as a lower social class feature, but the fronting of /u/ and /o/ is seen as an upper class feature. Finally, a diagnostic vowel difference separating the South from the rest of the United States is the merger of /ɛ/ and /ɪ/ before nasals, so that *gem, pen* and *Bengal* all have the vowel /ɪ/ (though words like *head* and *rest* are not affected).

Consonantal features that once were definitive of varieties of Southern English have mostly disappeared. This includes variations on interdentals similar to those found in some African-American speech (e.g. [f] for /θ/ at the ends of words like *both*) and the palatalization of /k/ and /g/ once found in coastal areas of the South as well as the Caribbean (R. McDavid 1979 [1955]). Use of [d] for /z/ in *wasn't* and *isn't* is still prevalent (Hazen 2000), but the distinction between /hw/ and /w/, which lingered longer in the South than in other parts of the United States, is no longer maintained by the generations younger than middle-aged (as is also the case for the ɑ/ɔ distinction, and the use of the aj [ay] sound in words like *tune* and *news*).

Perhaps the most distinctive consonant, or lack thereof, in the South has been the so-called 'postvocalic /-r/': any /r/ following a vowel as long as it does not precede another vowel. *Far* and *farther* would thus be subject to this deletion of /r/, but *foreign* would not be. This loss of /r/ was ubiquitous for generations born before World War II in the Lower South, for all classes and ethnic groups, but in the Piedmont is typical only of blacks and the upper social classes of whites, and uncommon in the Southern mountains (R. McDavid 1979 [1948]). The non-prevocalic loss of /r/ likely began at the time British English was losing the /r/, in the Atlantic port cities that maintained regular contact with England, such as New York, Boston, Richmond, and, most importantly for the South, Charleston. The fact that this feature spread much further inland in the South than in the Northeast can be attributed to the influence of speakers of African languages with a CV syllable structure, who would tend to delete the /r/ at the ends of syllables when they learnt English (Feagin 1997). This widely researched feature of Southern White and African American Englishes is disappearing quickly among whites; today it is heard occasionally from middle-aged males, but otherwise only from older speakers. It is still an element, however, of the stereotypical Southern accent used by television and movie actors, as discussed below, along with the drawl and monophthongized /ai/.

Morphology, Syntax and Vocabulary

The morphological forms used by speakers of standard Southern varieties are practically identical to speakers of standard varieties elsewhere, with a few non-systemic exceptions, such as *dived* being historically more common than *dove* in the South (it is less used today). Non-standard Southern speakers use a variety of non-standard preterites and past participles, but few if any are qualitatively different from non-standard verb forms used in English around the world, for example, *done* for *did* in 'I done it', *have drank* for *have drunk* (V. McDavid 1998). Likewise syntactical ways of expressing negation are virtually the same in the South as in the rest of the world, with use of *ain't* or double negation (e.g. 'He don't know nothing') common among non-standard speakers. That these non-standard grammatical forms are often considered by Southerners and outsiders alike to be particularly Southern is a result of excessive stereotyping of South-erners as uneducated. They do not seem to be more widespread in the South than in other regions of the United States among working class speakers. This section of the chapter will therefore focus on features that actually are distinc-tively Southern.

Three morphological forms found in Upper South speech are special posses-sive pronoun forms and contractions and 'a-prefixing' (*a-* is pronounced with a schwa). *A*-prefixing has been treated in several studies. *a -*, from *on* historically, as documented in especially the northern parts of the British Isles, is used with *–ing* participles in the present or past progressive. It is not used with adjectival or nominal *–ing* forms, and may not be used when the following verb begins with an unstressed syllable (Wolfram and Schilling-Estes 1998: 4–6). It is consid-ered old-fashioned, but is not uncommon. Less commonly heard are the pos-sessives that are recognized as non-standard. These possessive pronouns may be formed according to an analogy with *my* → *mine*, leading to forms like 'That's *yourn'* (*hisn*) (Wolfram and Schilling-Estes 1998: 76). In contrast, another form with regional distribution in the South Midland that is so widely used as to be unremarkable/standard is a special use of contractions. These are clauses where auxiliary verbs are contracted rather than *not*, as in other forms of American English. Examples are 'She'll not do it' and 'He's not been here'.

By far the most talked about contraction in standard Southern English variet-ies is *y'all*, likely a contracted form of *you all*, and its commonly heard possessive form, *y'all's*. It is used by speakers of all social classes across the South, in formal as well as informal contexts. (One study analysed its use by a judge in a court-room [Ching 2001].) It is often the first Southern speech feature acquired by in-migrants from other regions of the United States (Bernstein 2003). The rea-son it is so readily acquired is that it fills the second-person-plural gap in the English pronoun system. When it is used to a single addressee it is still semanti-cally plural (the 'associative plural'), referring to the addressee and his/her family, friends, colleagues or organization (Montgomery 2002). A fading South

Midland counterpart is *you'uns*, along with its extension *we'uns* (though the analogous *younuns* is part of the general Southern lexicon). Besides *you all*, the pronouns *what all* and *who all* are still common.

Two other well studied syntactic peculiarities of Southern English (white and black) are the double modals and *fixing to*. Though not allowed in other varieties of American English, some combinations of more than one modal verb are used in the South, those with *may* or *might* followed by *would*, *could* or *should*. By far the most common is *might could*, the equivalent of *might be able to* (Montgomery 1998). Far from being a stigmatized form, *might could* is used by educated speakers of Southern English in many social contexts, as is *fixing to*, meaning 'about to', as in 'I'm fixing to go'. *Fixing to* is often reduced phonologically (to [fɪksnə] and further to [fɪtnə] in black varieties); thus it can be seen as a grammaticalized aspect marker similar to *useta* in its syntax, though requiring a *be* auxiliary (Zeigler 2002).

White speakers of English in the American South use other syntactic strategies that have not been studied by linguists as much as those discussed above (for the following and other examples, see Montgomery 2004b). These include remote stressed *been* with past participles ('They've BEEN married') and completive *done* ('He's done left'), sometimes with *have* omitted, and copula deletion, especially in interrogatives ('You at home?'), all used by white speakers but to a much smaller degree than by African Americans (Cukor-Avila 2003). There is also the phonologically reduced *wasn't* with plural pronouns ('They [wəʔn] [NOTE: should be w-schwa-glottal stop-syllabic n] home'), the use of *one* to signal alternatives ('It was him or me one'), *like(d) to* meaning 'almost' ('I liked to fell'), and various inceptive markers like *go to, get to, commenced to* and others ('She got to (= started) talking about it'). These have a range of social distributions, from alternative *one* being part of standard varieties to completive *done* stigmatized as rustic.

Grammatical features that are marked as rustic or used to signal a rural identity are on the decline, in general, as are lexical items denoting referents that are or were part of rural life. These include words relating to animal husbandry and farming, especially using the labour of men and mules. Changes in technology, combined with the rise of agribusiness, have led to the loss of many terms or to their replacement with occupational jargon unknown to the general public. The demographic shift from a mostly rural society of small farmers to a mostly urban and suburban one was not complete until late in the twentieth century in the South. Thus words like *gee* and *haw* to direct a mule, or *tow sack* for a burlap bag have only died out with the last generation. At the same time, compulsory, publicly funded education did not become universal across the Southeast until almost mid-twentieth century. The concomitant increase in educational and literacy levels for all social classes has brought a host of educated terms into the general lexicon, many of which continue to exist alongside vernacular terms, for example, *firefly* and *lightning bug* Johnson 1996.

New directions in American popular culture affect the South as much as the rest of the country. In fact, the city of Atlanta is now a leader in the hip-hop music industry; it is the residence of many recording artists and the site of record labels and recording studios. Most of these artists are African Americans, but the language they are popularizing has an influence on the vocabulary of English speakers of all races around the world, reminiscent of the spread of the jazz vocabulary of an earlier era. Young, white speakers of Southern English receive, create and disseminate slang as much as any other group of young Americans, as documented by Connie Eble, whose books on college slang rely mostly on research done at Southern universities (1996, 2003a). Few of these terms, however, are limited to a regional Southern distribution.

Lexical items are spread across the South as well as nationwide via television and other media. The lexicon changes more readily than the grammar, and especially the phonology, in response to outside influences. Few regionally distributed words remain, and there are no longer sub-regions of the South distinguished by vocabulary (Johnson 1996). The only regional lexical items that are not fast becoming obsolete are terms for local foods or customs (e.g. *hush puppies, Brunswick stew,* catfish capturing or *noodling* and a *chicken stew* [an event]) or for plants and livestock that are limited in their range and related terms (e.g. *scuppernongs* or jargon limited to the large-scale production of poultry).

English Usage: Discourse Features

Discourse features that have been studied in Southern White English include indirectness and politeness, especially in the use of titles and honorifics such as *ma'am* and *sir* and in greetings and leave-takings (Davies 1997). These are addressed below after the foremost discourse topic, storytelling or narrative. The study of narrative in the Southeast has a long history. Besides linguists like Lisa Abney (1996) and Barbara Johnstone (1999), folklorists and storytellers have also been interested in Southern English narratives.

The classic linguistic study of narrative in the South is that of Shirley Brice Heath (1983). By employing discourse analysis to study educational anthropology, she was able to come up with several kinds of differences between African-American working class Southerners, upper and upper-middle-class white Southerners, and lower-middle and working class white Southerners in Piedmont Carolina. These cultures differed in who told stories, when they told stories, why they told stories and how children learnt to tell stories. Working class whites in the mill town section of a small Southern city used narrative for moralistic purposes. The story could not be told in the absence of the protagonist, or it would be gossiping, and it had to conform to a straightforward, agreed-upon version of the truth, or it would be lying. Working class white children had trouble using storytelling creatively and using verbal embellishments when these were required of them in the classroom.

Anyone who does not exhibit communicative competence in community sociolinguistic norms is often judged as rude. Adhering to norms of politeness is important in storytelling, but it is especially important in more fleeting exchanges between acquaintances and with strangers. The gallant notions of respect for elders, ladies and those in authority are encoded in the honorifics *ma'am* and *sir*. A person in a position of vulnerability is expected to respond to those in power with *yes sir* and *no sir*, or the consequences could be dire. This was especially critical in the past in interracial encounters, with blacks being subjected to punishments ranging from a mild rebuff to lynching for not demonstrating that they knew 'their place' by using honorifics with whites, avoiding eye contact while speaking and other deferential behaviours. *Sir* continues to be a requirement for many whites when facing a police officer or judge or in the case of children towards parents or teachers. In the case of addressing elders, adult whites in the Lower South have traditionally used *mister* or *miz* and the older person's first name, if white, *aunt* or *uncle* and the first name if black. ('Mrs.' was almost always pronounced [mɪz] by Southerners long before 'Ms.' was invented.)

Non-Southerners often find the rituals of Southern politeness to be hypocritical. Women often compliment one another, for example. Compliments are an expected part of language use, but they are not necessarily a sign of friendliness: the person offering the compliment may despise the other. Smiling and proclaiming oneself glad to see the other upon meeting and leave-taking are further language rituals. Speakers are 'sincere' about upholding the verbal traditions of the community, but not necessarily about the content. Finally, indirectness is another feature of politeness rituals in the South, with interlocutors taking time for several exchanges about the weather or the health of family members before addressing the real topic of concern.

Uses of English

English is used in every social context in the American South, the only exception being in the homes of the small but growing proportion of the population whose native language is something other than English and in the small businesses and workplaces of recent non-English-speaking immigrants. English is the language of government, education, public meetings and most religious services, sports events and businesses, especially offices and retail stores. Where immigrant communities are largest, other languages are beginning to be heard in the public sphere as well, however, including in the media.

In Texas there are Vietnamese and Chinese radio stations, and Atlanta has a Korean television station. The non-English language with the largest media presence (though a distant second to English) is Spanish. Spanish television stations are available throughout the region, and Spanish-language newspapers and radio stations are found in both large and small cities, and often even in rural areas.

Many varieties of English can be heard in the media, with even the newscasters at network affiliate stations showing a hint of a Southern accent. Upper class Southern speech is heard from politicians, lawyers and businessmen who are put on the air for news stories or other interviews. In some cases, television or radio voices are heard using non-standard or stigmatized features of Southern English, including in locally produced advertisements. Sports and religious shows usually demonstrate regionally identified speech, much of it non-standard. The more local the reach of the broadcast, the more Southern features appear in the speech of those who are heard on the radio.

One interesting arena for white Southern English speakers is in country music. Even non-Southerners try to sound Southern when performing country and western songs. Here the 'covert prestige' often associated with non-standard varieties becomes overtly acknowledged, with a great value placed on the masculine and rural associations of non-standard Southern speech.

Language Attitudes, Economic Trends and the Future of White Southern Englishes

The Southern accent is the most recognized and discussed of other regional dialects in the United States (Preston 1997). Unfortunately, most of the popular attention paid to the English of the South is negative, and Southern characters have long been used by fiction writers and screenwriters to portray the traits of stupidity, slovenliness and meanness by using a strong Southern white accent, thus strengthening the association in non-Southerners' minds between the way of using language and unpleasant personality traits (Johnson and Chastain 2001). Southerners are aware of the stigma their dialect places upon them when they go outside their home region. This leads to linguistic insecurity, and when white speakers of Southern varieties regularly travel or live outside the South, their speech changes, with the more salient shibboleths fading away. There is anecdotal evidence that this is happening within the region due to the influence of urban and suburban professionals moving into the South from other parts of the United States and bringing their disdain for Southern speech with them.

Variation studies find, however, that Southern English features are being maintained and in some cases strengthened, despite an awareness that there are many who consider Southern speech to be 'bad English' (Preston 1993). Southerners have traditionally had a strong sense of place, of being connected to the land, and their speech reflects their feeling of belonging, of being at home. A larger percentage of Southerners speak Standard English than ever before, but it remains a regional standard, spoken with a distinct Southern accent and sprinkled with common regional grammatical markers that, while differing from other types of English, are considered appropriate for use by educated speakers in most contexts in the South. Only written language and the most somber, 'frozen', oratorical styles omit Southern grammatical forms like *y'all* and *might could*. As instant messaging continues to vernacularize the written language, Southern syntax can be expected in that realm as well.

One reason for the persistence of distinct features in the speech of white Southerners is related to the economic trend that began in the late twentieth century that brought unprecedented growth to 'the Sunbelt'. The destruction of the region's economy resulting from the Civil War continued to make the South one of the poorest regions in the country, with its people and its natural resources vulnerable to economic exploitation, until World War II. While the effects of slavery linger on even today, the Civil Rights movement began to bring the South further into the modern economy, with the 1996 Olympics in Atlanta serving as a pinnacle for New South promoters. Business is booming.

Just as the speech of the poorest, least educated and stigmatized groups of people in our society is considered substandard, unworthy even of the label 'language', so the speech of the poorest regions of the United States has been judged to be substandard. If the economy of the Southeast continues to flourish in the twenty-first century, Southern varieties of English will become more prestigious and influential. White English speakers in the South will become less insecure about their speech. They will continue to use Southern pronunciations and grammar to display their regional identity, and they will create new regional features and norms along the way that may well spread to other parts of the United States.

Bibliography

Abney, L. (1996). 'Pronoun shift in oral folklore, personal experience, and literary narratives, or what's up with you?', *SECOL Review*, 20: 203–226.

Algeo, J. (2003). 'The Origins of Southern American English', in S. Nagle and S. L. Sanders (eds), *English in the Southern United States*. Cambridge: Cambridge University Press, pp. 6–16.

Anderson, B. L. (2003). 'An Acoustic Study of Southeastern Michigan Appalachian and African American Southern Migrant Vowel Systems.' PhD Dissertation, University of Michigan.

Bailey, G. (2001). 'The Relationship Between African American Vernacular English and White Vernaculars in the American South: A Sociocultural History and Some Phonological Evidence', in S. L. Lanehart (ed.), *Sociocultural and Historical Contexts of African American English*. Amsterdam: John Benjamins, pp. 53–92.

Bailey, G., Wikle, T., Tillery, J., and Sand, L. (1991). 'The Apparent Time Construct.' *Language Variation and Change*, 3: 241–264.

Bernstein, C. (2003). 'Grammatical Features of Southern Speech: *Yall, Might Could, and Fixin to*', in S. Nagle and S. L. Sanders (eds), *English in the Southern United States*. Cambridge: Cambridge University Press, pp. 106–118.

Bernstein, C., Nunnally, T., and Sabino, R. (eds) (1997). *Language Variety in the South Revisited*. Tuscaloosa and London: The University of Alabama Press.

Carver, C. M. (1987). *American Regional Dialects: A World Geography*. Anne Arbor: The University of Michigan Press.

Ching, M. K. L. (2001). 'Plural *You/Ya'll* Variation by a Court Judge: Situational Use', in *American Speech*, 76(2): 115–127.

Coles, F. (2001). 'The Authenticiy of Yat: A "Real" New Orleans Dialect', *Southern Journal on Linguistics*, 25(1 and 2): 74–85.

Cukor-Avila, P. (2003). 'The Complex Grammatical History of African-American and White Vernaculars in the South', in S. Nagle and S. L. Sanders (eds), *English in the Southern United States*. Cambridge: Cambridge University Press, pp. 82–105.

Davies, C. E. (1997). 'Social Meaning in Southern Speech from an Interactional Sociolinguistic Perspective: An Integrative Discourse Analysis of Terms of Address', in C. Bernstein, T. Nunnally, and R. Sabino (eds), *Language Variety of the South*. Tuscaloosa: The University of Alabama Press, pp. 225–241.

Eble, C. (1996). *Slang and Sociability: In-Group Language Among College Students*. Chapel Hill: University of North Carolina Press.

—. (2003a). *College Slang 101: A Definitive Guide to Words, Phrases and Meanings They Don't Teach in English Class*. Georgetown, Connecticut: Spectacle Lane Press.

—. (2003b). 'The Louisiana Purchase and American Speech.' *American Speech*, 78: 347–352.

—. (2003c). 'The Englishes of Southern Louisiana', in S. Nagle and S. L. Sanders (eds), *English in the Southern United States*. Cambridge: Cambridge University Press, pp. 173–188.

Feagin, C. (1979). *Variation and Change in Alabama English: A Sociolinguistic Study of the White Community*. Washington: Georgetown University School of Language, pp. 123–139.

—. (1997). 'The African Contribution to Southern States English', in C. Bernstein, T. Nunnally, and R. Sabino (eds), *Language Variety in the South Revisited*. Tuscaloosa and London: The University of Alabama Press.

—. (2003). 'Vowel Shifting in the Southern States', in S. Nagle and S. L. Sanders (eds), *English in the Southern United States*. Cambridge: Cambridge University Press, pp. 126–140.

Fischer, D. H. (1989). *Albion's Seed: Four British Folkways in America*. New York: Oxford University Press.

Fridland, V. (2001). 'The social dimension of the southern vowel shift: gender, age and class'. *Journal of Sociolinguistics*, 5: 233–253.

Hamann, E. T. (2002). 'Un Paso Adelante? The Politics of Bilingual Education, Latino Student Accomodation, and School District Management in Southern Appalachia', in S. Wortham, E. G. Murillo, Jr., and E. T. Hamann (eds), *Education in the New Latino Diaspora*. Westport, Connecticut: Ablex Publishing, pp. 67–97.

Hancock, I. (1986). 'On the Classification of Afro-Seminole Creole' in M. B. Montgomery and G. Bailey (eds). *Language Variety in the South*. Tuscaloosa and London: The University of Alabama Press, pp. 85–101.

Hazen, K. (2000). *Identity and Ethnicity in the Rural South: A Sociolinguistic View Through Past and Present Be*. Publication of the American Dialect Society 83, Tuscaloosa: University of Alabama Press.

Heath, S. B. (1983). *Ways with Words: Language, Life, and Work in the Communities and Classrooms*. Cambridge: The University of Cambridge Press, pp. 149–189.

Johnson, E. (1996). *Lexical Change and Variation in the Southeastern United States: 1930–1990*. Tuscaloosa and London: The University of Alabama Press.

—. (1997). 'Geographical Influence on Lexical Choice; Changed in the 20th Century', in C. Bernstein, T. Nunnally, and R. Sabino (eds), *Language Variety of the South*. Tuscaloosa: The University of Alabama Press, pp. 382–391.

Johnson, E. and Boyle, D. (2006). 'Learning Spanish in the North Georgia Mountains,' in T. E. Murray and B. L. Simon (eds), *Language Variation and Change in the American Midland: A New Look at "Heartland" English*. Philadelphia: John Benjamins, pp. 235–244.

Johnson, E. and Chastain, S. (2001). 'Two Views of One Place: The Dialect of Putnam County, Georgia, in the Works of Joel Chandler Harris and Alice Walker', *Southern Journal of Linguistics*, 25: 174–184.

Johnstone, B. (1999). 'Uses of Southern-sounding speech by contemporary Texas women.' *Journal of Sociolinguistics*, 4: 505–522.

Joyner, C. (1996). 'South Carolina as a Folk Culture.' Fifty-Ninth Annual Meeting Address of the University South Caroliniana Society.

Klingler, T. A. (2003). *If I Could Turn My Tongue Like That: The Creole Language of Pointe Coupee Parish*. Louisiana: Louisiana State University Press.

Kretzschmar, W. A., Jr., McDavid, V. G., Lerud, T. K., and Johnson, E. (eds) (1994). *Handbook of the Linguistic Atlas of the Middle and South Atlantic States*. Chicago and London: The University of Chicago Press.

Kurath, H. and McDavid, R. Jr., (1961). *The Pronunciation of English in the Atlantic States*. University: The University of Alabama Press.

Kurath, H. (1949). *A Word Geography of the Eastern United States*. Ann Arbor: The University of Michigan Press.

Kurath, H. (1977). *A Word Geography of the Eastern United States*. Ann Arbor: The University of Michigan Press.

Labov, W. and Ash, S. (1997). 'Understanding Birmingham', in C. Bernstein, T. Nunnally, and R. Sabino (eds), *Language Variety of the South Revisited*. Tuscaloosa: The University of Alabama Press, pp. 508–573.

McDavid, R. I. Jr., (1955). 'The position of the Charleston dialect', PADS 23.35–50, SC.

—. 1979a (orig. 1948). 'Postvocalic /-r/ in South Carolina: A Social Analysis,' *American Speech. Dialects in Culture: Essays in General Dialectology*. Alabama: The University of Alabama Press, pp. 136–145.

—. 1979b (orig. 1955). 'The Position of the Charleston Dialect', *Dialects in Culture: Essays in General Dialectology*. Alabama: The University of Alabama Press, pp. 272–308.

McDavid, V. G. (1998). 'Educational and Gender-Related Differences in the Use of Verb Forms in the South Atlantic States', in M. B. Montgomery and T. E. Nunnally (eds) *From the Gulf States and Beyond: The Legacy of Lee Pederson and LAGS*. Tuscaloosa, Alabama: The University of Alabama Press, pp. 201–215.

McMillan, J. B. and Montgomery, M. (1989). *Annotated Bibliography of Southern American English*, 2nd ed. Tuscaloosa: University of Alabama Press.

McNair, E. D. (2005). 'Mill Villagers and Farmers: Dialect and Economics in a Small Southern Town'. 'Annual Supplement to American Speech', Publication of the American Dialect Society, no. 90. Duke University Press for the American Dialect Society.

Montgomery, M. (1994). 'Introduction', in M. Montgomery (ed.), *The Crucible of Carolina.* Athens, Georgia: The University of Georgia Press, pp. 1–15.

—. (2002). 'The Stuctural History of *Y'all, You All* and *You'uns*', *Southern Journal of Linguistics,* 26(1): 19–27.

Montgomery, M. and Melo, C. A. (1990). 'The Phonology of the Lost Cause: The English of the Confederados in Brazil'. *English World-Wide,* 11: 195–216.

Montgomery, M. B. (1998). 'Multiple Modals in LAGS and LAMSAS', in M. B. Montgomery and T. E. Nunnally (eds), *From the Legacy the Gulf States and Beyond: The Legacy of Lee Pederson and LAGS.* Tuscaloosa, Alabama: The University of Alabama Press, pp. 90–122.

Montgomery, M. B. and Hall, J. S. (2004a). 'Grammar and Syntax of Smoky Mountain English' in *Dictionary of Smoky Mountain English.* Knoxville: The University of Tennessee Press, pp. XXXV–LXVI.

—. (2004b). *Dictionary of Smoky Mountain English.* Knoxville: The University of Tennessee Press.

Mufwene, S. S. (2001). *The Ecology of Language Evolution.* Cambridge: Cambridge University Press

—. (2003). 'The Shared Anscestry of African-American and American White Southern Englishes: Some Speculations Dictated by History', in Nagle, S., Sanders, S. L. (eds), *English in the Southern United States.* Cambridge: Cambridge University Press, pp. 65–81.

Mufwene, S. S. and Condon, N. (eds) (1993). *Africanisms in Afro-American Language Varieties.* Athens: University of Georgia Press.

Nagle, S. and Sanders, S. (eds) (2003), *English in the Southern United States.* Cambridge: Cambridge University Press.

Pederson, L. (1986). *Linguistic Atlas of the Gulf States: Handbook Volume 1.* Athens: University of Georgia Press.

Pederson, L. (1993). 'An Approach to Linguistic Geography', in D. Preston (ed.), *American Dialect Research.* Amsterdam/Philadelphia: John Benjamins Publishing Company, pp. 31–92.

Pederson, L., McDaniel, S. L., and Adams, C. M. (eds) (1991). *Linguistic Atlas of the Gulf States: Regional Pattern Volume 5.* Athens: University of Georgia Press.

Picone, M. D. (1997). 'Enclave Dialect Contraction: An External Overview of Louisiana French', in *American Speech,* 72(2): 117–153.

Preston, D. R. (1993). 'Folk Dialectology', in D. Preston (ed.) *American Dialect Research.* Amsterdam/Philadelphia: John Benjamins Publishing Company, pp. 333–376.

—. (1997). 'The South: The Touchstone', in C. Bernstein, T. Nunnally, and R. Sabino (eds), *Language Variety of the South.* Tuscaloosa: The University of Alabama Press, pp. 311–351.

Schneider, E. W. (2003). 'Shakespeare in the Coves and Hollows? Toward a History of Southern English', in S. Nagle and S. L. Sanders (eds), *English in the Southern United States.* Cambridge: Cambridge University Press, pp. 17–35.

Shores, D. L. (2000). *Tangier Island: People, Place and Talk.* Newark: University of Delaware Press.

Smith, B. E. (2001). *The New Latino South.* Memphis, Tennessee: Southern Regional Council.

Thomas, E. R. (1997). 'A Rural/Metropolitan Split in the Speech of Texas Anglos'. *Language Variation and Change*, 9: 309–332.

Tillery, J. and Bailey, G. (2003). 'Urbanization and the Evolution of Southern American English', in S. Nagle and S. L. Sanders (eds), *English in the Southern United States.* Cambridge: Cambridge University Press, pp. 82–105.

Tillery, J., Bailey, G., and Wikle, T. (2004). 'Demographic Change and American Dialectology in the Twenty-First Century', in *American Speech*, 79(3): 227–249.

Turner, L. D., Mille, K. W., and Montgomery, M. B. (2002) (orig. 1949). *Africanisms in the Gullah Dialect.* New ed. University of South Carolina Press.

Valdman, A. (ed.) (1997). *French and Creole in Louisiana.* New York: Plenum Press.

Wilson, C. R. (ed.) (2007). *The New Encyclopedia of Southern Culture, Volume 5: Language.* M. Montgomery and E. Johnson (eds). Chapel Hill: University of North Carolina Press.

Wolfram, W. (2003). 'Enclave Dialect Communities in the South' in S. Nagle and S. L. Sanders (eds), *English in the Southern United States.* Cambridge: Cambridge University Press, pp. 141–158.

Wolfram, W. and Christian, D. (1976). *Appalachian Speech.* Washington, DC: Center for Applied Linguistics.

Wolfram, W. and Schilling-Estes, N. (1997). *Hoi Toide on the Outer Banks: The Story of the Ocracoke Brogue.* Chapel Hill: University of North Carolina Press.

—. (1998). *American English.* Massachusetts: Blackwell Publishers, Inc.

Wolfram, W., Carter, P., and Moriello, B. (2004). 'Emerging Hispanic English: New dialect formation in the American South'. *Journal of Sociolinguistics*, 8: 339–358.

Wolfram, W., Hazen, K., and Schilling-Estes, N. (1999). 'Dialect Change and Maintenance on the Outer Banks'. Publication of the American Dialect Society 80, Tuscaloosa: University of Alabama Press.

Zeigler, M. B. (2002). '"Fixin(g) to": A Grammaticalized Form in Southern American English', *Southern Journal of Linguistics*, 26(1): 28–36.

Route of the African Seminoles

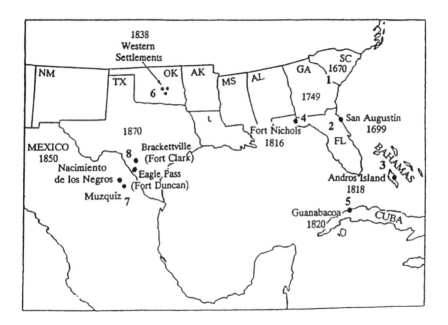

1838
Western
Settlements

NM

TX

OK   AK

MS   AL   GA   SC
1670
1

1749

6

1870

L

4

Fort Nichols
1816

2   San Augustin
1699

MEXICO
1850

Brackettville
(Fort Clark)

8

FL

BAHAMAS

Nacimiento
de los Negros

Eagle Pass
(Fort Duncan)

Andros Island
1818

3

Muzquiz   7

5

Guanabacoa
1820

CUBA

Chapter 3

Texas Afro-Seminole Creole

Ian F. Hancock

Introduction

A language sharing its origins with Sea Islands Creole (SIC, usually called *Gullah* or *Geechee*) continues to be spoken by a dwindling elderly population of fewer than three hundred in south Texas, central Oklahoma and northern Mexico[1]. Called *Seminole* ('shim-i-*no*-li') in the Brackettville, Texas community and *Mascogo* in the sister community in Nacimiento, Coahuila, Afro-Seminole Creole dates to the time of separation from Florida, following that territory being sold to the United States in 1821.

Sources of the African Maroons

During the Atlantic slave trade, the British took most of their African captives to Barbados, which they settled in 1627, before distributing them to their other colonies. By 1795, well over half of the *ca.* 2,000 Africans in South Carolina, which was founded in 1670, were from Barbados, though after 1698 they were being brought in more and more from Africa directly. South Carolina originally covered a huge area, which even included much of what is today Florida. Georgia was then Creek Indian country, and was considered to be free territory. When it became a colony by charter in 1732, it immediately tried to prohibit slavery, but because of pressure from South Carolina the attempt was unsuccessful.

Until 1749, Georgia had been getting its own slaves from Carolina, but after that date began to import them from elsewhere. Unlike Carolina, Georgia continued to bring slaves in from the West Indies, and until a halt was drawn to the importation of West Indian and African slaves in 1770, they were arriving from Jamaica, Antigua, Barbados, St. Croix, St. Kitts, St. Martin, St. Vincent, Montserrat, Nevis, Martinique, Guadeloupe, Grenada and Cuba, a pattern of settlement quite different from that in South Carolina.

Numbers of Black and Native American escapees from the English plantations in the seventeenth- and eighteenth-century Crown colonies of Carolina and Georgia were able to find refuge in Spanish Florida, where they were allowed to establish autonomous communities around St. Augustine and where they were known as *cimarrones*, a word meaning, roughly, 'fugitives'[2]. By 1821 there were already 34 Seminole settlements in northern Florida, three of which were African. According to Giddings (1858:3), the word 'Seminole' was first used to refer to the Black escapees into Florida, and was only later applied by the Creeks to the Indian fugitives.

In 1817, General Andrew Jackson and his army were sent to northern Florida to subdue the Seminoles and seize the land from Spain. They killed livestock, burned crops and destroyed the Black forts along the Apalachicola and Suwannee Rivers. At that time, the Seminoles, numbering an estimated 7,000, were welcomed by the Spanish government as they served as a buffer between themselves and the English. A royal decree from Spain dated 10th October, 1699 promised protection:

> . . . a todos los desertores negros de los ingleses que huyeron a San Augustin y que se convirtieron al catolicismo [*i.e.* to all Negro deserters from the English who fled to St, Augustine and became Catholics].

Porter (1971:164) writes of the Spaniards who were caught in Georgia and imprisoned for enticing slaves to leave Carolina and go to Florida. Those maroons did not, however, always join up with the Indian fugitives, though some did, especially later when aggression from the north became more severe. The migration of Africans to the fort in Florida had stopped by the mid-1760s:

> Spanish power in Florida, moribund for a score of years, had been extinguished . . . the British were at last in control and runaway Negroes from South Carolina and Georgia could no longer find refuge under the walls of St. Augustine (*op. cit.*, 171).

This did not mean an end to the settlement of Africans in Florida; it merely meant that the fugitives were establishing their own independent communities separate from both the Indians and the Spaniards:

> As late as 1774, blacks were apparently not living among the Seminole Indians. As slaves continued to escape from the American colonies, settlements of blacks sprang up in Florida, but their relations with the Indians were not always good (Littlefield, 1977:5).

This was going on even into the early 1820s. In a letter written at that time, Charles Pinckney (1757–1824) one of the drafters and signers of the Constitution of the United States (Powers 1998), complained about the numbers of slaves escaping from South Carolina into Florida, which by then had become US territory. Thus the Black maroons, or Afro-Seminoles, were seeking refuge in Florida between about 1690 and the 1820s; that they were mainly from Georgia during the earlier part of that nearly 140-year time span, and that most Georgian slaves were West Indian rather than directly African, supports the argument for the Caribbean origin for Afro-Seminole Creole. One clue to the early makeup of the Afro-Seminole population is provided by the words *Joo* and *Joomaican*, who are remembered as having been present during the early period.

At the time that Florida became US territory, slavery was still legal, and raids to capture free Africans (as well as Indians) created considerable problems for Governor Jackson in his efforts to develop the new territory, including further bloody conflicts; in December, 1835 Major Francis Dade and his troops were ambushed by 300 Seminole warriors near Fort King (Ocala), starting the Second Seminole War, an episode leading to the mass removal of Seminoles to Indian Territory in what is today Oklahoma. By 1834, 3,824 Indians had been removed to the west. The war lasted until 1842, by which time 4,420 Seminoles had surrendered and been sent West. From 1855 to 1858 the Third Seminole War (also known as the Bowlegs' War) took place, when Billy Bowlegs and his family were captured and deported to Indian Territory. Only about 300 Seminoles – almost all of them Indians – remained in Florida, where they had been granted five million acres of land further south in the Everglades. The first Indian Seminoles from British territory were Oconee people from Milledgeville, Georgia, who moved into Florida in 1750, over half a century later than the first African escapees. These were joined by the Muskogee (*cf. Mascogo* as a Seminole ethnonym), and following them were the Apalchicola, Chiaha, Hitichi, Sawokli and Tamathli, all of whom lived in the River Chattahoochee area in western Georgia, and all of whom spoke dialects of Hitichi. In 1767 they were joined by the Maskogee-speaking Eufala from Alabama, and in 1788 other Maskogee-speaking groups also joined them. Following the Creek War in 1813–1814, the number of Indian Seminoles tripled because of new arrivals from Georgia and Alabama – the Yuchi from Georgia, the Alabama (from Alabama), the Yamassee and the Apalachee. Today, the Indian Seminoles in Florida speak two quite distinct languages, both of them Mushkogean: Muskogee and Mikasuki. Groups of Black Seminoles left Florida for other places as well; some went to the Bahamas (Wood 1980, Howard 2002), some reportedly to Guanabacoa in Cuba, and others were invited to stay with the Cherokee. Still others decided to remain in Florida.

Oklahoma

In 1849, some of the Oklahoma settlers applied to the Mexican government for permission to go and live there, possibly because they believed they would be more at home in a Hispanic environment and perhaps could speak Spanish, but particularly because almost as soon as they had arrived in Indian Territory, the US government declared them legally to be slaves, while slavery had already been abolished in Mexico some twenty years before. A group of about 500 Black and Indian Seminoles left Oklahoma in the late fall of 1849, crossing Texas where they were joined by two hundred Kickapoo Indians in the Brazos river valley near Waco, and crossed into Coahuila, Mexico in July 1850. At first the Black Seminoles settled in Moral, not far from the Texas border, while the Indian Seminoles settled separately at La Navaja and the Kickapoo at Guererro. Later they moved a hundred miles further into Mexico to Musquiz, soon after that moving a few miles away to El Nacimiento de los Negros, with a few families going instead to Matamoros. The Kickapoo moved to the nearby colony of El Nacimiento de los Indios, but almost all of the Indian Seminoles decided to return to Oklahoma (Opala 1980).

Slave raids continued even in Nacimiento, however, led mainly by US Army Captain Warren Adams who was especially concerned with recapturing slaves who had escaped from Texas; some 3,000 were living as fugitives in the Sierra Madre mountains. While the effects of these raids hurt the Seminoles, much greater losses resulted from a smallpox epidemic brought back from an encounter with the Comanches in 1857, which left 74 people dead.

During their move West the Seminoles also encountered other Indian languages such as Cherokee and Biloxi; in Mexico and Texas they interacted with speakers of Kickapoo, Lipan and other languages; the word *ma:skô:ki* (Haas 1940:49, Loughridge 1964) is the Creek self-designation; people of African descent are called *(s)tilûsti* in that language. The Mascogos or Black Seminoles today do not speak any Indian languages, although individuals knowing some words and expressions were alive into the 1970s and have been recorded (e.g. *kokka-yenna* 'where are you going?' *kwa-he* '(I'm going) home') But the fact that they were employed as interpreters for the US Army a century before that is evidence enough that they were familiar with various Native American tongues.

Mexico

In Mexico, the Black Seminoles met another Creole-speaking group who were already there. These were the Black Creek who, like the Afro-Seminoles, were originally Africans who had become acculturated to the Indians they lived with without losing their Creole language. They were the Africans who lived with the Upper Creek in Georgia, and who had also been sent West to Indian territory. While the Afro-Seminoles, who lived with the Lower Creek and others in Florida, left Tampa Bay by boat for New Orleans and travelled to Indian Territory via the Mississippi River, the Black Creek reached Oklahoma overland. They were brought to Coahuila and left there by their Indian owners, who had been negotiating for land for them since 1834. In addition to these two groups, the community was also being joined by 'state-raise' men and women escaping from slavery in Texas via an underground railroad leading south into Mexico. Such families as the Gordons and the Shields descend from these fugitives. Although members of the Brackettville and Nacimiento communities recognize their various origins and are pretty well aware of which family is Black Creek and which is Seminole or one of the smaller contributing groups, the commonest designation used by everybody, especially with outsiders, is Seminole.

Texas

In 1870, following negotiations with Mexico, the American government sent US Cavalry Captain Franklin Perry to Nacimiento to recruit the Seminoles, because of their reputation as fighters and because of their familiarity with Native Americans, to come and help the US Army drive the Plains tribes out of West Texas so that settlement there would be less of a problem for the Whites. The Seminoles agreed, and garrisoned themselves under the leadership of General Bullis in Fort Duncan at Eagle Pass in Maverick County, and Fort Clark at Brackettville in Kinney County, in south Texas. They were successful, and continued to serve the United States until they were discharged in 1914. For three more years they lived on their own reservation at Fort Clark, but this was taken from them, and since 1917, they have lived across the highway in Brackettville. Some returned to Nacimiento, and others have gone to live in the neighbouring towns of Del Rio, Eagle Pass, Ozona and elsewhere. Some even live now in California, St. Louis and New York, and still make trips from time to time to Brackettville at New Year, on Juneteenth and for Seminole Day in mid September.

The Seminoles were never informed of their rights as American Indians, and later attempts to be included on the Seminole Register and to obtain land of their own were ignored. As Woodhull says,

> General Bullis was greatly honored, and his name and fame are held in reverence by the people of the Southwest frontier, but his scouts have been disbanded and their families have been moved off the Reservation at Fort Clark. They are not entitled to consideration as Indians, because they did not register under some provision of Congress, of which they knew nothing, and they get no consideration as negroes (1937:127).

On September 16th, 2007, a delegation from Oklahoma led by Representative Angela Molette (Tuscaloosa Ohoyo) officially confirmed the Black Seminoles as the United Warrior Band of the Seminole Nation (one of the so-called 'Five Civilized Tribes') in a ceremony in Brackettville, Texas at which Seminole Negro Indian Scout Association President William Warrior was sworn in as tribal chief.

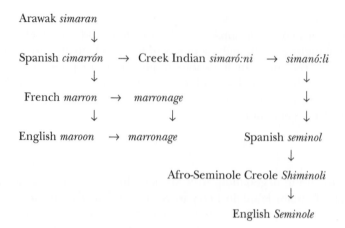

Arawak *simaran*
↓
Spanish *cimarrón* → Creek Indian *simaró:ni* → *simanó:li*
↓ ↓
French *marron* → *marronage* ↓
↓ ↓ ↓
English *maroon* → *marronage* Spanish *seminol*
↓
Afro-Seminole Creole *Shiminoli*
↓
English *Seminole*

The Language

The existence of the Seminoles' language was kept from outsiders until 1976. Joe Dillard, whose *Black English* was for many years the standard work on African-American speech reports that his field trip to Brackettville 'tended to confirm the notion that the dialect of the Black adults is essentially that of Black English everywhere in the United States' (1972:182). And Kenneth Wiggins Porter, who had surely worked more closely with the people for over a period of thirty or more years than any other outsider, expressed 'embarrassment and surprise' at having worked with the Seminoles for so long without ever having learnt of their language (personal communication, July, 1976). He had earlier called their speech 'perfectly understandable English' (Haynes 1976:3); thus two short stanzas in something that he called 'Seminole Speech' were reproduced in an article by Christopher Evans entitled 'A Scout's Honor' which appeared in the March 25th, 1990 issue of the *Fort Worth Star Telegram* on pages 7 and 8, but which in fact are written in an Uncle Remus-like English using impressionistic orthography, rather than in Seminole, of which Porter by his own admission was unaware:

An' den, ah wuz a trablin'	Ouah faith an' prayuhs dey wuh too weak
Wid a hoss atween mah knees	To sabe the body whole.
Back to Nacimiento	Ol' Satan 'stroy de libin' man,
To de springs and cypress trees!	But he could not tetch de soul!

In actual Seminole, these verses would be

En den ah binnuh trabble	We fait' en preh dem bin dess too weak
Wit hoss 'tween me knee	Fuh sabe de whole a we body

Back 'gen duh Nassum-yennuh   Ole Sadant 'stroy de natchul man,
Duh de worruh en cyp'uss chree!   But e nubbuh tetch e soul!

In his unpublished book on the life of John Horse, Porter (1947) likewise includes several samples of what he considered to be Seminole Creole; thus he has John Horse saying

'I spec's mebbe dey's Injuns likes 'em almos' as much as de w'ite folks! Suah seems lak dey's got mighty sca'ce, anyhow . . . seems lak dey day ain't no gophuhs lef' in dis whole country Ah k'n lay mah han's on! . . . dat boy heah again . . . de one wid de gophuhs'.

'Less'n de head ob dis-yeah snake catches onto he tail befo' he cross de ribbuh dis trick ain't gwine tuh wuhk! Lawdy lawdy! But dis am one smaht trick! To mahch we across behin' dat camp, across de ribbuh, back aroun', an' obuh again! Smaht as dat fiah-trick yestiddy—and not such hahd wuhk! Wonduh who t'ought dem up? Abraham? Dat ole John Caesar? Mebbe Jumpuh? Osceola hissef? Whoebbuh it wuh, he mighty smaht man—smaht lak Ah'd lak to be. Ah reckon dem w'ite folks'll stay in dey camp now—less'n dey 'cides go on back wheh dey come f'om an' wheh dey belongs! Lawdy lawdy! Wish't I had one ob dem fah-seein' things so Ah cud see de faces ob dem ossifuhs as we mahch past!'.

This is remarkable, in light of the fact that Dr. Porter lived with the Seminoles, on and off, for over thirty years.

Learning about Seminole

My own knowledge of the existence of the language began as a hunch. In 1975 I met a graduate student at The University of Texas who was writing a thesis on state military history. He told me he had visited Brackettville to tape-record an interview with a man, a 'Black Seminole', whose father had served as a scout for the Texas Rangers in the early nineteen hundreds. I had never heard of Black Seminoles, believing (like most people at that time) that Seminoles were Native Americans and that they lived in Florida. Assuming a connection with Florida on the basis of the name, my curiosity led me to the works of Arthur Wiggins Porter, which provided much of the history outlined here. The fact that the Black Seminoles were escapees from the Georgia plantations suggested the possibility that they were Gullah speakers, and that perhaps they had brought Gullah with them on their journey west. I asked to borrow the tape, and it was clear from listening to Caesar Daniels, who was being interviewed, that there was considerable interference in his English from another system, which I recognized as creole. I published a paper based on that tape before deciding to visit Brackettville for myself the following year (Hancock 1975).

In the summer of 1976 I drove to Brackettville, which is located about thirty miles from the Mexican border on Highway 90, and went straight to the town hall seeking information. I asked about language, and was told that the Seminoles did not have their own language, that they spoke English, but that some spoke Spanish too. I got the same answer again elsewhere, and finally found myself in Dimery's Bar, a local social centre frequented by the Seminoles. Here, not knowing that my visit was already expected thanks to a quick phone call, I casually led up to the topic of language with the lady standing behind the bar, Lilly-Mae Dimery – but I was again told that there was no special Seminole language. I decided at that point to say something in Sea Islands Creole, to see whether it would elicit a response: I thought that if I sounded like a lunatic it wouldn't really matter, because I'd be gone for good. In my best approximation of that language, I said 'is it really true that you don't have your own way of speaking among yourselves?' ('duh chrue fuh chrue say hunnuh nuh ha hunnuh own way fuh talk munks all a hunnuh?'). But instead Ms. Dimery set down her tray, pointed at me and told me to wait right where I was. The bar had become completely quiet. She got on the phone and within minutes a grim looking lady came striding in and I was asked to repeat what I had just said. It was the late Ms. Charles Emily Wilson, schoolteacher and historian for the Black Seminoles. She paused for a few seconds, then came back with a long response in Gullah that I understood perfectly. We continued like that for a while, and she asked me to come to a community meeting later that evening, because (she said) there were people who would be very interested to meet me. I learnt there that the Seminoles had been isolated for so long, that they were quite unaware that creole languages very much like their own were spoken elsewhere in the world by millions of people. Understandably they were puzzled as to how I, an outsider, could have known their language. On subsequent visits I invited Jamaican and Sierra Leonean friends along, and in 1995 I arranged for the Brackettville Seminoles to meet in Atlanta and talk to the Sea Islanders for the first time in perhaps more than two centuries. Their comment was that they sounded as though they were trying to speak Seminole, but were not getting it quite right.

In fact Afro-Seminole Creole (ASC) is not the same as SIC, but the two are closely related and descend from the same parent creole, for which I am reserving the label *Gullah*. Sea Islands Creole has increasingly metropolitanized under the influence of the English that surrounds it; ASC has undergone far less anglicizing influence, being spoken for much of its existence in the environments of Spanish and various Native American languages. Sea Islands Creole has African influences not found in ASC, traceable to the influx of (especially Sierra Leonean) peoples who were brought into Georgia and Carolina after the Seminoles had left that area for Florida. Afro-Seminole Creole is most like the SIC found in the writings of Jones. Aspects of its structure and lexicon have been described elsewhere (Hancock 1977, 1980, 1986, 1993, 1998, 2002), but a few characteristics of the language may be noted here.

First of all, it lacks the non-English allophones described by Turner such as [ɸ], [β], [ʝ], [ç], etc. and much of the Mende and other African-derived lexicon found in SIC. Nevertheless ASC contains about forty words of African provenance, some half of which are traceable to KiKongo/KiMbundu and the balance to languages of the Guinea Coast. On the other hand it has a number of words of American-Indian and Spanish origin not found in SIC. Some are given here; further examples and discussion are found in Hancock 1998.

With matches in Bantu: *oolah* 'bedbug', *pingy* 'cooking pot', *cootie* 'stunted pig', *teemuh* 'dig a hole', *zoondoo* 'a hammer'.

With matches in Twi: *Cuffy* 'male given name', *Cudjo* 'male given name', *kunkie* 'a tamal'.

With matches in Upper Guinea languages: *boontuh* 'buttocks', *chikka-bode* 'teeter-totter', *tabby* 'mud daub', *chooklah* 'girlfriend', *ninny* 'breasts'.

The English items match in the main those found in other Anglophone Atlantic creoles, pointing to both place (Southwestern England) and time (the eighteenth century).

From SW English dialects: *weekaday* 'weekday', *mole* 'fontanelle', *yeddy* 'hear', *leff* 'leave', *broke* 'break', *loss* 'lose', *ees* 'yeast', *ood* 'wood' (see Hancock, 1994).

From Scottish English dialects: *pit* 'put', *snoot* 'snout', *wurrum* 'worm', *gray-tuh* 'grate', *bresh* 'brush'.

Palatalization of initial velars in such words as *gyal, gyaad'n, gyaalic, kyandle* as well as the articulation of <oi> as [aI] in such words as *liyer, nize, spile, jine* and *piz'n* point to eighteenth century English phonology.

From Spanish: *banyuh* 'wash', *kwahah* 'make cheese', *matatty* 'grindstone', *soakettuh* 'mud', *beeoleen* 'violin', *calpintero* 'woodpecker', *treego* 'rice'.

From Indian languages: *suffki* 'corn porridge', *stammal* 'ground corn', *pol-eyjo* 'hominy', *polijotee* 'a corn-based drink'.

There are words for which no etymology have so far been found, such as *babba* 'carry on the back', or *skiffy* 'vagina' (though cf. Krio *bamba* 'carry on the back' and Bahamian Creole *skiff* 'young woman').

Similarities with other creoles

It has been argued by Haynes that ASC is not a creole (Haynes 1976), by Leap that it is 'Indian English' (referred to in Haynes), and by Drechsel (1976) that it is relexified Mobilian Yamâ (a Choctaw-based pidgin), who espoused the general polygeneticist argument that it is a product of local origin and development and not the result of diffusion from a common anglophone creole base. But it is a creole and, predictably, most like SIC. It differs from that language in a number of ways, probably due to retention of features lost or obsolescent in the latter, where the post-nominal plural *dem*, for example, now functions as an '& Co'. marker only: *John dem* 'John and his family/group' but additionally in Seminole *book dem* 'books'.

Early SIC texts show *no* as a preverbal negator, and this is the only means of negating in ASC: *E nuh shem* 'he didn't see her'. SIC now generally negates with *ain't* (*E ain' shum*). This hasn't happened in ASC since the future marker there is *en* (< *gwen* < *gwine* < *going*).

As in archaic Jamaican Creole (but not recorded for SIC) there are the forms *warrah* and *darrah* for 'what' and 'that'; like the Caribbean but not the African anglophone Creoles, ASC has the construction *Ah gi um worruh fuh e jrink* ('I gave him water (for him) to drink', *cf.* Krio *Ah gi am watta foh (leh e) drink*).

Atlantic anglophone lexical items widely found in related creoles include *lukka* 'like, as', *nuff* 'plenty of', *nummuh* 'only', *shoes* 'shoe', *yaze* 'ear', *teet* 'tooth', *wisseh* 'where', *do-mout* 'doorway', *big-yie* 'envious', *cut-yie* 'give a glance of anger', *yie-worruh* 'tears', *moon* 'menses', *day-clean* 'daybreak', *han* 'arm and hand', *foot* 'leg and foot'.

State of the language today

Unlike SIC, which appears to be disappearing due to anglicization, ASC is disappearing because it is not being transmitted to subsequent generations. Nor will its speakers reveal their knowledge of ASC to casual outside enquiry. When I was standing behind a bench in the cemetery at a dedication ceremony some time ago, a lady some distance away hailed a friend who was sitting right in front of me in English. When she reached her, she stooped to kiss her, and repeated the greeting in her ear, this time in Seminole. The oldest fluent speakers are now in their sixties, and while younger people can understand much of it, they cannot reply in the same language. Children can neither speak nor understand it. Influence from English is evident in the Texas community, though not in Nacimiento, where Spanish is now the main language of the village. But more African words are remembered and used there, and older pronunciations of some items, such as *choo-eh* 'spill', now *trowway* (< 'throw away') in Brackettville. In both communities, speakers claim that *their* parents and grandparents spoke an even more remote variety, which even they had trouble understanding.

There is ongoing discussion of seeking funding to establish a summer school in Brackettville, in order to teach the language and history to the present generation.

A Grammatical Description of Texas Afro-Seminole

Nouns and pronouns

Nouns do not usually change for plural by adding an *-s* at the end as in English; a few words like *day* and *ting* sometimes take a final *-s*, and the word *chile* has its own plural *chirren*, but the usual way to show that there is more than one of anything is to follow the word with *dem*:

De man-dem wey binnuh wuck dey
'The men who were working there'
Ah en talk tuh me frien' dem
'I'm going to talk to my friends'
If there is a number before the noun, the *dem* is not necessary:
Fo uh me frien'
'Four of my friends'

The same word *dem*, when placed after someone's name, means that person and his family or group of friends:

We duh gwen siddung long wit Louis-dem
'We're going to sit with Louis and his family (or Louis and his group)'
Kay-Kay-dem done eat up all we tettuhpoon
'Kay-Kay and her friends have eaten all our sweet potato pudding'

Possession is shown by putting the word for what is owned or possessed directly after the owner, without an apostrophe *-s*:

Pompey dahdy
'Pompey's father'
John Horse hoss
'John Horse's horse'
Me ahnty neighbuh Toyota
'my aunt's neighbour's Toyota'

Some groups of words which can go before nouns are:

Demonstratives

dis	'this'
dish-yuh	'this', close by
da	'that' (*dat* when emphatic)
darra	'that'

dem	'those'
dem-yuh	'these'
yanduh	'those', far away

Adjectives

big	'big'
lilly	'little'
hongry	'hungry'
State-raise	'non-Seminole'
Jellie	'jealous'
Hasty	'agitated, nervous'

Possessive pronouns

me, muh, my	'my'
you, yuh, hunnuh	'you' singular
e	'his, her, its'
him	'his, her, its', emphatic
we	'our'
hunnuh, yall	'your'
dem	'their'

Hunnuh is only a plural pronoun in most related creoles, but this is not the case in ASC. Possessive pronouns (and demonstratives) go before adjectives. If the possessive pronoun comes at the end of a sentence, it is followed by *own*:

> *Darra-dey cah duh we own*
> 'That car is ours'
> *E nuh look lukkuh e own*
> 'It doesn't look like his/hers'

The same word *own* can also go with a few other words:

> *Duh who-dat own?*
> 'Whose is it?'
> *Dishyuh mus be somebawdy own*
> 'This must be somebody's'

Articles

One, uh	'a, an'
De	'the' singular

| Dem, de | 'the' plural |
| Some | 'some' |

Pronouns that go before nouns (possessive pronouns) have already been listed above. Other kinds of pronouns are the ones that go in front of a verb (subject pronouns), and those which go after a verb (object pronouns). They have almost the same form as the possessive pronouns:

Subject pronouns

Ah, me	'I'
You, hunnuh	'you' singular
E, him	'he, she, it'
We	'we'
Hunnuh, yall	'you-all'
Dem	'they'

The word for 'I' is nearly always *Ah*, but *me* is sometimes used in emphatic constructions, and before negative *nuh*, especially in the expression *me nuh know* 'I don't know. *E* is also the commonest word for 'he' or 'she' or 'it', but *him* is used for emphasis very frequently.

Object pronouns

Me	'me'
You, hunnuh	'you'
Um, rum	'him, her, it'
We	'us'
Hunnuh, yall	'you-all'
Dem	'them'

The form of *um* [əm] with an *r*, i.e, *rum* [rəm], is only used when the word before it ends in certain vowels; this is the same in West African Krio and in Sea Islands Gullah:

G'am ([gæm] = gi um) tuh rum
'Give it to her'
Ah cyan' membuh rum
'I can't remember it'

Verbs

In English, the different forms of a verb are shown by adding different endings to it, *e.g.* walk, walk*s*, walk*ed*, walk*ing*. In Seminole, the basic form of the verb does not change like this. Instead of adding endings to it, separate words are placed in front of it. This is typical of creole languages everywhere.

In creoles, and therefore in Seminole, more importance is attached to the nature of something happening than to the actual time it happens. In Seminole there are two words to express the nature of the action (called its *aspect*) and two words to express the time of the action (its *tense*). These can be combined with each other to make more complicated structures. The aspect words are

Duh, uh   indicating that action is in progress
                 or happens usually or habitually,

and

Done   indicating that an action is completed.

Uh is the form of *duh* that is used after the tense word *bin*, listed below (*binnuh* = *bin duh*).

It is important to remember that these have no reference to time. *Duh* can be used with the tense words to indicate continuous action in the past or future, and *done* can refer to something that will be completed at some time in the future that has not even begun yet, or else was completed before some time in the past, also by being used with the tense words. The tense words are

Bin   indicating action before now,

and

En, gwen   indicating action in the future.

If action now (*i.e.* in the present) is expressed, it is done so with *duh* since if the time of the action is now, that action must be in the process of happening. When the verb alone is used, the time it refers to is past. This is not true of some verbs, which refer to actions which seem to be independent of time, like *know* or *want*.

The different combinations and meanings of these can be understood more easily in the following examples:

With no tense or aspect words

Ah chry fuh do um
'I tried to do it'
Ah tell de man dis mornin
'I told the man this morning'

Molly joog me good wit e pin
'Molly stuck me hard with her pin'
Ah know how fuh shet um
'I know how to shut it'
Wuh else yuh wan'?
'What else do you want?'

When the verb alone comes after the word *fuh*, and there is no subject pronoun, the *fuh* means 'to':

Ah bin too bex fuh talk tuh rum   'I was too angry to speak to her'

When a subject pronoun comes before *fuh* and a verb, then *fuh* means 'must' or 'should':

Ah fuh talk tuh rum	'I should talk to her'
Ah bin fuh talk tuh rum	'I should have talked to her'
Hunnuh nuh fuh jrink da worruh	'You mustn't drink that water'

With bin

Meck e bin churray um?	'Why did he throw it away?'
Dem bin nyus fuh talk Simanole	'They used to speak Seminole'
Dem bin pit e dahdy een jail	'They put his father in jail'

The last sentence would also be the translation of 'his father was put in jail', because there is no passive in Seminole:

Dem wale me	'I was beaten; they beat me'
Dem tief e car	'her car got stolen; they stole her car'

With en

The future word *en* has several other forms, such as *gwen, gwine, ennuh, gwunnuh* and so on. The pronunciation without the g-seems to be the most common, and probably existed in the creoles from very early on. In Trinidad Creole the future word *go* has another form *oh*, and in Saramaccan Creole spoken in South America, the only form now is *oh*. Even in American Black English, 'I'm gonna do it' has the variant pronunciation 'I'm 'onna do it' and even 'I'm uh do it'.

Hunnuh en fin' we deh	'You will find us there'
De sperrit-dem en kyah you 'way	'The spirits will carry you off'
Hunnuh gwine dead too	'You-all will die too'

With duh

Ah duh chry fuh do um	'I am trying to do it'
Molly duh cratch e so foot	'Molly is scratching her sore leg'
Ah fuh duh talk tuh rum	'I should be talking to her'
Dem duh jouk um	'They're teasing him'
Him duh go tuh school	'He is going to school'

Notice that in the last example, 'he is going to school' can have two different meaning, as in English. It can be the answer to 'where is that boy on his way to now?' and also to 'what is he doing these days? Some creole languages have different constructions for each of these.

With done

You done bruck um fuh chrue now	'you've really broken it now!'
Ah done tiyah fuh read	'I have become tired of reading'

Some verbs used with *done* can be translated with 'become' as well, when there is no object following:

E done fix	'It has become fixed'
E done cook	'It has become cooked'

Compare these with

E done fix um	'He has fixed it'
E done cook da poke	'He has cooked that pork'

Bin *with* done *and* duh

Bin duh is usually pronounced *binnuh* in ordinary speech:

All me peepil binnuh talk um	'All my people used to speak it'
Dem binnuh shout een de chuch	'They were singing in the church'
Ah bin done shet um suh tight	'I had shut it so tightly that I
tell ah couldn opin um 'gen	couldn't open it again'
E bin done tell me bout you befo	'She had told me about you before'
Ah bin done duh walk chree hour	'I had been walking for three
befo ah reach deh	hours before I reached there'

En *with* done *and* duh

By dis time tumorra hunnuh en	'By this time tomorrow, you'll
done spen two whole week yuh	have spent two whole weeks here'

Ah hope seh hunnuh en done	'I hope you'll have stopped
duh meck all da nize een a while	making all that noise in a while'
Hunnuh en uh see me, nuh worry	'You'll be seeing me, don't worry'

Duh becomes *uh* after *en*, in the same way as it does after *bin*.
In slow or careful speech, it stays as *duh*.

Some other verbs

Seminole has taken some other auxiliaries from English. These are *must, could* and *would*, and their combinations *mussa, coulda* and *woulda*:

Ah nuh bin know seh ah could do um	'I didn't know I could do it'
Ah shonuff would like fuh go too	'I'd sure enough like to go too'
Ah coulda tell you dat easy	'I could have easily told you that'
E woulda spile fuh chrue	'It would really have spoiled'

Two other verbs with characteristic pronunciations in Seminole are *ha* ('have') and *leh* ('let'):

Dem chillen nuh ha nuttin fuh do	'Those children have nothing to do'
E ha fuh git back fuh school	'She has to get back to school'
Leh we go, bubbuh!	'Let's go, sonny!'
You nuh bin ha fuh la'm go	'You didn't have to let him go'
Ah nen leh hunnuh een	'I'm not going to let you in'

The BE verb

'Be' here covers all the different forms of that verb – is, am, are, was, were, being and so on. In Seminole, there are different ways of saying this.

'Be' between nouns is duh *in the present tense,* (gw)en be *in the future, and* binnuh *in the past:*

Him duh de o'des one aroun yeh	'He's the oldest one around here'
Mr. Toughtry bin duh lyer	'Mr. Toughtry was a lawyer'
E bin wan' fuh be lyer	'He wanted to be a lawyer'
Duh da e en be	'That's what he's going to be'

Duh is also used as a 'highlighter' when certain words in a sentence need to be emphasized. In this case, they come at the beginning:

We wan' talk tuh John	'We want to speak to John'
Duh John we wan' talk tuh	'It's John we want to talk to'

Also with question words:

Duh wisseh hunnuh duh gwine?	'Where are you going?'
Duh who-dat bin call me name?	'Who called my name?'
Duh warruh e need?	'What does she need?'
Duh who-dat duh dey deh?	'Who's there?'
Duh wuh dem bin tell hunnuh?	'What did they tell you?'

Unlike the other creoles (except SIC), Seminole grammar does not allow verbs to be brought forward in the same way; both West African Krio and Jamaican Creole can say *duh buy you buy im* or *duh tief you tief im?* ('did you buy it or did you steal it'), but in Seminole it would have to be *you buy um or you tief um?*

'Be' in the sense of 'exist' or 'be in a place' (like Spanish estar), is dey:

Hunnuh book dem dey pun da cheer	'Your books are on that chair'
Muskittuh bin dey ebbawey	'Mosquitoes were everywhere'
Ah en dey een me room	'I'll be in my room'

'Be' in front of adjectives is not translated at all in Seminole

Whereas in English you would have to say 'I *am* hungry', 'they *were* noisy' and so on, this is left out in Seminole. That is because adjectives are really a kind of verb.

Adjectives

These behave just like verbs, except that without a tense or aspect marker they still can have a 'present tense'. It is difficult to think of adjectives having tenses, but it is one way to explain the difference between *dis leaf yalluh* and *dis leaf duh yalluh*; the first one means 'this leaf is yellow', a kind of permanent state which includes the present since it is yellow while you make the observation about it; the second one has *duh* which is the aspect word for action in progress, so it would mean 'this leaf is getting yellow', or 'this leaf is yellowing'.

Adjectives can be used with the other tense and aspect markers too, just like verbs:

Dis leaf en yalluh	'This leaf will be yellow'
Dis leaf ennuh yalluh	'This leaf is going to turn yellow'
Dis leaf bin yalluh	'This leaf was yellow'
Dis leaf binnuh yalluh	'This leaf was turning yellow'
Dis leaf done yalluh	'This leaf has turned yellow'

and so on.

Adjectives are made comparative by using the word *mo* in front of them, or if they are just short words, by adding *-uh* to them. Sometimes both *mo* and *-uh* are used together. The word for 'than' is *nuh*:

You ogliuh nuh me	'You're uglier than I am'
You mo ogliuh nuh me	'You're uglier than I am'
You mo tankful nuh me	'You're more thankful than I am'

They are made superlative by using the word *mos'* in front of them, or if they are just short words, by adding *-is* to the end. Sometimes both *mos'* and *-is* are used together:

You duh de odis' ooman	'You're the oldest woman'
You duh de mos' odis' ooman	'You're the oldest woman'
You duh de mos' tankful man	'You're the most thankful man'

Negatives

There are many examples of negative sentences in the earlier pages. Usually this is made by putting *nuh* (or *no* or *nah*) right after the subject noun or pronoun:

Me nuh sabby um	'I don't know him'
Me oncle nuh know	'My uncle doesn't know'
Me ahnty nuh bin wan' fuh know	'My aunt didn't want to know'
En ah n' en tell um	'And I'm not going to tell her'

When a sentence has two parts, *i.e.* a subject and an object, both are made negative, so it is correct Seminole grammar to say *we nuh see nuhbawdy en we nuh bin eat nuttin*, 'we didn't see anyone and we didn't eat anything'.

The verbs *could, would, coulda, woulda* and *kin* ('can') don't have negatives with *nuh*; the negative forms of these verbs are *couldn, wouldn, couldna, wouldna* and *cahn'* or *cyahn'*.

The aspect marker *done*, when made negative, is not *nuh done but *nabbuh*: *E nabbuh shem* 'he hadn't seen her'.

Joining sentences

Words and sentences can be joined together in different ways to make longer, more complicated constructions. Sometimes two complete sentences can be put together with a joining word, sometimes a sentence can be put inside another sentence, and sometimes a sentence can be put after a noun or a verb. When sentences are joined in any of these ways, they need joining words. Some of these are given below.

A sentence following another sentence

Me duh gwine en you fuh 'tay yuh	'I am going *and* you must stay here'
Josie wan' leff um dey buh	'Josie wants to leave it there *but*
you wan' fuh teck um wit you	you want to take it with you'
Ah en eat now, been' you n'en	'I will eat now, *since* you're not
dey home befo six	going to be home before six'
E say e nuh know how e en fine	'She said she didn't know how she'd
room fuh e seddown, nummuh	find room to sit, *except that* she
e en seddown somewey	was going to sit down somewhere

Following a noun

Dishuh yaze wey de doctor	'This ear that the doctor
bin fix still nuh right	fixed still isn't right'
Dem piece uh ood wey dey onneet	'Those bits of wood that are
da stove en ketch fire ef you	under that stove will catch fire
if nuh moobe um	you don't move them'

Following a verb or adjective

Duh chrue seh all two	'Is it true *that* both men
de man drown?	drowned?'
Ah bin yeddy seh duh lie	'I heard *that* it was a lie'
E ax um seh 'duh wuh you wan'?'	'He asked him "what is it
	that you want?"'
E gie um ansuh seh 'nuttin'	'He answered him
	"nothing"'

More about fuh

Two different uses of the word *fuh* have been given already, namely as the indicator of a verb when it has no subject (*to* run, *to* jump, *to* eat, etc.) and as a word meaning 'must' or 'should' when the verb does have a subject ('I *must* run', I m*ust* jump', etc.): *fuh run, ah fuh run; fuh jowmp, ah fuh jowmp*, etc. Fuh can be used this way by itself, as in these examples, or together with *ha* ('have'), to give *haffuh*: *Ah haffuh run*.

Together with *bin*, *bin fuh* means 'should have', as in *dem bin fuh go* 'they should have gone', but sometimes it is mistakenly used as though it meant the same thing as *bin duh* (*binnuh*).

In sentences of the kind 'something for you to eat', or 'a song for them to sing', which need a 'to' before the verbs in English, there is no need to use *fuh*:

Sometin fuh you eat	'Something for you to eat'
One song fuh you sing	'A song for you to sing'

It is also not necessary to use *fuh* after *wan'* ('want'):

Ah wan' go	'I want to go'

Dey pun *and* studdeh

Dey pun means to be engaged in some action, as in *e dey pun fool*, 'he's acting the fool (at this time)'. The word *studdeh* can also have a similar meaning, and signifies that the action of the verb is repetitive or continuous: *E studdeh binnuh watch de gyal* 'he was steadily watching the girl'.

Adverbs

Regular adverbs have the same form as the adjectives they are related to; it is their position in the sentence which makes them adverbs:

De poodie gyal duh sing	'The pretty girl is singing'
De gyal duh sing poodie	'The girl is singing prettily'

Some other adverbs, not derived from adjectives, are

How	'how'
Meck, meck-so	'why'
Wisseh, wey	'where'
Wuh-time, win	'when'
Tuhday	'today'
Turruh-day	'the other day'
Soon	'soon',
Soon een de monin	'early in the morning'

Adverbs are also whole phrases which tell you how, why, where or when:

Behime de do	'Behind the door'
Tru de do-mout	'Through the doorway'

Puntop we roof   'On our roof'
Wit e pent-bresh   'With his paint-brush'
Kezz e bin wan' fuh   'Because he wanted to'
Nice de winduh   'Near the window'

Tags

Tags are little words added to the end of a sentence to give it a particular tone. Two common tags in Seminole are *enty* and *nuh*:

Nuffuh peepil bin deh dey, enty?
'Plenty of people were there, weren't there?'
Dem en come back, enty?
'They'll come back, won't they?'

Enty can also come at the front of a sentence:

Enty dem yie bin shet?
'Weren't their eyes closed?'

With *nuh*:

Nuh loss um, nuh
'Don't lose it, will you'
Gie me, nuh
'Give it to me, won't you?'

Notes

[1] *Pace* S. Romaine (2001:V.160) who believes that Afro-Seminole Creole is extinct.
[2] Although the popular association of the word *Seminole* today is with the Indian population in Florida, according to Giddings (1858:3) it was first used to refer to the African escapees into that region, and was only later applied by the Creeks to the Indian fugitives. 'Seminole' has generally been supposed to derive from a Native American word *cima* meaning 'a type of wild grass', but more recently another etymology in the Arawak word *símaran* meaning 'bow and arrow' has been proposed by José Arrom (1986). The Indians themselves pronounced *cimarrón* as *cimalon* or *cimanol* transposing the 'm' and the 'l', hence the name Seminole – pronounced [sɪmə'noʊl] by most Afro- Seminoles today, but in the more conservative creole of the oldest speakers, pronounced [ʃɪmɪ'noʊli].

Bibliography

Arrom, J. J. (1986). '*Cimarrón:' Apuntes sobre sus Primeras Documentaciones y su Probable Origen*, Ediciones Fundación García-Arévalo, Serie monográfica, No. 18. Santo Domingo, Dominican Republic.

Drechsel, E. (1976). *Pidginization and creolization in North American Indian languages: Mobilian Jargon and Afro-Seminole Creole*. Unpublished report to the National Science Foundation.

Giddings, J. R. (1858). *The Exiles of Florida*. Follett: Columbus. Reissued by Black Classic Press, Baltimore, 1997.

Haas, M. (1940). *Creek Vocabulary*. Unpublished manuscript.

Hancock, I. (1975). 'Creole features in the Afro-Seminole speech of Brackettville, Texas'. *Caribbean Linguistic Society Occasional Paper*, No. 3.

—. (1977). 'Further Observations on Afro-Seminole Creole'. *Caribbean Linguistic Society Occasional Paper*, No. 7.

—. (1980). 'The Texas Seminoles and heir language'. Working Paper of the Afro-American Studies and Research Center of The University of Texas at Austin, Spring, p. 29.

—. (1986). 'On the Classification of Afro-Seminole Creole', *in* M. Montgomery and G. Bailey (eds), *Language Variety in the South: Perspectives in Black and White*. Alabama University Press, pp. 85–101.

—. (1993). 'Mortars and Metates', in P. Seitel (ed.), *Festival of American Folklife*. Washington, DC: Publication of the Smithsonian Institution, pp. 59–61.

—. (1994). 'Componentiality and the Creole Matrix: The South-West English Contribution', in M. Montgomery (ed.), *The Crucible of Carolina: Essays in the Development of Gullah Language and Culture*. Athens and London: University of Georgia Press, pp. 94–114.

—. (1998). 'History Through Words: Afro-Seminole lexicography', in L. Fiet and J. Becerra (eds), *Caribbean 2000: Identities and Cultures*. Rockefeller Foundation Publication, University of Puerto Rico, pp. 87–104.

Haynes, L. (1976). *Candid Chimaera: Texas Seminole*. Term paper, Department of English, New Mexico State University, Las Cruces.

Howard, R. (2002). *Black Seminoles in the Bahamas*. Gainesville: University Press of Florida.

Littlefield, D. F. (1977). *Africans and Seminoles*. Westport and London: Greenwood Press.

Loughridge, R. M. (1964). *English and Muskokee Dictionary*. Baptist Home Mission Board, Okmulgee.

Opala, J. (1980). *A Brief History of the Seminole Freedmen*. Occasional Paper No. 3 of the African and Afro-American Studies and Research Center, Austin: The University of Texas.

Porter, K. W. (1947). *Freedom Over Me: The Story of John Horse (Gopher John, ca. 1812–1882)—Seminole Negro Chief and His People in Florida, the Indian Territory, Mexico and Texas*. Unpublished typescript.

—. (1971), *The Negro on the American Frontier*, New York, Arnos Press.

Powers, B. E. (1998). 'A founding father and Gullah culture', *National Parks*, 72(11/12): 26–29, November/December 1998.

Romaine, S. (2001). 'Afro-Seminole Creole', in J. Algeo (ed.), *The Cambridge History of the English Language. Vol. 6, English in North America.* New York: CUP, p. 160.

Wood, D. E. (1980). *A Guide to the Seminole Settlements at Red Bays, Andros 1817–1980.* Nassau: The Bahamas Government Printing Department.

Woodhull, F. (1937), 'The Seminole Indian scouts on the border', *Frontier Times,* 17(3), 118–127.

American West

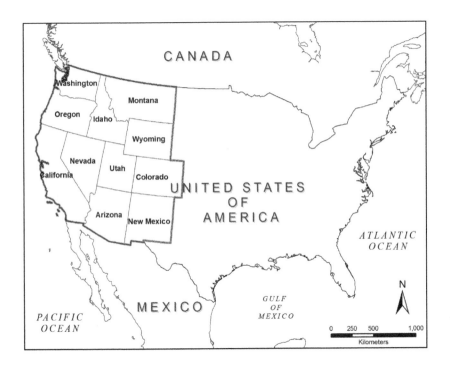

Chapter 4

Midwest American English

Beth Lee Simon

Midwest as a Conceptual Linguistic Place

Both within and outside the United States, people refer to an *American Midwest* as if it were a findable and knowable place, and to *Midwestern* as an identifiable linguistic variety, but when we claim there is a Midwest or Midwestern American English, what do we mean? Is there a core set of linguistic items that is statistically significant within a geographic area (even allowing for change in the significance of any individual item)? Is it possible to establish a set of linguistic items indexical of language users, real or imagined, within an identifiable region?

As a child, my untroubled sense of Midwest mirrors that of a Michigander's (sic) hand-drawn map locating varieties of English within the United States (Preston 1996a, 307): a large, central area including all of Indiana, Illinois, Iowa, Michigan, Minnesota and Wisconsin. My Midwest ended in Ohio on the east, included a bit of Nebraska and Kansas on the west, and stopped around the Iowa – Missouri border. My sense of the language matched that Michigander's as well: 'Midwestern English (normal)'.

This chapter establishes the Midland dialect and region and shows it as co-extensive or overlapping with the conceptual American Midwest. Initially confined within a relatively limited geographic area, the Midland dialect has expanded not only in the sheer number of defining phonological, grammatical and lexical items, but also in the perception of where this 'middle of America' is. Folk linguistic research on American English (Preston 1996a, 1996b, 2005) has been useful in demonstrating how non-linguists overlay value-laden designations onto US geographic regions, and *Midwest* is consistently one of those regions, although where this Midwest is and what it includes depend on where surveyees are located. Nonetheless, there is a significantly convincing collection of linguistic items in the corpus that validate a Midland variety of American English, and at the same time, there are enough shared presumptions or responses to suggest that for these 'folk . . . language has a cognitively exterior reality' (Niedzielski and Preston 2009, 372) indexing social and cultural values that map a Midwestern dialect and identity.

Research represented in such publications as the *Dictionary of American Regional English* (*DARE*) points to three major US dialect regions east of the

Rocky Mountain Range: *North, South* and *Midland*. Within this grouping, much of the Upper Midwest lies in the traditional *North* dialect region, but the dialect region people commonly mean by Midwest is often *Midland*. Because of the historical pathways of settlement as well as ongoing economically motivated migrations from rural to urban areas, the linguistic Midland is a porous territory such that, as we shall see below, items iconic of Midland groups occur beyond the Midland, and non-Midland areas adjoining the Midland are perceived as 'Midland'.

Regionality as an organizing concept is not limited to self-conscious children. It functions as an administrative tool to subdivide demographically complex nation-states (Beal 2006, 1–2) into workable units. US agencies from the Census to the National Endowment for the Humanities account for data or administer awards by regional sectors, one of which is the *Midwest*.

Region has cognitive reality and social saliency; we think about ourselves, and we tell about ourselves and others, in terms of region, and there are real-world outcomes to the ways people conceptualize the presumed 'links between linguistic forms and socio-geographic phenomena' (Irvine and Gal, 2009: 375). Lexical items, phonological representations and the morphosyntactic features used to construct characters in popular movies, television, music, literature and web-based media are taken as indexical of *midwesternness* (1). The value spectrum may range from forthrightness to anti-intellectualism embodied as Iowa movie farmers where baseball-players manifest out of a believer's failing cornfield, or TV's Illinois small town residents where financially strapped working-class families parse social issues in diners. Midwesterners show up as desperate but resilient isolates in novels, and as limited small-town lovers in the popular music lyrics. Again and again, *where* we are is established by the interaction of recognizable phonological, morphosyntactic, lexical or prosodic features with the iconography of agricultural and small town life. These serve to reify the Midwest. (2)

This is said by way of introduction because, from childish musings to functional abstractions, from identity performance to identity imputation, region matters (Simon 2006, ix) in understanding language varieties. It is formative of who we are and normative for who we think we are. This chapter offers a linguist's description of the Midland regional dialects of American English while keeping in mind popular conceptions of Midwest English and what forms the core of that notion.

Origins of American English in the Midwest

In the categorization of the Mouton World Atlas of Variation in English (Kortmann, (ed.) 2012), Midwest American English is a 'high contact L1 variety', that is, one of the varieties of 'transplanted L1 Englishes'. This is an English first 'transported' and then 'indigenized' within North America with 'native speakers who, from earliest settlement times, represent a diverse set of linguistic backgrounds'.

The 'original colonial hearth areas' (Kretzschmar 2004) of seventeenth-century North American settlement were distinguished by separate colonies developing 'cultural differences early on, including linguistic differences' (Kretzschmar 2004: 258). These differences were significant enough that by 1782, Thomas Jefferson perceives four 'cultural areas—North, South, Pennsylvania, and New York', which he discusses in a letter to a French correspondent, F. J. Chastellux who had, earlier in the year, labelled the language of the new country *Americain* (Pederson 2000).

The Pennsylvania colony, the natal bed of Midland dialects, was founded by charter granted in 1681 to William Penn by Charles II, establishing it as a refuge for groups fleeing religious and political conflict in England, Germany and elsewhere. Unlike other Atlantic settlements, the great majority of seventeenth-century English-speaking immigrants to Pennsylvania, the Quakers, other English and Welsh, were not from southern England, and by the beginning of the eighteenth century, they were joined by substantial numbers of Palatine Germans and Scots-Irish from Ulster. From there, these groups

> found their way into the interior, and their descendants were among the most mobile in American history, moving westward and southwestward, reaching northern Virginia and then the piedmont of North and South Carolina by the mid eighteenth century. (Montgomery 2001: 124)

One of the most significant developments allowing mobility was the discovery of the Cumberland Gap in 1750. The Wilderness Road (later replaced by the National Road) through the Gap opened westward migration onto the Middle West frontier. From 1790 to 1840, the Wilderness Road was the principal route into the Shenandoah, across the Appalachians and north, up into Tennessee, the Kentucky bluegrass and the Ohio River. 'Southern uplanders resettled to the west, across the Appalachians to central Kentucky and Tennessee, and then on to southern Ohio, Indiana, and Illinois during the first decades of the nineteenth century'. (Ash 2006). Some of the linguistic features identified with American Southern dialects are a result of this early migration from North Carolina, Tennessee and Kentucky into Ohio, Indiana and Illinois, and the blurring of the southern portions of the Midland with the Upper South-east to the Carolinas is evidence of this history.

There were other important lines of immigration beginning in Pennsylvania. Scots-Irish from Ulster and Palatine Germans begin to arrive in the 1830s and their numbers increased dramatically thereafter. Like other colonial dialect origins, Midland varieties developed from a British English base, but in the case of Pennsylvania, Swedish and Dutch communities were already present and were joined by French, Scots-Irish, Welsh and German settlers. Settlement of the upper reaches of the Middle West frontier began in 1833, when the US government opened part of the land following the end of the Black Hawk Wars. There were two main streams of settlers. On the one hand, Northerners from western New England and New York State moved west along a route just south of the Great Lakes, through northern Indiana and Illinois to the Mississippi River. In a second stream, Midlanders from New Jersey, Pennsylvania and northern Virginia moved west across Ohio, Indiana and central Illinois. Some settlers also came from the Carolinas, Virginia and Tennessee across Kentucky and into southern Indiana and Illinois, then on into southern Iowa and Nebraska. (Ash 2006)

This is the historical core of the modern Midwest, Ohio, Indiana and Illinois, that then expanded west to Iowa and Nebraska. This is the hub for the multiplicity of migration routes from the mid-Atlantic south moving west and north through middle Tennessee and Kentucky that is still a pathway for linguistic items associated with the upper South into the southern Midwest. At the same time, there continues to be an extension or spread of primarily the socially transparent phonological and grammatical features of Midland through the Mountain West to the Pacific.

In brief, settlements from western Pennsylvania and the Delaware Valley into Ohio, the northern two-thirds of Indiana and Illinois, compose the original Midland dialect area, and it is here, in varying frequencies of use, that we find the features of the related set of varieties we can call Midwest American English.

Linguistic Features of the Midland Dialects

The first use of *Midland* occurs relatively late in the development of major North American dialects. George Hempl, using an extensive data set, divides the United States into a four regional dialect areas (1896). Based on contrast of /s/ and /z/ in *grease* and *greasy*, he distinguishes a distinct Midland that 'separat[ed] the North from the South and extend[ed] from the Atlantic to the Mississippi' (438) (3), and from this vantage point, the area suggested by Hempl is impressively accurate.

'Kurath considered Pennsylvania the seedbed for a larger region (which he called the 'Midland'). He was responsible for articulating and propounding this idea, but decades earlier a little-known study made a similar case for Pennsylvania. . . . N.C. Burt (413) . . . 'The dialect of Pennsylvania is mainly Scotch-Irish'. . . . He first and alone cited *whenever* in its Ulster meaning of 'as soon as' (Montgomery 2001).

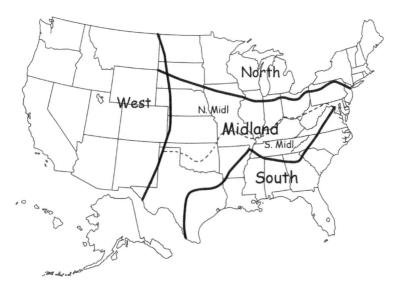

FIGURE 4.1 Major US dialect areas with midland boundaries and subdivisions.
Source: © 1996 Duke University Press. Adapted with permission. Murray, T. E., T. C. Frazer, and B. L. Simon. 1996. *Need* + Past Participle in American English. *American Speech*, 71:259.

Then, in the 1949 publication of *A Word Geography of the Eastern United States*, Hans Kurath set out the dialect areas of the eastern United States: North, Midland and South.

By Kurath's definition, the Midland was a region centred around Philadelphia, extending west across most of Pennsylvania and northern Maryland and Delaware. Later studies (Davis 1948, Shuy 1962, Dakin 1966) extended these boundaries west, delimiting the Midland as a region that includes all but the northernmost strip of Ohio, Indiana and Illinois, plus all of Appalachia west of the Allegheny Mountains (Ash 2006: 34).

At the time Kurath's postulation of a Midland dialect was based on rather lean data, the presence of relatively few features and the absence of features found elsewhere; that is, Kurath's Midland was 'where the South stopped being the South in some cases and the North stopped being the North in others' (Montgomery 2005). Others, using more robust phonological, morphosyntactic and lexical data, confirm Kurath's hypothesis. In 1987, Craig Carver, using the lexical materials collected at *DARE*, reiterates the northern boundary, (although he sees this as the division between the Upper and the Lower North), and Labov, Ash and Boberg, '[a]ttacking the problem of defining dialect areas . . . based primarily on phonological data' (but also including likely grammatical and a very few lexical items), prove that boundary again. Indeed, Ash (one of the designers and editors of *Atlas of North American English* (*ANAE*) points to 'the rather precise line between the North and the Midland' as 'one of the most lasting and deepest borders in the ecology of American language'. (2006, 34).

While the regional distinction exists, and continues beyond the Mississippi River, through the Plains States to the Pacific West, a number of the features traditionally used to distinguish Midland from Northern varieties have been or are becoming lost. For instance, vowel merger to /ɛ/ in *Mary ~ merry ~ marry* and to /o/ in *hoarse ~ horse* is as typical among younger Northern speakers as among Midland speakers.

Linguistic features of the present-day midland

Many of the widespread defining features of Midwest American English pass unnoticed because they are sociolinguistically unremarkable and stylistically transparent, perhaps one reason that Midwesterners self-identify based on perceived 'negative' evidence (as the Ohio speaker in the film *American Tongues* says, 'We're bland'.). Yet, as we see below, defining features can be subdivided socio-regionally into those that are in widespread, acceptable use and those with localized, limited, conscious or disfavoured use (such as those examined in Hazen's study of Heritage Language in West Virginia's Appalachian Midland. (4). As Kretzschmar points out regarding 'Standard American English' pronunciation, 'the most highly educated speakers in formal settings tend to suppress any linguistic features that they recognize as marked, i.e., regionally or socially identifiable' (2004, 261). Thus, marked items such as epenthetic or 'intrusive' /r/ are noticed (and individuals work to suppress it), while low-back vowel merger goes unnoticed, even in local areas where it does not predominate. Specific variants, and variation itself, are often below the level of consciousness both for individual speakers and within areas of use, and perhaps this is at least partly the reason that several phonological and morphosyntactic features arising in the Midwest and linguistically diagnostic of the Midland are currently expanding beyond their original boundaries.

What follows are the defining and most salient distinctions of Midwest American English. Within each category, I order them most to least widespread.

Phonology

From *ANAE* data, the defining phonological characteristic of Midland dialects would not be the presence of a single feature or set of features, but a more absolute contrast, that is, an absence of occurrence, language use exhibiting none of the 'defining features of either Northern Cities Shift (NCS) or Southern Shift' (Labov, Ash, and Boberg 2006). One foray into the question of NCS limits and whether the North – Midland boundary is as impervious as some studies claim appears in a master's thesis (James 2003), which offers evidence of

NCS among high school students in Fort Wayne, Indiana, an urban economic gravitational centre for southern Michigan.

Individual features that are associated with Midland speech and contribute to establishing Midland phonological boundaries are presented below.

Low back vowel merger

The most widespread, unmarked, non-salient phonological distinction identifying Midland dialect is the 'low back vowel merger', that is, the loss of a phonemic distinction between the low vowel (something close to /ɑ/) in *cot* or *Don* and the back vowel (something close to /ɥ/) in *caught* or *dawn*. It is, as well, perhaps the earliest phonological distinction noted; Webster (1789) observes '/ɑ/ in soft, drop', associating it with Scots-Irish. (in Montgomery 2001, 141). Originating in western Pennsylvania, the merger spreads to the north and south as it moves west.

Kurath and McDavid find it in the western United States, and research of the last ten years demonstrates its expansion among younger, urban speakers (see for instance Gordon 2004 on the merger in St. Louis, at the western edge of the Midland region). While the merger itself is widespread, the resultant vowel for individual speakers may differ from one locality to another, and from one age group to another (Gordon 2004, 342).

Vowel mergers and near mergers before liquids

Historically, vowel mergers and near mergers before liquids /r/ and /l/ were a Midland feature in contrast to the distinctive vowels of the North dialect. The contemporary situation is that, regardless of region, most American English speakers

FIGURE 4.2 Low-back vowel merger, *cot – caught*.
Source: Compiled from Labov, Ash, Boberg, (2006).

age fifty-five or younger have complete vowel merger before /r/ such that the original three-way vowel contrast in *marry, Marry, merry* is realized as /mɛri/.

Vowel merger or near merger before /l/, on the other hand, distinguishes Midwest American English, and it is found in the West as well. Before /l/, mergers of /i/ and /ɪ/, /u/ and /ʊ/, and /e/ and /ɛ/ 'result in homophones for pairs such as *feel* and *fill*, *fool* and *full*, and *fail* and *fell*. The phonetic quality of the merged vowel approximates to the lax member of each pair; i.e., [ɪ], [ʊ], [ɛ]'. (Gordon 2004, 344).

Like the low back merger above, vowel merger before /l/ appears to be expanding. It is now found among younger speakers in areas which historically exhibited clear vowel separation, and where older speakers continue to do so. (Thomas 2001, Gordon 2004).

Front lax vowel mergers, /ɪ/ and /ɛ/

Front lax vowel merger of /ɪ/ and /ɛ/ is a feature of the core region, particularly associated with the Southern Appalachian area.

FIGURE 4.3 Front vowel merger, *pin – pen*.
Source: © 2006 John Benjamins. Adapted with permission. Ash, S. 2006, p. 41. The North American Midland as a dialect area, in Murray, T. and B. Simon, *Language Variation and Change in the Midland; a new look at 'Heartland' English.*

The resultant vowel may be either /I/ or /ɛ/, even within the same locality, such that of two north central Indiana speakers of the same age and sex, one has merger to the high front lax (pɪn ~ pɪn) and the other to the mid front lax (pɛn ~ pɛn).

Morphosyntactic Features

A set of affixes, pronominal and verb forms, and phrasal constructions compose a core grammar of the Midland dialect of American English. (5). As maps and discussion below indicate, some items are more prevalent in areas of the South Midland, others, in the North Midland, and several distinctly Midland items; the strong past tense verb form of *dive*, as well as *need/want* + phrasal constructions, and *positive anymore*, are currently in dynamic expansion of use and acceptability throughout and beyond the Midland.

This grammatical set (6) is subdivided into two groups: those in widespread, unremarkable use in the Midwest, and those found primarily in defined Midland areas, with less frequent occurrence, and deemed non-acceptable or non-standard outside the Midwest, and often within the Midland but outside areas of use.

Regionally widespread; usage unremarkable and/or acceptable

1. *all the* + adjective, adverb, singular count noun, one
2. positive *anymore*
3. *dive* past tense forms
4. *need/want/like* + [past participle]
5. *need/want* + [prepositional adverb]
6. *quarter till* [the hour]
7. *sick* [preposition] *the stomach* (as in *sick at/on/to the stomach*);

Regionally limited; usage considered non-standard; use remarked, deemed unacceptable or disfavoured

8. *wait on* (wait for)
9. *wakened* (as the past participle of *wake*);
10. *whenever* 'at the time that; as soon as' (e.g.);
11. *you'ns* (second person plural personal pronoun).
12. *come/go with*

This set forms a core Midland grammar in the way that Kurath first pointed out more than 50 years ago, that is, a grammar based on combinations of these features found among different communities of Midwesterners rather than all of these features being exclusive to the Midwest. These are 'largely affixation, function words, pronominal usage, verbal ellipsis, and distinctive syntactic patterns — in short, to aspects of language which have too often been overlooked . . . to a certain extent, in dialect study overall', (Murray and Simon 2006), in other words, the kinds of features that are particularly useful for revealing dialect because they are more stable than lexical and even phonological features. Neither users nor non-users notice occurrence, and only those specific to or associated with Appalachian English are mentioned or condemned in usage handbooks. (see Montgomery 2008 and Montgomery and Hall 2004, for an annotated list of Appalachian English morphosyntactic features.) Midwesterners are often surprised to learn that at least the first seven are one of a set of possibilities.

all the far, all the farther, all the further, all the [singular count noun/one]**

These phrases share the same syntactic structure and are used to express maximum degree. For this reason, the first and last are included here, rather than below with the items more limited geographically and sociolinguistically. Of these, **all the far* and variants with a base adjective or adverb ('That's all the far she can throw it', 'That's all the fast it can fly',) and **all the* with a singular count noun or *one* ('That's all the coat he has', 'Is this all the one you have?'), are part of the Scots-Irish inheritance and found primarily among speakers of Southern and South Appalachian dialects.

In contrast, the comparative *all the farther* and *all the further* are widespread throughout the Midwest, from Pennsylvania west to Iowa.

The *DARE* Questionnaire prompt, Question LL34, When a road is blocked: 'this is all _____ we can go', clearly constrains the range of likely responses. Nonetheless, the number of respondents and the high level of education (49 per cent of those responding 'all the farther' and 40 per cent of those responding 'all the further' were college-educated) indicates a sociolinguistic and stylistic transparency. Phrases such as 'That's all the faster he can run', and 'That's all the farther I've read' occur throughout the Midwest, occur frequently, and without comment. Indeed, *all the* phrases with a comparative adjective and adverb form is one of the features of Midwest English that produces wonder at the suggestion of variant expressions.

Positive anymore

In contrast to negative or interrogatory use, *anymore* has developed the 'positive' sense of nowadays, lately, or currently, as in 'We always use coupons anymore when we shop', and the area of this type of usage is expanding rapidly. Originally, occurrences of positive *anymore* were limited to western Pennsylvania, Appalachia and the Ozarks. Now, use has greatly expanded. (For a complete discussion, see Murray in Frazer 1993. Occurrences are documented

FIGURE 4.4 Responses of *all the farther/further* and variants to *DARE* questionnaire prompt.
Source: Compiled from Hall, von Schneidermesser (2004). Responses to *Dictionary of American Regional English (DARE)* Questionnaire prompts and material from *DARE* files compiled from data provided by Joan Hall and Luanne von Schneidermesser.

throughout the Midwest, it is found in the adjoining Inland North and in the South (see Ash 2006) and is moving rapidly across the Mountain States (Colorado, Nevada and Idaho) on to the West Coast (Murray 2004).

DIVE *past tense*

Two past tense forms for the verb *dive* predominate in American English: *dived* and *dove*. The *Oxford English Dictionary*, which describes *dove* as North America and English dialect, cites Longfellow 1855 and an 1882 edition of the *New York Herald*, sources that indicate that this strong form of the past tense was unremarkable among literate Americans. *The Oxford English Dictionary* (1989, Vol. IV, 883).

Development of the innovative form *dove* contrasts with the general analogic trend for past tense verb forms to transform from strong to weak. Although initially identified with the North dialect region, it has expanded into the Midwest. Indeed, from Iowa east to Indiana, *dove* is increasingly predominant.

The maps show a *dived ~ dove* predominance contrast shifting across a Midland - North dialect boundary from Pennsylvania at least through northern

FIGURE 4.5   *dived (in)*

FIGURE 4.6   *dove (in* or *off)*. Responses of *dove (in* or *off)* to *DARE* Questionnaire prompt.
Source: Compiled from Hall, von Schneidermesser (2004).

Iowa and South Dakota of the Upper Midwest. The *dove* form predominates in areas adjoining the Upper Midwest, is an inheritance of western movement along the northern tier (see Kurath, Hansen, Hanley, Lowman, and Bloch 1939–1943, Map 580 and also Atwood 1953, with both *dived* and *dove* in northern, central and eastern Pennsylvania and northern Ohio). While *DARE's* 1965–70 data give *dived* predominance in the Midland and *dove* in the North, recent evidence suggests *dove* is replacing *dived.* In northwestern Ohio–northeastern Indiana, *dove* predominates especially among younger speakers. Moving west, where the Inland North–North Midland boundary runs across the middle of Iowa, a state that reflects sociohistorical patterns of the Upper Midwest, *dove* is almost exclusive. In the Indiana case, Northern *dove* is spreading into the Midwest. In the western Midwest, north of Interstate 80, the *dove* form has always predominated. Results from recent informal college surveys in the northern Indiana point to *dove* as the unremarkable and sole choice.

Need/ Want/Like + *past participle*

This set of constructions is part of the Midwest inheritance of Scots-Irish settlement, and like other features of Scots-Irish origin, they are unremarkable within areas of use. The *need + past participle* construction has widespread use and acceptability within the Midland and the range of acceptable use appears to be expanding.

In contrast, the other two, *want* (or) *like + past participle*, occur in limited areas. Each is marked outside of specific areas of use, not only outside of the Midland, but within the Midland, and rejected as grammatically or stylistically acceptable. As the maps show, areas of use for these syntactically, semantically and pragmatically similar phrases are geographically nested within each other.

Established with the Scots-Irish settlement, the *need + past participle* construction is one of the defining items of Midland grammar in the core area of Ohio and Indiana (perhaps bolstered by German settlement where the construction may seem to reflect analogous German forms) where it is sociolinguistically and stylistically transparent (Murray, Frazer and Simon 1996, Murray and Simon 2002), In Indiana, the construction is used in formal written documents such as legal briefs and on news broadcasts by leading local newscasters. Telephonic survey responses for the *Atlas of North American English* show use and acceptance expanded across the urban Midwest (Ash 2006, 48).

The area of non-remarked usage is expanding. Ulrey (2009) using the Access World News [AWN] database, found written tokens in all states except Hawai'i and Alaska. Until the mid-1990s, documented written usage was limited to the Midland with the concentration within the historical heart of the Midland, but AWN corpus analysis shows a substantial increase in the number of occurrences outside of the Midland.

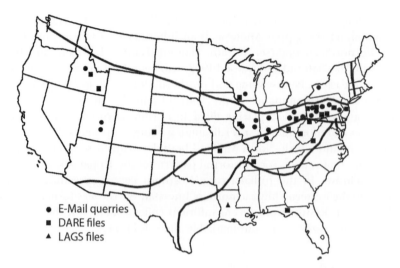

FIGURE 4.7 Attestations of *need + past participle* from *DARE* and *Linguistic Atlas of the Gulf States* files and discussion list queries; symbol size indicative of multiple responses.
Source: © Duke University Press; adapted with permission. Murray, T. E., T. C. Frazer, and B. Simon. 1996. *Need* + Past Participle in American English. *American Speech*, 71: 159.

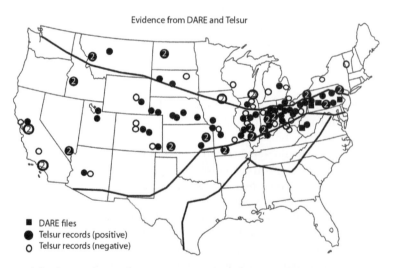

FIGURE 4.8 Attestations of *want + past participle* from *DARE* files and Telephonic Survey (Telsur) data; symbol size indicative of multiple responses.
Source: © Duke University Press; adapted with permission. Murray, T. E. and B. L. Simon. 1999. *Want* + Past Participle in American English. *American Speech*, 74.

Use of phrasal *want* + past participle is nested within the *need* + past participle area although, as is clear from Figure 4.8, *want* + past participle remains fairly restricted to its original settlement areas. Such a limited area contrasts sharply with the Midwest-wide, unremarkable *want* + adverbial particle (Figure 4.9 below) constructions with which *want* + past participle has strong surface similarity.

Syntactically and semantically mirroring *need* + past participle, statements such as 'the cat wants fed', 'the pie wants sliced' indicate the speaker's intention to cause other participants to fulfill a third party's need or lack.

Of these three, *need/want/like, like* + past participle has most limited geographic range of use. Within areas of use, statements such as 'The baby likes cuddled', and 'Infants like picked up', (the former was produced by a trained medical staff person, the latter by an honors linguistics student during a formal presentation) are grammatically acceptable and unremarkable. At the same time, this construction is deemed unacceptable and non-standard by non-users within the inclusive *need* + past participle areas.

FIGURE 4.9 Responses of *want off/out/in* to *DARE* Questionnaire prompt.
Source: © Sage Publishing; adapted with permission. Benson, Erika J. 2009. Everyone Wants In: *Want* + Prepositional Adverb in the Midland and Beyond. Journal of English Linguistics. 37: 33.

FIGURE 4.10   Responses of *quarter till* to *DARE* Questionnaire prompt.
Source: Compiled from Hall, von Schneidermesser (2004). Responses to *Dictionary of American Regional English* (DARE) Questionnaire prompts and material from *DARE* files compiled from data provided by Joan Hall and Luanne von Schneidermesser.

need/want + *prepositional adverb*

This construction, like its counterpart want + prepositional adverb, occurs with a number of adverb possibilities (-down, -in, -off, -out as most frequent), and the level of acceptance depends on the adverb as well, in some uses, with the pronoun (Benson 2005, Paules and Benson) This phrasal unit shows surface structural similarities with *need/want/like* + past participle, and as with those constructions, came into the Midland with Scots-Irish settlement.

want + *prepositional adverb*

Phrases such as *'I want off at the next stop'*, *'The cat wants out'*, *'Do you want down?'* *'The dog wants in'* have been documented in speech and writing throughout the Midwest since the late nineteenth century (1887, 1892, in Benson 2009: 30), in contexts suggesting awareness of the construction as peculiar to the 'Middle West'. Wentworth's *American Dialect Dictionary* offered the following set of reported occurrences culled from sources published between 1914 and 1944: *want down, -in, -into, -off, -out, -through, -up.*

In contemporary usage however this construction, especially with adverbial *off, in* or *out*, is so transparent and unmarked that Midwesterners are hard put to find an alternative expression or even consider it as a variant. Like elliptical *need* + past participle, *want* + *off*, *-in*, *-out* is part of the core Midland grammar. It is in widespread use in the Midland, with some variants, particularly *want in* and *-out*, and perhaps *-off*, expanding beyond the original territory.

Recent surveys show a concentration of use in the Midland, a wide range of acceptability judgements depending on the prepositional adverb, and sociolinguistic transparency (Benson 2009).

Quarter till (the hour)

This form for saying fifteen minutes before the hour or *quarter to* is so common throughout the Midwest that people are unaware of other possible variants, even when they use other variants. Indeed, along with the construction *need* + past participle, *quarter till* is one of the strongest, least marked items of Midland grammar.

As with other Midwest-defining items, this is a Scots-Irish inheritance. Kurath labelled it Midland, and others document this throughout the Midwest into Southern Appalachia and the upper South, and throughout the Great Lakes.

Sick at/in/on/to the stomach

These vary in distinct regional patterns, but two, Midland *sick at* and Northern *sick to* overlap in adjoining areas.

These often coexisting phrases for stomach discomfort indicate some of the complexities of Midwest language use and how presence, transparency and acceptability of competing variants is a general feature of Midland English. Here, of the four variants, *sick at -, sick in -, sick on-,* and *sick to the stomach*, the first and last, *sick at* and *sick to*, are both Midland, but with different centres of use. Like *dove, sick to the stomach* is an inheritance from North resettlement in the Upper Midwest. *DARE Questionnaire* responses of *sick* (or *upset*) *at* were widespread except for the North.

Of the features in the second group of morphosyntactic items, all but one came into the Midwest and American English with Scots-Irish immigrants, but unlike those above, these are or are becoming geographically and socially limited. Perhaps in consequence, almost all are judged non-standard or unacceptable even by users within areas of use.

Wait on (wait for) *verb phrase*

Of this group, the well-established *wait on*, 'wait for', is the least unacceptable or least remarkable among Midland language users. The *English Dialect Dictionary* labels it southern Scots, northern Ireland, Ulster and Wight, and the earliest American occurrence is 1817, in William Sewall's *Diary*. While usages such as 'We're waiting on a bus that's 10 minutes late', once had widespread currency in the South and the Midwest, *wait on* appears to be giving way or has given way

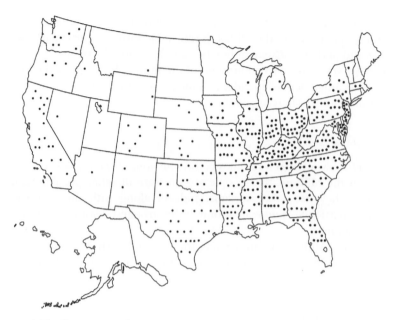

FIGURE 4.11   Responses of *sick at his stomach* and variants to *DARE* Questionnaire prompt.
Source: Compiled from Hall, von Schneidermesser (2004). Responses to *Dictionary of American Regional English* (DARE) Questionnaire prompts and material from *DARE* files compiled from data provided by Joan Hall and Luanne von Schneidermesser.

to the more common *wait for*, especially as one moves west from the Midwest core area.

DARE materials show *wait on* as 'widespread but more frequent' in the South and Midwest, but both actual use and acceptability appear to be diminishing. While most frequent, unremarkable use is in the southern Appalachian area and among speakers in Ohio and Indiana, it co-occurs with the non-regional *wait for*. Indeed, this Midland item is in a state of transition. Within areas of use it is in competition with non-regional *wait for*. In everyday use, it passes unremarked, but when presented as an isolate form on questionnaire surveys, it is evaluated as unacceptable or ungrammatical.

wakened *(up) past participle*

The form *wakened (up)*, a past participial variant of *awakened*, is documented in Scotland, Ireland and the north of England. As the map shows, *wakened (up)* responses to the *DARE* questions about waking at night are few, but clearly focused in the original Midland dialect area of western Pennsylvania and Delaware Bay, Ohio, Indiana and Illinois.

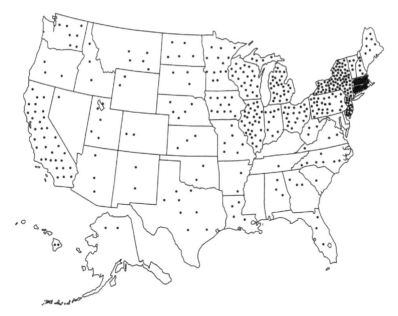

FIGURE 4.12 Responses of *sick tot his stomach* and variants to *DARE* Questionnaire prompt.
Source: Compiled from Hall, von Schneidermesser (2004). Responses to *Dictionary of American Regional English* (DARE) Questionnaire prompts and material from *DARE* files compiled from data provided by Joan Hall and Luanne von Schneidermesser.

whenever adverb

The adverb *whenever* in the sense of 'as soon as', came into Pennsylvania with Scots-Irish immigrants from Ulster. (Montgomery 2001: 125). An 1878 entry in a Pennsylvania diary notes 'Thus it will be said that, "whenever the carriage came, the lady got in"', and the more recent, 'Whenever I first heard the news, I about fell over', show it as descriptive of a one-time event, but it is used as well for extended duration in the past or a periodic event (Montgomery and Kirk 2001).

you'ins 2nd person pronoun

First noted in Margaret Van Horn Dwight's 1810 journal entry, 'Youns [sic] is a word I have heard used several times, but what it means I don't know, they use it so strangely', it is possible that *you'ins*, like past tense *dove*, is an American innovation, although use is predominately within the Scots-Irish settlement areas of western Pennsylvania and southern Appalachians.

FIGURE 4.13   Responses of *wakened (up)* to *DARE* Questionnaire prompt.
Source: Compiled from Hall, von Schneidermesser (2004). Responses to *Dictionary of American Regional English* (DARE) Questionnaire prompts and material from *DARE* files compiled from data provided by Joan Hall and Luanne von Schneidermesser.

Come/go with

While occurrences of the phrasal verb '*Do you want to come with?*' or '*Do you want to go with?*' are unremarkable in areas with historically dense concentrations of German settlement (both urban and rural), use is limited almost entirely to those areas.

Lexicon

Of the components of language, it is the lexicon that is most responsive to and reflective of change, and for that reason, it is most volatile. As culture, technology, demographics, environment, economics and other aspects of life change, lexical items that were distinctive of a particular territory or settlement group pass into and out of common use.

Mitigating against a stable Midwest lexicon are three patterns of change. First, many Midwest lexical items formerly noted as contrastive with Northern or Southern American English no longer exist in ordinary speech or writing. For instance, Northern *darning needle* in contrast with Midlands *snake feeder* for dragon fly, and Northern *whiffletree* in contrast with Midlands *singletree* for the pivotal crossbar on a draft animal, are moribund or extinct. Second, formerly regional contrasts such as *pail* with *bucket* have become interchangeable or occur only in specific collocations, *wooden bucket* and *tin pail*. Finally, regionally distinct items have been superseded by technological and social change; for instance while Northern *bag* co-occurs with Southern *sack*, (demonstrating that the Midwest is where the North exchanges with South) it is more likely that shoppers now choose between non-regional *plastic* and *paper*.

Thus, of the items Pederson (2000) lists as distinguishing Midland from North, *snake feeder* v *darning needle* (dragonfly), *stone fence* v *stone wall*, *bucket* v *pail*, *slop* v *swill*, *seesaw* v *teeter-totter*, *spicket/spigot* v *faucet*, *seed* v *pit* (of a cherry or peach), *lightening bug* v *firefly* and *singletree* v *whiffletree*, few are in regional variation among speakers under the age of sixty-five. Again, of those distinguishing Midland from South, *green beans* v *snap beans*, *red worm* v *earthworm*, *fireboard* v *mantelpiece*, *tow sack* (for *burlap bag*) v *crocus sack*, *peanut* v *goober*, perhaps only *green beans* v *snap*, and *peanut* v *goober* remain significant.

FIGURE 4.14 Carbonated drink: *pop, soda, coke/cola*.
Source: © 2006 John Benjamins. Adapted with permission. Ash, S. 2006, p. 47. The North American Midland as a dialect area, in Murray, T. E. and B. L. Simon, *Language Variation and Change in the Midland; a new look at 'Heartland' English*.

Nonetheless, Linn and Regal's reanalysis (2006, 250–252) of Midland and Northern items in the Linguistic Atlas of the Upper Midwest, published in the 1970s but representing responses from thirty or more years earlier, reveal significant regional and social variation although the linguistic items themselves have all but vanished from contemporary use or are no longer regionally distinct.

What this suggests is that while, on the one hand, the rapidity with which the lexicon as a dynamic repository reflecting changes in social, cultural and technological environments makes static listings less than useful over time, on the other, tracking change in the lexicon is fruitful, as we see in the case of Midland *pop* v North *soda*.

One might think that the speed with which local changes in language use and awareness globalize would vitiate regional specificity, but that has not been the case. While colas and their advertising are part of global commerce, one of the most remarked lexical contrasts in American English, the Midland *pop* vs the North *soda*, remains regionally diagnostic. A website is devoted to collecting attestations of these variants for a cola drink. Here, as data collected from urban speakers for *ANAE* shows, who drinks what, and where they drink it, is documentedly regional.

The 'pop' vs 'soda' regional contrast interests more than just linguists. As a demographer of this item of popular culture, Matthew Campbell maps self-reported tokens of 'pop', 'coke', 'soda', and other generic soft drinks (http://popvssoda.com:2998/countystats/total-county.html), showing county-by-county distribution and locality variation across the United States (2003). The sheer robustness of the data not only validates regional distinctions predicted by dialect surveys, but also shows a high level of consciousness regarding regionality and identity.

Conclusion

The shared sense of Midwest American English, and the demonstrable *Midland* American dialect, which it overlays, is distinctive in phonology and grammar, as well as in lexicon, although what that lexicon consists of depends on time and place. The Midland dialect of the American Midwest has received and/or benefited from less scholarly examination and less popular representation than other varieties. This may be the case because a significant number of the defining phonological and grammatical features of the Midland are neither stylistically determining nor socially stratifying. They are items that are perceived as standard or transparent in daily use. Some of these, in particular, *need* + past participle, positive *anymore* and some formulations of *want* + prepositional adverb (want + in, off, out), all having strong Midland concentration, are found in unmarked use outside the Midland, in a range of stylistic levels, and across social groups.

Notes

1. Discussed in Bailey, 2006: 165, 176–7.
2. While thinking about the cover for *Language Variation and Change in the American Midland*, I emailed a contributor to ask his idea of an appropriate image. 'Fields of grain', he emailed back.
3. For a complete discussion of the methodological issues, history of, and continued debate related to determining a Midland dialect in American English, see Simon, and Murray and Simon, in Murray and Simon 2006.
4. Among the features of the Appalachian Heritage Language Hazen examines for currency beyond areas of Appalachian speech, only sociolinguistically transparent positive *anymore* shows evidence of expanding use. In contrast, while multiple modals and especially 'intrusive' 'r' are Midland features, Midland speakers label them as 'Southern' and 'rural' respectively.
5. This set emerges from review of the following materials (grouped according to type):
   1. Published regional Linguistic Atlas projects: *Linguistic Atlas of New England*, (1939–43); *Linguistic Atlas of the Mid- and South Atlantic States* (1998); *Linguistic Atlas of the Gulf States* (1986–92); *Linguistic Atlas of the North Central States*; (Marckwardt and Kretzschmar, 1978-); and *Linguistic Atlas of the Upper Midwest* (1973–76), as well as Alva Davis' dialect study of the Great Lakes region (1951).
   2. *DARE* (Cassidy 1985; Cassidy and Hall 1991, 1996; Hall 2002, and the unpublished corpus referred to as *DARE Files*).
   3. *Atlas of North American English*, which included a set of likely syntactic and lexical variables to provide points of dialectal comparison for the extensive phonological data also being collected).
   4. *The English Dialect Dictionary* (Wright, 1898–1905); *The Scottish National Dictionary* (Grant, 1931–1975); *The Dictionary of Smoky Mountain English* (Montgomery and Hall, 2004).
   5. Surveys conducted with Thomas E. Murray (the specific methodological details of which can be found in Murray, Frazer, and Simon (1996); Murray and Simon, (1999, 2002); and Simon and Murray, (1999).) Between 1984 and 2004, approximately 12,000 L1 English language users from throughout the United States but primarily from Ohio, Indiana, Illinois, Missouri, Kansas, Iowa, Nebraska, the Dakotas, Minnesota, Wisconsin, and Michigan, were contacted either in person, by telephone or US mail, or by posting queries on language- or culture-oriented electronic bulletin boards.
   6. The present list is a reconsideration of a list of 17 individual items first proposed in Murray and Simon 2004, and discussed more thoroughly in Murray and Simon 2006.

   7 *Linguistic Atlas of the Gulf States.*

Acknowledgements

I am grateful to Erika Wyss of Indiana University Purdue University, who digitally generated all of the map figures for this chapter.

All map figures were generated by Erica Wyss to whom I am grateful.

Figure 4.1. Murray, T. E., T. C. Frazer, and B. Simon. 1996. *Need* + Past Participle in American English. *American Speech*, 71:259.

Figure 4.2. Labov, W., S. Ash and C. Boberg. 2006. *Atlas of North American English*. www.ling.upenn.edu/phono_atlas/.

Figure 4.3, 4.14. Ash, S. 2006, p. 41, 47. The North American Midland as a dialect area, in Murray, T. and B. Simon, *Language Variation and Change in the Midland; a new look at 'Heartland' English*.

Figure 4.4, 4.5, 4.6, 4.10, 4.11, 4.12, 4.13. Responses to *Dictionary of American Regional English* (DARE) Questionnaire prompts and material from *DARE* files compiled from data provided by Joan Hall and Luanne von Schneidermesser.

Figure 4.7. Murray, T. E., T. C. Frazer., and B. Simon. 1996. *Need* + Past Participle in American English. *American Speech*, 71:159.

Figure 4.8. Murray, T. E. and B. Simon. 1999. *Want* + Past Participle in American English. *American Speech*, 74.

Figure 4.9. Benson, Erika J. 2009. Everyone Wants In: *Want* + Prepositional Adverb in the Midland and Beyond. *Journal of English Linguistics*. 37:33.

Bibliography

Allen, H. B. (1973–76). *The Linguistic Atlas of the Upper Midwest*. 3 Vols. Minneapolis: University of Minnesota Press.

Ash, S. (2006). The North American Midland as a Dialect Area, in T. E. Murray and B. L. Simon (eds), *Language Variation and Change in the American Midland*, 33–56.

Atwood, E. B. (1953). *Survey of Verb Forms in the Eastern United States*. Ann Arbor: University of Michigan Press.

Bailey, R. W. (2006). Standardizing the Heartland. In T. E. Murray and B. L. Simon (eds), *Language Variation and Change in the American Midland*, 165–178.

Beal, J. C. (2006). *Language and Region*. New York: Routledge.

Benson, E. J. (2009). Everyone wants in: want + prepositional adverb in the Midland and beyond. *Journal of English Linguistics*, 37(1): 28–60.

—. (2005). Need down, in, off, out? Paper Presented at the American Dialect Society, Albuquerque, New Mexico.

Cambell, M. (2003). Names for Generic Soft Drinks, by County. http://popvssoda.com:2998/countystats/total-county.html

Carver, C. (1987). *American Regional Dialects*. Ann Arbor: University of Michigan Press.

Cassidy, F. G. (ed.) (1985). *Dictionary of American Regional English*, Vol. 1. Cambridge: Belknap Press of Harvard University.

Cassidy, F. G. and Hall, J. H. (eds) (1991/1997). *Dictionary of American Regional English*, Vols 2, 3. Cambridge: Belknap Press of Harvard University.

Dakin, R. F. (1966). The Dialect vocabulary of the Ohio River Valley: A survey of the distribution of selected vocabulary forms in an area of complex settlement history. PhD dissertation, University of Michigan.

DARE Files. Unpublished materials of the *Dictionary of American Regional English*. Madison Wisconsin: University of Wisconsin-Madison.

Davis, A. (1951). Dialect distribution and settlement patterns in the Great Lakes region. *The Ohio State Archeological and Historical Quarterly*, 60: 48–56.

Frazer, T. C. (2000). Are rural dialects endangered like island dialects? *American Speech*, 75: 347–349.

Gordon, M. J. (2004). The West and Midwest: phonology. In *A Handbook of Varieties of English* Vol. 1, 338–350.

Hall, J. H. (ed.) (2002). *Dictionary of American Regional English*, Vol. 4. Cambridge: Belknap Press of Harvard University.

—. (2004). Personal email communication: Index by region, usage, and etymology to the *Dictionary of American regional English*, Vol. IV.

Hazen, K. (2006). The Final Days of Appalachian Heritage Language. In T. E. Murray and B. L. Simon (eds), *Language Variation and Change in the American Midland*, 129–150.

Hempl, G. (1896). 'Grease and greasy', *Dialect Notes*, Vol. 1 (1890–96), Duke University Press, North Carolina, 438–444.

Irvine, J. T. and Gal, S. (2009). Language-Ideological Processes. In N. Coupland and A. Jaworski (eds), *The New Sociolinguistics Reader*. Palgrave/Macmillan: New York, London, 374–378.

James, C. M. (2003). Fort Wayne and the Northern Cities Vowel Shift. Unpublished paper, Ball State University, Muncie, Indiana.

Kortmann, B. (ed.). (2012). *The Mouton World Atlas of Variation in English*. Berlin: Mouton de Gruyter.

Kortmann, B. and Schneider, E. W. (eds) (2004). *A Handbook of the Varieties of American English*. Berlin: Mouton de Gruyter.

Kretzschmar Jr., W. A. (2004). Standard American English pronunciation. In *A Handbook of Varieties of English*, Vol 1. Berlin, New York: Mouton de Gruyter, 257–269.

Kurath, H. (1949). *A Word Geography of the Eastern United States*. Ann Arbor: University of Michigan Press.

Kurath, H., Hansen, M. L., Hanley, M. L., Lowman Jr., G. S., and Bloch, B. (eds) (1939–1943). *The Linguistic Atlas of New England*. 3 Vols. Providence Rhode Island: Brown University Press and the American Council of Learned Societies.

Labov, W., Ash, S., and Boberg, C. (2006). *The Atlas of North American English*. Berlin: Mouton de Gruyter.

Linn, M. D. and Regal, R. (2006). The Midland Above the Midland. In T. E. Murray and B. L. Simon (eds), *Language Variation and Change in the American Midland*, 245–262.

Mellencamp, J. (1982). 'Jack and Diane'.

Montgomery, M. B. (2001). British and Irish Antecedents. In J. Algeo (ed.), *The Cambridge History of the English Language, Vol 6: English in North America*. Cambridge: Cambridge University Press, 86–153.

Montgomery, M. B. (2008). Appalachian English: Morphology and Syntax. In
E. Schneider (ed.), *Varieties of English, Vol 2: The Americas and the Caribbean*. Berlin,
New York: Mouton de Gruyter, 428–467.

Montgomery, M. B. and Hall, J. S. (2004). Dictionary of Smoky Mountain English,
Knoxville: University of Tennessee Press.

Montgomery, M. B. and Kirk, J. M. (2001). 'My mother, whenever she passed away,
she had pneumonia': the history and functions of whenever. *Journal of English
Linguistics*, 29: 234.

Murray, T. E. (1993). Positive *anymore* in the Midwest. In T. C. Frazer (ed.), *'Heartland' English: Variation and Transition in the American Midwest*. Tuscaloosa: University of Alabama Press, 173–186.

Murray, T. E. and Simon, B. L. (eds) (2006). What Is Dialect? Revisiting the Midland. *Language Variation and Change in the American Midland*, 1–30.

—. (2004). Colloquial American English: Grammatical Features. In B. Kortmann,
K. Burridge, R. Mesthrie, E. W. Schneider, and C. Upton (eds), *A Handbook of
Varieties of English: Volume 2: Morphology and Syntax*. Berlin, New York: Mouton de
Gruyter.

—. (2002). At the intersection of regional and social dialects: The case of *like* + past
participle in American English. *American Speech*, 77: 32–69.

—. (1999). *Want* + past participle in American English. *American Speech*, 74(2): 140–166.

—. (2006). *Language Variation and Change in the American Midland: A New Look at
'Heartland' English*. Amsterdam: John Benjamins.

Murray, T. E., Fraser T. C., and Simon, B. L. (1996). Need + past participle in
American English. *American Speech*, 71(3): 255–271.

Niedzielski, N. and Preston, D. R. (2009). Folk Linguistics. In N. Coupland and
A. Jaworski (eds), *The New Sociolinguistics Reader*. Basingstoke/New York: Palgrave/
MacMillan, 356–373.

Oxford English Dictionary, 2nd ed. (1989). Vol. IV. Clarendon Press: Oxford, 883.

Pauls, G. and Benson, E. J. I need out because he wants in the house: the subject
pronoun in want and need phrasal constructions. *minds.wisconsin.edu/bitstream/
handle/1793/.../PaulesSpr09.ppt?*

Pederson, L. (2000). Regional Patterns of American Speech. In *American Heritage
Dictionary of English*, 4th edition. http://www.bartleby.com/61/5.html

—. (2001). Dialects. In J. Algeo (ed.), *The Cambridge History of the English Language, Vol
6: English in North America*. Cambridge: Cambridge University Press, 253–290.

Pederson, L. A., McDaniel S. L., Bailey, G., Bassett, M. H., Adams, C. M., Liao, C.,
and Montgomery, M. (1986–1992). *The Linguistic Atlas of the Gulf States*. 7 Vols.
Athens: University of Georgia Press.

Preston, D. (1996a). Where the Worst English is Spoken. In E. Schneider (ed.) *Focus
on the USA*. Amsterdam/Philadelphia: John Benjamins, 297–360.

—. (1996b). Whaddayaknow?:The Modes of Folk Linguistic Awareness. *Language
Awareness*, 5: 40–74.

—. (2005). What is Folk Linguistics? Why Should You Care? Lingua Posnaniensis.
Review of General and Comparative Linguistics, 47: 143–162.

Simon, B. L. (2006). Introducing the Midland: What Is It, Where Is It, How Do We
Know. In T. E. Murray and B. L. Simon (eds), *Language Variation and Change in the
American Midland: A New Look at 'Heartland' English*, ix–xii.

Smiley, J. (1991). *A Thousand Acres.* New York: Knopf.

Thomas, E. (2001). *An Acoustic Analysis of Vowel Variation in New World English.* Publication of the American Dialect Society 85. Durham, North Carolina: Duke University Press.

Ulrey, K. S. (2009). Dinner needs cooked, groceries need bought, diapers need changed, kids need bathed: trackin the progress of need + past participle across the United States. Unpublished master's thesis, Ball State University, Muncie, Indiana.

Webster, N. (1789). *Dissertations on the English Language, with Notes, Historical and Critical.* Boston: Isaiah Thomas. Reprint.

Wentworth, H. (1944). *American Dialect Dictionary.* New York: Thomas Y. Cromwell.

Wright, J. (1855–1930). *English Dialect Dictionary.* London: Frowde.

Chapter 5

Chicano English

Carmen Fought

Background of Chicano English in the United States

Terminology

Before beginning the description of Chicano English in the United States, it is important to discuss the ethnic terms used in this chapter. The label 'Latino' is used to identify the ethnic groups on which this chapter focuses, people whose ethnic origins are in the Spanish-speaking parts of Mexico, Central America or South America. Other terms used in the literature include particularly a) 'Hispanic' (the term used by the census), and b) 'Mexican-American', 'Dominican-American', etc. (where the specific place of origin is identified). 'Latino' seems to be emerging in many geographic regions as the term preferred by speakers within the ethnic groups it identifies, particularly in contrast with 'Hispanic' which is sometimes viewed as being associated with the government, the academy or other out-groups.

The term 'Chicano English' identifies the variety that was first described in the Southwestern part of the United States, and spoken primarily by people of Mexican-American origin. However, where relevant, information about other dialects spoken by Latinos and Latinas in the United States will be brought into focus since Chicano English forms part of a larger tapestry of Latino varieties of English.

Moreover, the term Chicano English will be singularly reserved for the variety spoken only by native speakers, most of whom were born in the United States. In theory, one could use the label 'Chicano English' to encompass any dialect spoken by people of Mexican origin in the United States, including both varieties that are identical to those of Anglos in the area, and varieties spoken by adult immigrants for whom English is a second language; however, my preference is not to embrace this use of the term in this chapter. Santa Ana (1993) discusses the importance of reserving the term Chicano English for the variety used by native speakers:

Chicano English is an ethnic dialect that children acquire as they acquire English in the barrio or other ethnic social setting during their language acquisition period. Chicano English is to be distinguished from the English of second-language learners . . . Thus defined, Chicano English is spoken only by native English speakers. (1993:15)

Chicano English, then, as discussed in this chapter, is a non-standard variety of English, influenced by contact with Spanish, and spoken as a native dialect by both bilingual and monolingual speakers.

Demographic Information

In the decade between 1990 and 2000, census figures show that the US Latino population (the census uses the term 'Hispanic') increased by more than 50 per cent, from 22.4 million to 35.3 million (Fought 2003). In January of 2003, the US Census released data indicating that Latinos and Latinas had replaced African-Americans as the largest minority ethnic group in the United States. They also represent the largest group of current immigrants to the United States. Because Latino immigrants are predominantly Spanish speakers, this process ensures that Chicano English continues to be a dialect flourishing in situations of language contact between English and Spanish.

The largest Latino subgroup consists of people of Mexican origin. Because census questions relating to Latinos and Latinas have changed over the decades, however, it is not possible to trace the long-term growth of this population in detail. The Latino population also has a distinctive demographic profile: it is younger than other groups. Its median age in 2000 was 25.9 years, compared with 35.3 years among the larger population. In addition, native-born Latinos have outnumbered immigrants historically by a large margin, a fact which would appear to have many social and linguistic implications. In 1990, for example, there were 14.0 million Latinos who were born in the United States versus only 7.8 million who were born in other countries (Fought 2003).

Geographically, the 2000 census showed that 76.1 per cent of Latinos in the United States lived in one of the following seven states: California, Texas, New York, Florida, Illinois, Arizona and New Jersey. California and Texas have had the largest Latino populations historically, especially in counties on or near the Mexican border. Many families have been living in these areas continuously, since before there was any European-American settlement of the area.

More recently, other regions of the United States, including rural regions in the coastal parts of the South, have begun experiencing a sharp increase in the number of Latinos and Latinas who have migrated to the area. As an example, between 1990 and 2000, North Carolina experienced a higher percentage of growth in its Latino population than any other state, and it now has the largest percentage of monolingual Spanish speakers of any state in the United States (Wolfram, Carter and Moriello 2004). These newer communities provide linguists with a unique opportunity to track the emergence of new Latino English varieties in situations of language contact.

Linguistic background and contacts

As noted above, Latino settlement in the Southwest predates European-American settlement. In linguistic terms, this means that English-speaking and Spanish-speaking populations have been in close contact throughout the history of the region. The types of speakers represented in Latino communities, both historically and at present, include foreign-born Latinos who are Spanish-dominant, as well as native speakers of English. The foreign-born speakers may represent various stages of learning English, or may be primarily Spanish speakers. Similarly, the native English speakers may or may not be bilingual, and if they do speak Spanish, their level of fluency may vary considerably.

Language proficiency and preferences are strongly tied to generational status. A 2002 National Survey of Latinos by the Pew Hispanic Center found that the individuals in the first generation of Latino immigrants to the United States spoke mostly Spanish (62 per cent) or were bilingual (37 per cent). In contrast, second-generation Latinos and Latinas rarely reported speaking predominantly Spanish (6 per cent), and were more likely to be bilingual (74 per cent) or monolingual in English (21 per cent). Fought (2003) found that third generation speakers in Los Angeles had a strong tendency to be monolingual in English. Second-generation speakers ranged in fluency from those whose Spanish was rated as native-like, to those whose Spanish ability was extremely limited. In addition, a number of other codes may be present in a particular community; Fought (2006) identifies 10 separate linguistic codes that may be present in Latino communities, including multiple varieties of Spanish and English, as well as code-switching.

Chicano English emerged historically from the context described above, in which English and Spanish were in constant contact, both across the community and within the competence of individuals. Early Latino immigrants to the Southwest learnt English as a second language. This non-native variety, as would be expected linguistically, included phonological, syntactic and semantic patterns influenced by Spanish. The first generations born in the United States generally grew up using both Spanish and English, and as the relevant Latino communities became more stable and settled, a new variety, Chicano English, emerged. It should be noted that non-native English is still a variety that can also be found in the community, due to the continued influx of adult immigrants from Spanish-speaking countries. Notes on the structure of this variety will be provided later.

As Wald (1984:21) notes, the emergence of Chicano English (and other varieties like it) shows many parallels with the course generally followed in the development of pidgin and creole languages. In settings where there is a pidgin, it is generally spoken as a second language by adult speakers, with significant inter-speaker variability, simplification and so on. However, among succeeding generations of children, the pidgin quickly becomes more elaborated and grammaticized, developing into a creole. Similarly, the non-native inter-language of adult Latino immigrants exhibits a high degree of inter-speaker variability, and lacks certain grammatical and linguistic functions. This unstable inter-language, however, provided the historical basis for the fully developed dialect which developed among the younger generations: Chicano English.

In addition to Spanish and non-native (immigrant) English, there are other varieties which have been in historical contact with Chicano English. One of these is African-American English (AAE). Fought (2003) describes a number of features of AAE that are shared by Chicano English speakers in California. Overall, however, it seems that Chicano English has been less influenced by AAE than, for example, Puerto Rican English in New York City (cf. Urciuoli 1996, Zentella 1997).

Often in sociolinguistic research, the potential influence of European-American regional varieties on Latino varieties has been discounted. In general, minority ethnic varieties have been viewed as following a separate linguistic course in which the local sound changes taking place in European-American varieties played little or no role. More recent research, however, shows that there can, in fact, be an influence of regional sound changes on Latino variet-ies, both at the individual and community levels. Fought 2003 found that Chicano English speakers in Los Angeles exhibited two sound changes typical of the California Anglo population: /u/-fronting and /ae/-backing. In addi-tion, the same study found the use of *like* as a discourse marker, as well as *be like* and *be all* as quotatives, semantic features characteristic of the local European-American dialect. Gordon (2000), in contrast, found that Mexican-American speakers in Indiana were generally not taking part in the Northern Cities Chain Shift. However, individual speakers with many European-American contacts did exhibit the variants associated with the change in progress.

Chicano English, then, can be seen as a contact variety, based on historical contact between English and Spanish. However, we must also take into account region-based influences for the particular area in which it is spoken. Further-more, as with all dialects, we must allow for sociolinguistic variation within Chicano English, related to age, gender, social class, local affiliations and other factors related to the construction of identity.

Linguistic description of Chicano English

The linguistic description provided in this section is based on a number of works, including Penfield and Ornstein-Galicia 1985, Santa Ana 1991, Wald 1993, Wald 1996, Mendoza-Denton 1997, Fought 2003, and Fought 2006. In addition, in each section, a few examples of the ways in which Chicano English differs from the non-native English variety discussed earlier will be provided.

The features cited here are characteristic of Chicano English, and help to distinguish it from other dialects. However, as is the case with all dialects, there exists considerable variation within the community in terms of the particular features used by individual speakers, as well as the frequency of their use. Some speakers may use almost all of the forms listed here, while others may use only a few. Some of the types of sociolinguistic differences found among Chicano English speakers will be addressed later.

Phonology of Chicano English

Chicano English differs significantly from other English dialects in the areas of phonetics and phonology, and such differences often play a more important role than grammatical features in marking an individual as a speaker of a Chicano English dialect. Some phonetic differences involve a slight shift in vowel quality towards a corresponding Spanish phoneme, although Spanish influence cannot account for all of the variation (cf. Godinez 1984). Intonation and stress patterns also play a role in giving Chicano English a unique rhythm and prosody (Fought and Fought 2002, Fought 2003:70ff). These qualities can be perceived as signalling a separate dialect of English, even in the absence of marked phonetic or grammatical differences. As with any community of speakers, phonetic elements vary among individuals and within the speech of a single individual, depending on context. In particular, there are quantitative differences in the application of certain phonological rules, such as the reduction of unstressed vowels. Below are some of the most salient features of Chicano English phonology.

VOWELS

Less frequent vowel reduction

Chicano English speakers tend to reduce vowels in unstressed syllables less often than speakers of other American English dialects. For example, the first vowel in *together* would usually be schwa [ə] in many dialects, but in Chicano English, this word would often be pronounced [tʰugɛðəɹ]. Also the direction of movement for unstressed vowels may be different in Chicano English.

Lack of glides

Chicano English speakers often have more monophthongal versions of vowels than speakers of other American English dialects. For example, the high vowels, [i] and [u], tend to be realized as [ij] and [uw] by speakers of many dialects of English, but Chicano English speakers have monophthongal vowels for these phonemes, similar to the corresponding vowels in Spanish. The same can be found with Chicano English versions of the diphthongs [ej] and [ow], which sound more like [e] and [o].

Tense realization of /ɪ/

In a limited set of contexts, Chicano English speakers use [i] as a phonetic variant of /ɪ/. This occurs most often in the linguistic environment of the morpheme –ing, so that *going* is pronounced [gowin]. It is important to note that in many other contexts, however, Chicano English shows a clear contrast between the phonemes /i/ and /ɪ/, in contrast with the English spoken by Spanish-speaking learners, who do tend to neutralize the distinction.

[ɑ] vs [a]

European-American dialects in the Southwest exhibit a merger of [ɔ] and [ɑ], so that the vowels in both *caught* and *cot* would generally be realized as the low back vowel [ɑ]. For Chicano English speakers, these vowels are also merged. But for many of them, the vowel used in these contexts is slightly fronted, more like the [a] of Spanish.

Centralized realization of [ʊ]

For [ʊ], the vowel in *book*, some Chicano English speakers have a high central rounded variant, so that, for example, *look* is pronounced [lʉk]

Other Chicano English speakers have an unrounded variant of this vowel, that is, [lɨk], which parallels a tendency in California Anglo varieties to front back vowels.

CONSONANTS

Stops for interdental fricatives

Chicano English frequently substitutes alveolar stops [t] and [d] for the interdental fricatives [θ] and [ð], so that *then* becomes [dɛn], for example. This feature is not unique to Chicano English, and occurs in a number of non-standard varieties, such as AAE, as well, although it does not appear to be typical of non-standard European dialects in California. Interestingly, stopping of interdental fricatives can often be found even among Latino speakers whose dialect is otherwise very standard overall in terms of grammar and phonology.

Loss of final consonants

As with all dialects of English, Chicano English tends to reduce consonant clusters. What sets Chicano English apart from European-American varieties in the area is that final consonants can be deleted even when they do not occur in a cluster. For example, the word *night* can be pronounced [naj]. AAE also seems to allow this type of reduction (Bailey and Thomas 1998), but it appears to be even more frequent in Chicano English.

Glottalization of final voiceless stops

Where final voiceless stops do occur in Chicano English, some speakers produce them as glottalized. Often these types of stops are also preceded by creaky voice in the vowel. Sometimes there is full substitution of a glottal stop for the expected consonant, [p, t, k], which may contribute to the perception of 'lost' final consonants, as well.

PROSODY

In addition to these segmental features, Chicano English, as noted earlier, has a very distinctive prosody. Some of this distinctiveness reflects the historical influence of Spanish on the dialect. To begin with, CE speakers occasionally place the stresses within a word (particularly a compound word) distinctly from speakers of other varieties, as in the following example (from Fought 2003):

mòrning   síckness

The dominant stress here, at the phrasal level, was on *sick-*. In other dialects, this compound would have a strong stress only on the first syllable, and if a secondary stress was present on *sickness*, it would be a very weak one.

This alternate pattern of stresses combines with a tendency towards syllable-timing in Chicano English (versus the stress-timing typical of Standard English). Fought and Fought (2002) found that there was a difference between Chicano English speakers and European-American speakers in California, such that the Chicano English speakers produced a more even-timed rhythm pattern, particularly at the beginnings of utterances. The pattern of less frequent vowel reduction discussed above also contributes to making this dialect sound more syllable-timed than other varieties of American English.

The combination of these features (prosodic and segmental) makes Chicano English sound more like Spanish than other dialects of English, given the nature of the vowels, the preference for open syllables created by the loss of final consonants, and the syllable-timed prosodic patterns. For this reason, Chicano English is often mistaken for non-native learner English by speakers outside the community. Many people hear a speaker of Chicano English and assume that the individual must be a native speaker of Spanish, when in fact, depending on the generation, this person may be completely monolingual in English, with little or no knowledge of Spanish.

Earlier, it was mentioned that in the Latino communities where Chicano English is spoken, one also finds, as part of the community repertoire, a non-native variety of English, spoken by recent immigrants or those who came to the United States as adults. While Chicano English undeniably shows the historic influence of Spanish, it is also clearly distinct from this second-language variety. Spanish-dominant speakers, for example, collapse certain phonemic distinctions in English such as between [i] and [ɪ], between [æ] and [ɛ], between [tʃ] and [ʃ], and between [ə] and [ɑ] (Fought 2003:81–3). Chicano English speakers have clear distinctions for all these pairs. Therefore, it is not accurate to say that Chicano English is simply a 'Spanish accent', although it may be mistakenly perceived this way by those outside the community.

Morphological and syntactic features of Chicano English

The syntax of Chicano English, in general, is not as distinctive as the phonology. In AAE, for example, one finds an elaborate aspectual system that contrasts with that of other English varieties. In Chicano English, however, a majority of the syntactic and morphological features that distinguish it from Standard American varieties are also shared by other non-standard varieties, such as AAE or working-class European-American dialects. There are a small number of features, however, that appear to reflect the influence of Spanish or to have developed independently.

It should be noted that it is not always possible to assign an unambiguous origin to particular non-standard features. Multiple negation, for example, is characteristic of AAE, of non-standard European-American varieties, and also of (standard) Spanish. So it may not be possible to determine whether this feature in Chicano English reflects the influence of one of these sources, a confluence of several of them, or an independent development.

Below are listed a number of syntactic and morphological features of Chicano English. Not all of these features would be used by any particular speaker of Chicano English. As would be expected, non-standard syntactic features are most characteristic of the working-class variety of Chicano English, although some, like negative concord, occur frequently among middle class speakers also.

Features common to many non-standard dialects

Regularization of irregular past tense forms:

> *It spinned.*
> *. . . most people that I hanged around with.*
> *I haven't wrote in a long time.*

Lack of –s marking on 3ʳᵈ person singular forms:

*(If) somebody else just **come** and take your life.*
*Otherwise, she **don't** know Brenda.*

was/were alternation:

*Everybody knew the Cowboys **was** gonna win again.*

Use of ain't:

*My name **ain't** exciting either.*

Regularization of possessive pronouns:

*. . . have to start supporting **theirselves** at early ages.*
*. . . he's a guy, he could take care of **hisself.***

Resumptive pronouns in relative clauses:

*The guy that um, that they knew **he** was doing it.*

Negative concord (multiple negation):

*Things **ain't** gonna **never** change in L.A. **no** more.*
***None** of the girls **don't** like her*

Subject-auxiliary inversion in embedded questions:

*. . . then they asked them **where did they live.***
*I don't know **what color are we**, but it doesn't matter.*

Features shared specifically with AAE

In comparison with other Latino varieties in the United States, Chicano English seems to have assimilated relatively few syntactic features specific to AAE, and such features are most commonly found among speakers who have more contact with African-Americans in their neighbourhood or peer group. In contrast, studies of Puerto-Rican English (Wolfram 1974, Zentella 1997) and of Dominican-American English (Bailey 2000) find a much wider range of features from AAE used among these groups. In addition, as noted earlier, some CHE features might have AAE as one of multiple sources.

Habitual be:

*The news **be** showing it too much.*
*Me and my mom **be** praying in Spanish.*

Expletive it:

> *It's four of us, there's two of them.*

Perfective had:

> *The cops **had** went to my house . . .*

Features particular to Chicano English

As with other non-standard dialects, it is the particular group of syntactic features used, rather than any one element, that make the Chicano English grammar unique. However, there are some non-standard features that are not commonly found among dialects other than Chicano English, and these are found particularly in the area of modals. Two such structures are listed below.

Use of would in if- clauses:

> *If **he'd be** here right now, he'd make me laugh.*

Use of the modal could to signal 'competence':

> *He **could** talk, like, smart, y'know . . . he's like a straight-A student.*
> *I learned that people that are left handed **could** draw better than people who are right handed.*

Semantics of Chicano English

As is true of dialects generally, there is much more inter-speaker variability for Chicano English in the area of lexical items and semantics than in the syntactic or phonological systems. The focus here is on contexts where the semantics of a particular item in Chicano English differs from its use in other dialects of English, and on lexical items that specifically signal contact with other varieties. As with the other sections of this chapter, no claim is made that the features on this list are exhaustive, or exclusive to Chicano English.

Use of non-standard prepositions

The non-standard use of prepositions in Chicano English is one of the very few features that seem to reflect unambiguously the influence of Spanish. There is a wide range of alternate prepositions used in Chicano English instead of those that might be expected in other varieties. Examples include:

> ***For** my mom can understand. **For** she won't feel guilty.*
> *We're really supposed to get out of here **on** June.*

*We all make mistakes **along** life.*
*He was **in** a beer run.*

Use of tell for 'ask'

*If I tell her to jump up, she'll **tell** me how high.*
*She was telling my aunt to **tell** them, you know, what, I mean, what's the reason?*

Use of barely to mean 'just recently':

*He just **barely** got a job you know back with his father.*
*I just **barely** checked in.* (= speaker has been there only 3 weeks)

Use of brothers to mean 'siblings':

*To my **brothers** I usually talk English.* (Speaker has four sisters and one brother.)
*My **brothers** don't want to l- don't want me to leave because they love the baby.* (Speaker has one sister and two brothers.)

Many of the syntactic and semantic features that have been discussed are found also among speakers of the non-native English variety found in Latino communities. In particular, the use of non-standard prepositions is particularly characteristic of this group. On the other hand, the extension of the semantics of *barely* seems to be a more recent and independent development in the dialect.

Use of Chicano English in the Community

In the Latino communities where Chicano English has been studied, it is always found in the context of a repertoire of other varieties, as discussed above. As might be expected, the selection of language varieties or styles plays a central role in the construction of ethnic identity. Not all of the varieties will be available in every community. As mentioned earlier, for example, the availability of AAE as a linguistic model is variable across different regions of the United States, and within individual Latino communities. In the Puerto-Rican American community studied by Urciuoli, contact with AAVE speakers was the norm (1996:65). On the other hand, speakers in the Mexican-American community of Los Angeles had less contact with African-Americans due to high inter-ethnic tensions (Fought 2003:95–6).

Furthermore, a variety may be available to some community members and not others. A good example is the wide range of fluencies in Spanish found among young Chicano English speakers in Los Angeles (Fought 2003). For some of these speakers, Spanish was not available as a regular code, although brief 'emblematic' uses of Spanish lexical items were still sometimes found among even the monolinguals. In general, then, individual community members will draw from the linguistic repertoire of the community in different ways, as they construct and reproduce ideologies about language.

Chicano English and Standard English

The usual patterns with respect to standard and non-standard varieties are evident in the Chicano English-speaking communities that have been studied. Varieties labelled as 'correct' English or 'pure' Spanish are privileged in the ideology over non-standard varieties of either, as well as over code-switching or AAE. This does not mean that other varieties, such as Chicano English, are not valued by community members, but they are often subject to overt criticism both within and outside the community.

As a result, those members of the community who speak both Chicano English and a standard variety are more likely to select the standard variety in formal or professional situations. Chicano English, like most non-standard varieties, is more likely to be used among friends and in-group members, in relatively informal situations. On the other hand, while the standard varieties are seen by many as a way to 'get ahead', they can nonetheless carry negative connotations of their own. In particular, standard varieties of English are often associated with European-Americans (cf. Urciuoli 1996), and therefore with a rejection of ethnic identity.

Chicano English and Spanish

As might be expected, given the dominant US ideology that values English and associates Spanish with the poor and uneducated, attitudes towards Spanish in Latino communities are often mixed. One Chicano English speaker from Fought's (2003) study comments about Spanish: 'I think it's very important. Very. Cause, you know, you're Mexican, you have it in your blood' (Fought 2003:200). Speakers in this study also pointed out the practical benefits of speaking Spanish, such as being able to translate for others in the community or to communicate with monolingual grandparents.

At the same time, though, there is a clear and increasing language shift to English in most of the communities where Chicano English is spoken, and retention of Spanish beyond the second generation is unusual (Veltman 1990, Zentella 1997, Fought 2003). This pattern suggests that despite the positive affirmations of the role of Spanish in Latino ethnic identities, Spanish is being lost by subsequent generations. It is even possible that in the future, Chicano English may become the only variety spoken by US-born Latinos and Latinas.

Despite the increasing number of monolinguals who speak Chicano English, however, the myth that Chicano English represents a 'Spanish accent' persists.

Children in the school system who speak Chicano English, for example, are often given tests designed for students whose native language is something other than English, because teachers often erroneously associate Chicano English with dominance in Spanish.

Chicano English and Code-switching

There have been many studies of code-switching in Latino communities where Chicano English or some other Latino variety is spoken. Although myths about code-switching persist, linguists have firmly established that code-switching is a rule-governed system, and that it signals fluency, rather than lack of fluency, on the part of the speakers (see Zentella 1997). Still, in the educational system, for instance, code-switching is often treated as an aberration or a language problem.

Attitudes towards code-switching in Latino communities can be complex. A speaker in the Puerto-Rican community studied by Urciuoli summed the conflicting attitudes up: 'Don't mix, it's awful—well, it don't sound to me awful, but it would sound awful to a teacher' (1996:97). In general, older speakers in these communities tend to have more conservative attitudes, as would be expected. However, among younger speakers, code-switching, usually referred to by the term 'Spanglish', seems to be experiencing a reclaiming. Teenage Mexican-American speakers in Fought (2003) expressed almost uniformly positive attitudes towards code-switching. Some speakers even felt that code-switching was what distinguished the ethnic identity of Mexican-Americans born in the United States from that of adult immigrants from Mexico. The recent release of a movie entitled 'Spanglish' suggests that at least some of these positive values are beginning to influence mainstream norms. The fact that the movie is a comedy, though, indicates that Spanglish is still seen as having a humorous rather than serious value.

Code-switching is often conflated with Chicano English, both inside and outside the community. However, linguistically, the two constitute completely separate varieties. Middle class speakers, for example, may code-switch between standard varieties of English and Spanish. Conversely, an individual who is monolingual can speak Chicano English without any code-switching at all.

At the same time, there is an inherent social relationship between these two varieties in Latino communities. Both represent important elements of how speakers in such communities signal their ethnic identity. Furthermore, as mentioned earlier, even monolingual English speakers will sometimes throw in 'emblematic' switches to Spanish. So in many places, the group of Chicano English speakers who never code-switch is relatively small. In this sense, code-switching might be considered a stylistic option that plays an important role in defining the range of Chicano English.

Media Use of Chicano English

The use of Chicano English in the media is a relatively new topic. There are a number of general studies available of how Mexican-Americans are portrayed in films, such as Berumen 1995, Flores and Holling 1999, and the collection of articles *Latin Looks*, edited by Rodriguez (1997). These studies trace a number of the stereotypes that can be found in media portrayals of Latinos and Latinas historically. Both in terms of feature films and in terms of television, though, studies of Latinos and Latinas lag behind those of African-Americans in terms of breadth and quantity.

Fought (2003) is one of the few studies to explore linguistic representations of Mexican-Americans in the mass media. The study focuses on five films that feature predominantly Mexican-American characters and actors: *Boulevard Nights* (1979), *Born in East L.A.* (1987), *La Bamba* (1987), *American Me* (1992), and *Mi Vida Loca* (1994). These films were chosen because they all had a relatively widespread distribution.

The study found that these movies present a fairly realistic portrayal of Chicano English. Rather than inaccurately representing all Latino characters as speaking non-native speaker 'broken' English, or, conversely, as all speaking standard dialects, the films presented a range of varieties. Some characters used vernacular styles of Chicano English with a great deal of non-standard grammar (e.g. the character of 'Santana' in *American Me*). Other characters used varieties that were relatively standard in their syntax, but had clear Chicano English phonology and prosodic features (e.g. 'Rudy' in *Born in East L.A.*). The films as a whole also showed a number of Mexican-American characters code-switching, which again, as discussed above, fits well with the usage patterns of real communities.

At a more detailed level, Fought found that 81 per cent of major characters and 77 per cent of minor characters were represented as speaking Chicano English. Only the character of 'Richie' in *La Bamba* used a completely standard variety. Characters who were shown as speaking non-native learner English were almost all played by older actors. The percentage of characters who code-switched was also quite high, at 77 per cent for major characters. It is difficult to say whether widespread representations of Chicano English and code-switching in feature films, including a number that have been released since the study discussed here was concluded, will have a positive effect on general attitudes about these varieties.

In addition, in markets such as the Los Angeles area, there are now an increasing number of television programmes and stations featuring Latinos. The largest of the corporations targeting this market (Univision and Telemundo particularly) have traditionally featured Spanish-language programming as their main staple. However, Telemundo recently launched a new network, mun2 – a wordplay on *mun* + *dos* ('two') as *mundos* ('world'). This new network features bilingual programming targeted at a younger audience. In November 2006, Apple announced that programming from Telemundo and mun2 would be available for purchase and download on their popular online entertainment site, the iTunes Store (http://www.macnn.com/articles/06/11/01/itms.adds.spanish.tv/).

Additionally, *The George Lopez Show*, one of the few sitcoms to focus on a working-class Latino family, premiered on ABC in 2002. The show ended production in 2007, but is widely seen in syndication. It stars George Lopez, one of the most successful Latino comedians of all time. Lopez uses a great deal of Spanish, code-switching, and Chicano English in his standup routines. The show, however, is quite conservative in terms of language, in that: a) there is almost no use of Spanish, b) some characters, such as Lopez's daughter on the show, speak a completely standard variety of English, and c) those who speak Chicano English use mainly phonology and very little of the grammatical and other features that would mark this variety in a typical working-class home. In addition, there is practically no use of code-switching on the show. Lopez himself commented on this anomaly in an early interview:

I don't think we've progressed far enough for me to be speaking Spanglish on ABC. It's not acceptable yet. Maybe in the fourth year, we'll have an episode with Spanglish and subtitles, but now I can't. It's baby steps, man. (Gallaga 2002)

In general, television tends to be more conservative than films in terms of language (cf. Fought and Harper 2004). Only time will tell how much use of Chicano English, with or without code-switching, future generations of television viewers will encounter.

Current Trends in the Study of Chicano English

In studying Latino varieties of English, and the current trends associated with those varieties, there are several promising avenues of research that have emerged in the last decade or so. One is the study of incipient communities of Chicano English speakers in regions of the United States that have not historically had as large a population of Latinos and Latinas as in the Southwest. As mentioned earlier, North Carolina is one such location (see Wolfram, Carter and Moriello 2004).

Research on the history of Chicano English in the Southwest has had to rely on indirect methods, since the relevant settlement of Mexican immigrants in that region took place before the establishment of sociolinguistic research methods. The newer communities of Mexican-Americans in places like North Carolina, however, offer an opportunity to study dialects of Chicano English as they develop. In essence, as a new generation of Chicano English speakers emerges in these regions, linguists will be able to study a variety that is tied to ethnicity as it develops.

Among other things, this type of research could allow for comparison of Latino varieties in different regions. For example, we might explore how the new Southern varieties are similar to or different from Chicano English, based on the descriptive studies that have already been done in the Southwest. In addition, the varieties associated with European-Americans and African-Americans in these areas are quite different from those in the Southwest. This divergence in the surrounding dialects could allow us to track nuances of how other English varieties in the region influence Chicano English as it develops. Such studies could have implications not only for the study of Latino varieties, but for the study of situations of language contact more generally, as well as the development of contact varieties.

Another interesting area of research involves the changing trends in the field of sociolinguistics generally. Where the earliest sociolinguistic studies tended to assign people to categories (e.g. ethnic categories, such as 'Latino') without much exploration of diversity within those categories, newer studies tend to take a more constructionist approach. In general, the current practice in sociolinguistic research is to view identity in general, and ethnicity in particular, as a process that the individual undertakes and recreates on a daily basis, a process that can be more variable and fluid than was previously assumed.

This approach has many implications for the study of Chicano English. First of all, we expect different community members to use slightly different varieties of Chicano English. Some will be more standard than others. Some will show a stronger influence from other dialects, such as AAE, while others may show little direct influence of this type. In addition, we will need to look at differences in how particular community members view and construct their identity, both in relation to other elements of identity such as gender, and in relation to the specifics of their personal histories and group memberships.

A number of recent studies have approached the linguistic variation within Latino communities in exactly this way. Mendoza-Denton (1997), for example, looks at Chicano English in Northern California among various groups of high school girls. To begin with, rather than simply assigning them to groups based on social class and so forth, she conducts ethnographic research to reveal the categories that are relevant within the community, which include groups such as *fresas*, Latina Jocks or gang members from the Norteñas or Sureñas gangs. These locally relevant categories were crucial to understanding the patterning of the tense /I/ variable in the dialect of Chicano English that the girls spoke.

Similarly, Fought (2003) looks at /u/-fronting and other phonological variables in the Chicano English of Los Angeles. This study is unusual in that it focuses on the use of variables from the local European-American community and the extent to which these do or do not appear in Chicano English. In order to explain the pattern of variation in /u/-fronting in this community, it is necessary to examine how clusters of social factors besides ethnicity (including gender, gang status and social class) interact in determining who uses this sociolinguistic variable.

A final relevant study is Gordon 2000, which studied the variables of the Northern Cities Chain Shift (an important set of sound changes taking place in a large inland northern section of the United States) across speakers of various ethnicities in Indiana. Gordon found that Mexican-American speakers generally did not exhibit many of the features of this vowel shift. However, one out of the five Mexican-American speakers he studied showed rates of all the features that were quite high, higher than some of the European-American speakers. Gordon explains that this speaker grew up in a predominantly white neighbourhood, and mostly has white friends, in contrast to the other participants. This individual also did not emphasize the importance of Mexican ethnicity to her identity in the way that the other Mexican-American speakers did.

Gordon also includes a small number of mixed-ethnicity speakers in his study. Very little study of speakers who identify with multiple ethnicities has been done in sociolinguistics to date, despite the fact that these speakers form a growing proportion of the population of many communities. Several of the speakers in Gordon's study showed high usages of the Northern Cities Chain Shift features, at a level comparable to the European-American speakers in the sample. In general then, the trend in research on Chicano English, and Latino varieties more generally, is to study how these linguistic varieties contribute to the construction of ethnic identity in complex but interesting ways.

Social, Political and Economic Impact of Chicano English

As a non-standard dialect, Chicano English is subject to the same prejudices and stereotypes that affect other similarly marked varieties such as AAE. Speakers of Chicano English are often judged as speaking 'incorrectly' or 'brokenly.' In addition, and particular to this variety, there is the mistaken assumption that a person who speaks Chicano English is a native speaker of Spanish, making 'mistakes.'

One of the contexts where such prejudices have the most detrimental effect is in the school system. Children who speak Chicano English may be judged as having poor verbal abilities, for example. In the school where my fieldwork was conducted, children who reported that Spanish was spoken in their homes, even if they did not speak it themselves, were often tested and then classified as 'LEP' (Limited English Proficient). This category is intended to identify children whose native language is something other than English; due to the nature of the test, however, Chicano English speakers often score poorly and are classified as LEP even if they are completely monolingual in English and speak no Spanish at all. An interesting question for the future, then, is how school systems can help speakers of Chicano English acquire the skills they may need later, without challenging their right to use a variety associated intimately with their personal and group identity.

One approach that has proved useful for speakers of Chicano English (as well as other vernacular dialects, such as AAE) is teaching Standard English through some modified form of contrastive analysis. This technique, which has a long history in ESL classes, involves highlighting contrasts in form between standard and non-standard varieties and helping children to identify the rules that apply to each set of patterns.

An illustration of the use of this method with Chicano English-speaking children can be seen in the PBS documentary **Do You Speak American?** It shows a teacher in an elementary school classroom in Los Angeles playing a Jeopardy-style game with his class, in which teams of students get points for being able to 'translate' AAE or Chicano English forms into Standard English forms. At least in this example, the students seem highly motivated, and have clearly made progress in learning standard forms, free from any negative discourse about the non-standard varieties. Giving children the opportunity to learn Standard English, while still validating and respecting Chicano English, would have important social and political repercussions. Unfortunately, these new methods have not yet gained clear acceptance within educational administrations and school boards.

As far as the economic impact of Chicano English is concerned, the situation in the Southwest is an interesting one. Despite social prejudices, Chicano English speakers are increasingly being recognized as a 'hot' new market for advertising dollar. As was discussed earlier, the media in general are expanding to target young, Latino audiences. In that sense, there exists a potential for economic growth associated with the use of Chicano English. The addition of a new broadcast channel, mun2, targeting this group is particularly significant. The (correct) perception that Latinos form a significant and rapidly growing segment of the consumer population fosters the potential association of Chicano English with positive economic outcomes.

Future Implications of Chicano English within the Southwest

One issue that the cited studies of Latino varieties seem to agree on is that such varieties are a key part of the construction of ethnic identity for many speakers within Latino communities. Given the crucial role of Chicano English in the linguistic expression of identity, particularly for speakers born here who know little or no Spanish, it is likely that this variety will continue to thrive and prosper within the Southwest region of the United States. We would also expect other, similar varieties to emerge and develop in areas where there are newly-formed Mexican-American communities, as discussed earlier.

In addition, as media sources become more diverse in an attempt to reach Latino audiences, more speakers outside the community will have access to Chicano English as well as code-switching. Just as AAE can now be heard in movies and on sitcoms, Chicano English may someday be easy to find on broadcast and cable television. It is possible, for example, that **The George Lopez Show** will be the first in a series of sitcoms revolving around Latino families, just as there are now a much wider range of sitcoms with primarily African-American casts than were available even a decade ago. Certainly, popular stand-up comedians such as Lopez, Carlos Mencia and others serve to bring Chicano English to all types of audiences who may not live in communities where Chicano English is spoken.

Though it has long been established that we model our speech on our peers and not on television actors, still the presence of a variety in the media gives it a certain cultural authority, both within and outside the group. This media presence can be expected to grow and expand as new regions of the country begin to have established Latino communities, where the varieties discussed here are spoken. If in addition, linguists can continue to dispel the myths that devalue Chicano English, code-switching and other non-standard varieties, then in the future we may hear Chicano English spoken in an even wider variety of places.

Bibliography

Bailey, B. (2000). 'Language and negotiation of ethnic/racial identity among Dominican Americans', *Language in Society*, 29: 555–582.

Berg, C. R. (1997). 'Stereotyping in films in general and of the Hispanic in particular', in C. E. Rodriguez (ed.), *Latin Looks*. Boulder, CO: Westview Press, pp. 104–120.

Berumen, F. J. G. (1995). *The Chicano/Hispanic Image in American Film*. New York: Vantage Press.

Flores, L. and Holling, M. (1999). 'Las familias y las Latinas: Mediated representations of gender roles', in M. Meyers (ed.), *Mediated Women*. Cresskill, NJ: Hampton Press, pp. 339–354.

Fought, C. (2002). 'Ethnicity', in J. Chambers et al. (eds), *The Handbook of Variation and Change*. Blackwell Publishers.

—. (2003). *Chicano English in Context*. New York: Palgrave/Macmillan Press.

—. (2006). *Language and Ethnicity*. Cambridge and New York: Cambridge University Press.

Fought, C. and Fought, J. (2002). 'Prosodic patterns in Chicano English'. Paper delivered at NWAVE XXXI, Stanford, CA.

Fought, C. and Harper, L. (2004). 'African-Americans and Language in the Media: An overview'. Paper delivered at NWAVE XXXIII, Ann Arbor, MI.

Godinez Jr., M. (1984). 'Chicano English phonology: Norms vs. interference phenomena', in J. Ornstein-Galicia and A. Metcalf (eds), *Form and Function in Chicano English*. Rowley, MA: Newbury House, pp. 42–48.

Gordon, M. J. (2000). 'Phonological correlates of ethnic identity: Evidence of divergence?', *American Speech*, 75: 115–136.

Mendoza-Denton, N. (1997). 'Chicana/Mexicana identity and linguistic variation: An ethnographic and sociolinguistic study of gang affiliation in an urban high school'. Stanford University dissertation.

Ornstein-Galicia, J. ed. (1984). *Form and Function in Chicano English*. Rowley, MA: Newbury House.

Peñalosa, F. (1980). *Chicano Sociolinguistics: A Brief Introduction.* Rowley, MA: Newbury House.

Penfield, J. and Ornstein-Galicia, J. (1985). *Chicano English: An Ethnic Contact Dialect. Varieties of English around the World,* vol. 7. Amsterdam: John Benjamins.

Santa Ana, O. (1991). 'Phonetic simplification processes in the English of the barrio: A cross generational sociolinguistic study of the Chicanos of Los Angeles'. University of Pennsylvania dissertation.

—. (1993). 'Chicano English and the nature of the Chicano language setting', *Hispanic Journal of Behavioral Sciences,* 15: 3–35.

Silva-Corvalán, C. ed. (1994). *Language Contact and Change: Spanish in Los Angeles.* Oxford: Clarendon.

Urciuoli, B. (1996). *Exposing Prejudice: Puerto Rican Experiences of Language, Race, and Class.* Boulder, CO: Westview Press.

Veltman, C. (1990). 'The status of the Spanish Language in the United States at the beginning of the 21st century', *International Migration Review,* 24: 108–123.

Wald, B. (1984). 'The status of Chicano English as a dialect of American English', in J. Ornstein-Galicia and A. Metcalf (eds), *Form and Function in Chicano English.* Rowley, MA: Newbury House, pp. 14–31.

—. (1993). 'On the evolution of *would* and other modals in the English spoken in East Los Angeles', in N. Dittmar and A. Reich (eds), *Modality in Language Acquisition/ Modalité et acquisition des langues.* Berlin: Walter de Gruyter, pp. 59–96.

—. (1996). 'Substratal effects on the evolution of modals in East LA English', in J. Arnold et al. (eds), *Sociolinguistic Variation: Data, Theory, and Analysis: Selected Papers from NWAV 23 at Stanford.* Stanford, CA: Center for the Study of Language and Information, pp. 515–530.

Wolfram, W. (1969). *A Sociolinguistic Description of Detroit Negro Speech.* Washington, DC: Center for Applied Linguistics.

—. (1974). *Sociolinguistic Aspects of Assimilation: Puerto Rican English in New York City.* Washington, DC: Center for Applied Linguistics.

Wolfram, W. and Dannenberg, C. (1999). 'Dialect identity in a tri-ethnic context: The case of Lumbee American Indian English', *English World-Wide,* 20: 179–216.

Wolfram, W., Carter, P., and Moriello, B. (2004). 'Emerging Hispanic English: New dialect formation in the American South', *Journal of Sociolinguistics,* 8: 339–358.

Zentella, A. C. (1997). *Growing up Bilingual.* Oxford: Basil Blackwell.

Websites used:

http://pewhispanic.org/files/reports/15.9.pdf

http://usinfo.state.gov/scv/Archive/2005/May/13-395879.html

http://www.macnn.com/articles/06/11/01/itms.adds.spanish.tv/ 'iTMS Adds Shows From Telemundo, mun2'

http://www.terribly-happy.com/georgelopez.html [online version of: Right now is a great time to be George Lopez . . . Omar L. Gallaga Published in the Austin American-Statesman 25 July 2001

Chapter 6

African American English

Charles E. DeBose

Background of the Speech Community

Although a number of different languages are spoken in the United States, the language of everyday public interaction is, with few exceptions, a highly uniform variety of English. According to the US Census bureau, approximately 82 per cent of the population of the United States five years of age and above speak only English. Over half of the remaining 18 percent who report speaking a language other than English at home identify that language as Spanish, and less than half of those report speaking English less than 'very well' (www.census. gov). Such statistics support the characterization of the language situation in the United States as essentially monolingual (DeBose 2005).

The vernacular English of native-born Americans of diverse backgrounds has essentially the same basic vocabulary; the same inventory of phonemes and the same basic sentence patterns. Notwithstanding its uniformity, however, certain marked features of vocabulary, pronunciation and grammar support the designation of three major regional dialects of American English: northern, midlands and southern. The variety commonly known as African American English (AAE) is a social variety of American English (AE) which originated under conditions in which persons of African descent were isolated from the mainstream of American society by barriers of slavery and colour caste. It survives today in predominantly Black neighbourhoods and communities throughout the nation.

An estimated 12.8 per cent of the total US population of nearly 300 million are 'Black or African American' (www.census.gov). In different regions of the country they constitute as much as 56.8 per cent of the population (District of Columbia) and to 0.4 per cent (Idaho). The percentage of Black Americans in the total population is higher in the southern states: Mississippi, 36 per cent; Louisiana, 32.5 per cent; Georgia, 29.2 per cent; South Carolina, 28.5 per cent, than in the northern and western states such as New York, 15.3 per cent; Illinois, 14.5 per cent; Michigan, 14.0 per cent; Ohio, 11.5 per cent; Pennsylvania, 10.1 per cent and California, 6.1 per cent. In absolute numbers, however, most African Americans presently reside in major metropolitan areas outside the South. An unknown percentage of all African Americans speak AAE.

AE speakers of all regions of the United States exhibit features of vocabulary, pronunciation and grammar that are indicative of their socio-economic status. Certain features associated with low social class and lack of education are proscribed by rules of prescriptive grammar, and tend to elicit strong and visceral reactions from cultivated persons. AAE has a number of distinctive features of vocabulary, pronunciation and grammar, which contrast markedly with corresponding features in the English of other American groups. Some features cited by linguists as typical of AAE overlap with typical features of southern regional speech, while others are general markers of low socio-economic status. Taken together they contribute to an overall distinctiveness, reflected in, among other things, the ability of many Americans to accurately identify persons as African American on the basis of their speech alone.

In the following pages, the distinctiveness of African American language is discussed in a way that informs some of the main issues that have engaged scholars since the first studies of 'Black English' emerged in the sixties, (Bailey 1965; Stewart 1967; Fasold 1969; Labov 1969; Wolfram 1969; Dillard 1971, 1972) including the question of what it should be called. The most common formula for naming the variety has been to combine the preferred group name for African Americans, as it changes over time, with, *English*, or an appropriate typological label, for example, *Negro dialect*, *Black English*. A few names occur as the title of works by particular scholars, for example, *Black Street Speech* (Baugh 1983); *Spoken Soul.* (Rickford and Rickford 2000).

The name Ebonics has existed since 1973 when it was coined at a caucus of African American scholars attending a conference in Saint Louis on 'cognitive and language development of the black child'. The psychologist R. L. Williams is credited with having created the word *Ebonics* as a blend of 'Ebony' and 'phonics', intended to evoke the idea of 'black sounds'. In the introduction to a collection of articles on the subject, Williams describes the immediate context in which the Ebonics concept crystallized:

> A significant incident occurred. . . . . The black conferees were so critical of the work on [Black English] done by white researchers, many of whom happened to be present, that they decided to caucus among themselves and define black language from a black perspective (Williams ed. 1975 ii).

Ebonics was not widely used by linguists or the general public until it was popularized in the controversy over a resolution of the public school board of Oakland, California, recognizing Ebonics as a language (Baugh 2000; Rickford and Rickford 2000; DeBose 2005). In the following discussion, the term African American English is used in reference to varieties of AE associated with the *dialect features* discussed below, and Ebonics (EB) in reference to claims made by academic scholars who insist that EB is not non-standard English and should not be used as a synonym for AAE (Smith 1998). Ebonics is also used in reference to linguistic behaviour that draws upon the communicative resources of African American verbal culture to *talk Black*, as a marked choice; in contrast to AAE, which is produced by speakers following the rules of their internalized competence as an unmarked choice. Otherwise, the name preferred by this writer, African American (AA), is used.

Linguistic background and contacts

A central focus of scholarly debate on the origin of AAE has been the claim that it evolved to its present form from an earlier creole, the so-called 'creolist hypothesis'; which posits, among other things, that the first African slaves on North American plantations shifted from their African ancestral languages to an English-lexified creole which subsequently lost many of its distinctive creole features through a process of convergence with dialects of AE spoken by whites. The opposing 'dialect divergence' view posits that the Africans quickly shifted to varieties of British colonial English, which diverged from those dialects to attain their present form.

Evidence from a variety of indirect sources has been cited in support of the creolist position, including travellers' accounts; fictional representations of the language of Black characters in written texts of earlier times; the sociohistorical context of European colonialism and the African slave trade. Certain AAE dialect features, discussed in detail below, have served as crucial evidence in scholarly debate of the origin of AA. While creolists cite the features in support of their position, noting their similarity to corresponding features of English-lexified creoles, their detractors attempt to refute such evidence by noting similar features in dialects of British English.

DeBose (2005) alludes to 'Two often unstated premises' that underlie much of the debate over the origin of AA:

1. That the slave ancestors of present day African Americans arrived in North America speaking a number of different African languages that were given up in rather short order, and
2. That AA is presently a dialect of American English, marked by certain distinctive features that set it apart from other varieties.

Creolists and dialect divergence advocates alike subscribe to the above premises, whereas Ebonics scholars take issue with the second premise in claiming that EB is not English, but an English-relexified member of the Niger-Congo family of West African languages. Other linguists call attention to features of AAE that reflect the influence of African languages on the lexical, phonological and grammatical structure of AAE, without questioning the view that it is a dialect of AE. DeBose and Faraclas (1993) contribute to an *Africanist* approach to the nature and history of AAE that calls attention to correspondences with West African languages as well as Caribbean creoles in the AAE 'tense-mood-aspect and copula systems.' Africanist scholars, as well as the above-mentioned creolists, tend to differ from dialect divergence scholars on the issue of how different present day AAE is from other varieties of AE in its 'deep structure'.

An archaic variety of AAE spoken on the Samaná peninsula of the Dominican Republic by descendants of free Africans who migrated there from the United States early in the nineteenth century has recently been studied as a relic variety, that preserves features of early AAE that have since died out (DeBose 1983, 1988, 1994; Poplack and Sankoff 1987). (See Table 6.1).

DeBose (1983) notes three features of Samaná English (SME) that support creolists' claims that AAE originated through a process of convergence of an earlier creole with British-derived dialects of AE: absence of post-vocalic /r/ in words such as /hi/, /hye/ 'here'; absence of the final consonant of clusters such as /st/, for example, /priys/ 'priest', /hows/ 'host'; and invariant word order in statements and questions, for example, Why I didn't see you? The categorical occurrence of such features in SME marks it as more divergent from Standard AE than present day varieties of AAE, in which the same features occur variably. Poplack and Sankoff argue that earlier AAE was less divergent from British colonial English than present day AAE citing SME data showing a lower frequency of copula absence than is typical of present-day AAE. Hannah (1995) attempting to replicate those results finds a higher incidence of copula absence.

The multilingual nature of the areas of West and Central Africa from which slaves were typically taken constitutes particularly strong evidence in support of both the creolist and Africanist positions. The lack of a common language among typical groups of captives heightens the likelihood that they would resort to pidginized varieties of European languages as a means of emergency communication, which would eventually creolize, as children born in captivity acquired the pidgins as their native languages. A frequently cited practice of slave traders of deliberately separating slaves from the same African ethnic groups, who might speak the same African languages, in order to weaken their ability to plot insurrection added, no doubt, to the pressure felt by the Africans to abandon their ancestral languages in favour of creoles lexified by European languages.

The typical multilingual composition of slave society was highly conducive to the emergence of creole varieties lexified by European colonial languages.

Table 6.1   TMA Marker of Gullah, Samaná English and African American English

CATEGORY	GULLAH	SME	AAE
COMPLETIVE	done	done	done
NON-COMPLETIVE	d∂	-s; -in	-s, -in
ANTERIOR	bin	bin, had, was	had, was
FUTURE/IRREALIS	go, gwine	gwine, gon'	gon'

In the newly created slave communities, the diversity of African languages that had served the captives as a means of everyday communication in their former lives were frequently unknown to their new neighbours. Typically, the only language they had in common with other Africans was a limited knowledge of the European language of the slaveholders. Such limited knowledge of English, or other European language would serve as input to newly emerging pidgins. As those pidgins assumed ever increasing roles as the primary means of everyday communication, and knowledge of them spread to increasingly younger members of the community, they would eventually have creolized.

Structural Features

In addition to the sociohistorical conditions in which the African American language was formed, additional evidence for prior creolization is found in the similarity of African American language to acknowledged creoles in its internal linguistic structure. Because of the established practice of using lists of isolated features to describe the grammatical structure of African American language, however, it has proved difficult to demonstrate conclusively to a sceptical audience that selected features of the variety are remnants of the grammar of a prior creole.

Three features that have been extensively discussed in connection with the claim that it evolved from an earlier creole are the verb suffixes -s and -ed, and present tense copula/auxiliary forms *is* and *are*, all of which tend to be absent in environments where they would be expected to occur in varieties of American English spoken by whites. Evidence of the similarity of AAE to creoles, with respect to such features, is easily countered with evidence of the same or similar features in British dialects.

In debating the pros and cons of the creolist hypothesis, scholars have based their arguments on the implications of certain features, which came to be regarded as crucial evidence. Several of the dialect features discussed below have been cited by creolists as evidence of the similarity of AAE to acknowledged English-lexified creoles of the African diaspora.

Recent studies have tended to strengthen claims of the creolist position by making explicit the systems underlying isolated features, and calling attention to corresponding systems in creole varieties. Such systematic correspondences have also been established between AAE and languages spoken in areas of West Africa from which the slaves were taken; strengthening in turn 'Africanist' accounts of the origin of AAE and a heightened interest in the detection of genetic relationships among AAE, creoles and West African languages (DeBose and Faraclas 1993; S. W. Williams 1993). Smith (1998) posits membership of Ebonics in the Niger-Congo family of African languages and the status of EB as a separate language in the notion of 'African Language Systems'.

The question of AAE origins is informed by the occurrence of cognate forms in language varieties spoken by persons of African descent in Canada, Liberia, the Bahamas, Sierra Leone and the Sea Islands of the Southeastern United States, referred to in the following discussion as *diaspora communities*. It has been shown that their languages are genetically related, based not only on the existence of numerous correspondences at all levels of linguistic structure, but also by social conditions surrounding their establishment which support the claim that the various languages maintained throughout the diaspora are the result of normal transmission of a proto-variety of Early African American (EAA) to their present locations (DeBose 2005).

The diaspora varieties all differ from Standard English in as many ways as they resemble one another; a fact which strongly suggests that the English input received by first generations of speakers of EAA underwent considerable restructuring. Evidence of such restructuring may be found in correspondences between linguistic features of the diaspora varieties and languages spoken in areas of West Africa from which African slaves were taken.

Linguistic Description of the Variety

The most widespread and common way of describing AAE is with reference to features of pronunciation and grammar commonly observed in empirical samples of AA speech that contrast with what would be expected in Standard English (SE) and varieties spoken by other American groups. Examples of such features are offered in this section, starting with those that characterize AAE pronunciation. Such features often represent variable absence of a phonemic segment that is typically present in other varieties, and are commonly described as *deletions*. The most frequently cited such 'deletion' affects the last member of a final consonant cluster such as /st/, /sk/ or /nd/.

The so-called *deletion of final consonant clusters* affects a number of frequently occurring words such as /mos/ 'most', /tæs/ 'task' and /fayn/ 'find'. Although such variation may be seen in all varieties of AE, it tends to occur in AAE at a higher frequency than other varieties, and in a wider range of phonological environments. Speakers of other dialects, for example, would be likely to delete the final /t/ of a word like *best* when it occurs before a following consonant as in /bes pærz/ 'best pears'; but not before a following vowel, (e.g. /best æplz/ 'best apples'. AAE speakers, however, tend to 'delete' the final consonant of *best* before a following vowel as well, for example, /bes æplz/. A tendency for some speakers to pluralize words such as *test, desk* and *ghost*, with the /iz/ variant of the plural morpheme, for example, /tesiz/, /desiz, /gosiz/, has led some observers to comment that for such speakers the words in question do not have a final /t/ or /k/ in their dictionary form, and consequently should not be described as 'deleted'. Two other consonantal variables commonly characterized as deletions involve post-vocalic /r/ and /l/.

AE shares the post-vocalic /r/ feature with a number of other non-rhotic American and British dialects. It differs to some extent, however, in its frequency of occurrence, the extent to which /r/ is 'deleted' rather than vocalized, for example, /tow/ 'tore', versus /toə/, and association with particular lexical items. Black persons from geographically rhotic areas will typically pronounce certain words (e.g. /mərdər/ 'murder') in a rhotic manner, and other words such as /šo/ 'sure' without post-vocalic /r/. The feature or r-absence is often referred to in lists of dialect features as *r-lessness*. In a similar manner, the term *l-lessness* is used to describe a tendency for the consonant /l/ to be absent from words in which it is expected in the etymological source. Speakers who tend to 'delete' /l/ may be observed pronouncing the word *bowl* in a manner that rhymes with *bow*. In certain words, such as /towld/ 'told' an /l/ may occur in a final consonant cluster in a way that results in deletion of both members of the cluster, producing dialectal homophones of words like *told, toll* and *toe*. (Labov 1972: 16)

Word segments pronounced in other varieties with one of the interdental fricative sounds, commonly spelt TH, may occur in equivalent AAE forms as either an alveolar stop, /t/ or /d/, or an interdental fricative /f/ or /v/ depending on its position in the word. A stop sound may occur in initial position, resulting in the pronunciation of words like *these*, as /diyz/. The sound /t/ often substitutes for the final consonant of *with*, that is, /wit/. The sounds /f/ and /v/ may replace t̲h̲ sounds in medial or word final position, for example, /məvə/ 'mother', /mawf/ 'mouth'.

Variation in AAE pronunciation involving vowels tends to be associated also with southern regional speech. One such feature involves neutralization of the difference between /i/ and /e/ so that pen is pronounced like *pin*. In a like manner, sets of words like *ten* and *tin* are pronounced in AAE as homonyms. In words in which the vowel /e/ occurs, in other varieties, before a cluster such as /nd/, sets such as *send/sin*; and *bend/Ben/bin* are homophonous in AAE. Other features of vowel pronunciation are discussed below as identity markers.

The greatest difference between AAE and other varieties of AE is found in the verb phrase, especially in the system of marking tense, mood and aspect. Differing accounts of particular features of the AAE verb phrase lie at the heart of long-standing controversies over such questions as whether or not AAE has the same underlying grammar as other varieties, and the creolist hypothesis discussed above. Much of the debate over those issues has centred on the variable absence of present tense forms of *be*, either in the function of main verb or auxiliary, (commonly referred to in AAE studies as *zero copula*) as illustrated by the following sentences.

1. *She my big sister.*
2. *We at home.*
3. *He kinda tall.*
4. *They walkin.*

Labov accounts for copula absence in sentences such as 1–4 by postulating 'underlying' forms, which are first 'contracted' and then 'deleted'. He also claims that copula absence occurs in AAE in the same environments in which it may undergo contraction in other varieties (Labov 1969) and identifies the following environments before which zero forms of the copula occur in empirical samples of AAE:

__ NP, for example, *She a fox;*
__ PA, for example, *We cold;*
__ LOC, for example, *They at home,*
__ V + in, for example, *She workin,*
__ gon, for example, *We gon be late;* and
__ not, for example, *They not at home.*

Such data have been cited in support of the claim that AAE has the same underlying copula constructions as other varieties and differs mainly in having a copula deletion rule that operates on the output of the contraction rule common to other varieties.

There are notable exceptions, however, to Labov's generalizations. One concerns the first person singular form *am*, which is rarely 'deleted', and contrived instances of which are ungrammatical, for example,

5. **I his big brother.*
6. **I walking home.*

While present tense forms of *is* generally occur in empirical samples of AAE, with high frequency, zero variants of *is* rarely occur following the pronouns *it*, *that* and *what*. Furthermore, the final /t/ of those pronouns is not pronounced in etymologically 'contracted' forms of those words in AAE speech, for example, /is/ it's, /ɖæs/ 'that's, and /hwəs/ 'what's.

Another problem with Labov's claims about AA copula variation concerns the form *gon*, /gõ/, 'will' related etymologically to the standard English *be going to*, construction. Listing it as an environment in which the copula is eligible for contraction and deletion is questionable insofar as neither full nor contracted forms of *be* ever occur in that environment in empirical samples of AAE.

Contrived examples in which they are placed are unacceptable to native speakers, for example, **we're gon' be late.*

Recent accounts of AAE copula variation treat zero copula constructions as the output of an AAE grammar that differs from the system common to other varieties in ways that permit NP, PA and LOC constructions to occur as nominal complements directly juxtaposed, as well as linked by means of a copula, to the subjects to which they are linked. V + in forms are classified, not as inflected verb forms, but rather as participles that function as nominal complements of the subject (DeBose and Faraclas 1993; DeBose 2001c, 2005). Those studies account for the unacceptability of predicate nominals directly juxtaposed to *I*, *it, that* and *what* by treating the etymologically contracted forms *I'm, it's, that's* and *what's* as mono-morphemic pronouns that occur in complementary distribution with the basic pronouns. The form *gon* is treated as a future marker, and one of a set of AA forms discussed further below that function as markers of tense, mood and aspect.

Other dialect features of AAE grammar that have been extensively studied are the variable absence of the verb suffixes *–s* and *–ed* (examples 7, 8 below); use of the stem form of the verb *be* to mark a sentence for habitual aspect (example 9); and use of the form *done* to lend a completive aspect interpretation to a predicated event (10):

7. *She cook fish all the time.*
8. *She cook fish yesterday.*
9. *She be cookin fish all the time.*
10. *She done cook some fish.*

Creolists (Bailey 1965; Stewart 1967; Dillard 1971) allude to the patterns represented by sentences 7 and 8 – as well as frequent zero realization of the copula – as aspects of a pervasive similarity of AAE to English-lexified creoles of West African and the Caribbean. The same scholars argue that AA differs synchronically from other varieties of AE in the grammar of the verb phrase.

Labov and his associates treat the patterns represented by 7–10 in a similar manner to Labov's account of copula variation, arguing that the patterns in question result from 'deletions' and other minor variations in an AAE system that it is essentially the same in its underlying structure as other varieties of AE. They characterize the feature represented by example 9, and referred to in the literature as *habitual* or *invariant be*, (Fasold 1969; Fasold and Wolfram 1975) as a different form than the inflected copula/auxiliary form *be*, and labelled, *be2*; which is used in AAE to mark the sentence in which it occurs for habitual aspect. That is, in addition to the general rule that AE syntactic predicates have the form of a finite verb phrase marked for past or present tense, AAE, offers its speakers the additional option of using *be2* to mark a sentence explicitly for habitual aspect.

DeBose and Faraclas (1993) account for the invariant *be* feature, not as an exception to the common AE system of marking verb tense, but, rather, in terms of a fundamentally different system in which

> Verb forms similar to the English infinitive, simple present, simple past and past participle frequently occur.., but .. [do] not play a primary role in the tense-mood-aspect interpretation of BE sentences. . . (p. 368)

According to DeBose and Faraclas, sentences such as (7) above are not instances of the AE simple present tense construction, but of a distinctive AA construction in which a stem form of any verb, including *be*, occurring directly after the subject, lends a non-completive aspect interpretation to a predicated event. The suffix -*s* may be attached, optionally, to the verb in this construction, regardless of the person of the subject, e.g,

11. We cooks fish every Saturday.
12. It bees kinda hard to get it open.

Similarly, DeBose and Faraclas do not treat sentences such as 8 above as instances of the simple past construction common to other varieties of AE, but as realizations of the AA nonstative predicate, which has a default completive aspect interpretation. Sentences such as 10 above in which the particle *done* precedes the main verb are treated similarly, as explicated below.

The *done* construction has long been acknowledged as a dialect feature of AAE grammar. Although it is amply attested in empirical samples of AAE data, explanations of its relationship to Standard English vary considerably. Fasold and Wolfram (1975) describe it as a completive aspect marker.

> The completive aspect is formed from the verb *done* plus a past form of the [main] verb. Because of the uncertain status of the past participle in the grammar of the dialect, it is difficult to determine whether this form is the past participle or not. (66)

According to Labov,

> *Done* has for all intents and purposes become an adverb, functioning sometimes like *already* or *really*, and lost its status as a verb. (Labov 1972: 56)

Labov's analysis of *done* is consistent with his position on the same versus different system issue, alluded to above, to the effect that Black English and Standard English 'do indeed form a single system'. (Labov 1972: 63) DeBose 1977 analyses the feature as 'a *perfect* construction' in which 'the particle *done*' is followed by a form of the main verb similar to the standard English past tense or past participle form; explaining that '[t]his construction takes the place of both the simple past and present perfect of acrolectal English. The particle *done* may sometimes be omitted' (468). Sentences 11 and 12 illustrate those options.

11. (with *done*) *John done broke his leg.*
12. (without *done*) *They gone home.*

DeBose and Faraclas (1993) allude to a 'lexical stativity parameter' (Mufwene 1983) which assigns tense, aspect and modality interpretations to AA sentences based on the value assigned to predicates for the feature [stative] in classifying *done* + V-EN as a 'derived verbal predicate' and marker of 'RESULTATIVE STATE' (368).

Green (2002) treats *done* as a member of the lexical category, aspect marker, a category unique to AA grammar, which occurs in the environment__V- *ed*, and 'marks a completed eventuality or an eventuality that is over (occurred in the past)' (2002. 25). Green also classifies the invariant *be* feature, and a feature discussed further below, known as 'remote been' (Rickford 1977), as aspect markers.

DeBose 2005 classifies *done* as a marker of completive aspect, which takes a V-EN participle as a complement. Since V-EN participles directly following the subject also have a completive aspect interpretation, the particle *done* redundantly reinforces that interpreation. DeBose 2005 also calls attention to the fact that cognates of *done* function as markers of completive aspect in English-lexified creoles of the African diaspora. (See Table 6.1).

The features discussed thus far are the most likely to be included in a list of typical AAE features. Other features sometimes included in such lists are characteristic of General Nonstandard (GNS) AE.

Recent studies call attention to the inadequacy of typical descriptions of Black language as lists of features. One point developed in this chapter in support of that view is that AAE is – first and foremost – a system of *linguistic competence* (Chomsky 1965) intuitively known and unconsciously followed by its speakers, many of whom claim it as their native language. It is amenable to study by formal methods of grammatical analysis, (c.f. Green 2002) as well as statistical analysis of recurring features of empirical data sets. The features documented by such empirical studies do not correspond to the internalized competence of AAE speakers, who perceive language thus marked as normal.

Accounts of dialectal variation in AE tend to focus primarily on regional variation and ignore the fact that class variation exists among speakers of all dialects. When one takes due note of that fact, some of the issues raised by Ebonics scholars about the nature of AA are clarified.

Just as the list of features identified with AA overlaps with features of GNS, it also overlaps with certain characteristic features of various regional dialects; for example, the variable absence of /r/. Several features associated Southern dialect, which play a major role in the distinctiveness of AA, are characterized here as *identity markers*. It is interesting to note that many of the features included in that discussion are situated in the lexicon, in contrast to the tendency for commonly cited AAE dialect features to be phonological or grammatical in nature.

While AA participates to a very high degree in the uniformity of AE, there are a number of words that may qualify as uniquely AA. They include the words joog /jug/, 'to stick, prick or poke' (DeBose 2005, p. 181), and *saditty*, 'affected, considering oneself superior' (Mitchell-Kernan 1972, 166), 'snooty; uppity acting' (Smitherman 1994, 198). While the word *joog* is clearly derived from the same African language source as *juke* of *juke box*, and includes in its range of meanings, 'engage in the sex act', as does the GAE synonym, *poke*; the etymology of *saditty* is unknown.

A number of AA lexical items have AE cognates, but are pronounced in a distinctively AA manner and have extended their meaning to include distinctively AA senses. A case in point is the word *sister*, which, when pronounced /sʊstə/ may be used with the extended meaning of an 'African American female'. Similarly, the word *brother*, has the extended meaning of 'African American male', especially when pronounced in a distinctively AA manner, i.e, /bruɗə/ or /bruvə/. As such it qualifies as an identity marker.

Other words that have special extended meanings in AA are /po/ 'poor, emaciated'; *fine*, 'attractive, good-looking', and *(high-) yellow* 'light-skinned Black person' (DeBose 2005). DeBose (2005) cites a number of lexical items that contribute to the distinctiveness of AA, notwithstanding its participation in the uniformity of AE:

> [A]lthough African American language participates considerably in that uniformity, it has, nevertheless, a distinctiveness that cannot be fully described by lists of features representing points at which it diverges from what would be expected in Standard English. (178)

The words in question include such content words as *saditty*, and others cited above, as well as, *can't*, pronounced /keynt/ and other forms classified as 'function words' and 'closed word classes'; for example, the pronouns *I*, *my* and *your*, pronounced /a/ /ma/ and /yo/, respectively. They also include the marked second person plural form *yall*, and distinctive qualifiers such as *kinda* pronounced /kana/ and *sho nuff* meaning 'certainly' (182, 3). One other important set of AA function words referred to as tense-mood-aspect markers, were introduced above.

In addition to the lexical forms just cited as examples of identity markers, there are features manifest primarily at the level of phonology that AA speakers access for indexing their identity (discussed in next section). The feature of /r/ absence, first cited as a dialect feature, can be seen as leaving an historical trace on such lexical forms as *chitlins*, the possessive pronoun /yo/ and the Hip-Hop word /ho/ 'whore'. The pronunciation of the pronouns *I* /a/ and *my* /ma/ are consistent with the typical southern regional pronunciation of words in which the diphthong /ay/, alternates with the monophthong /a/. One other noteworthy sound variable that serves as a resource for indexing AA identity involves words such as *on*, pronounced in other varieties with a low back and unrounded vowel, that is, /an/ has a higher rounded pronunciation, for example, /own/ in markedly Black speech. Such pronunciation features also have historical implications of the kind that are discussed further in the next section.

Such lexical items are not commonly found on lists of AAE features, for a number of reasons. First and foremost, they do not inform such hotly debated issues of AAE scholarship as the creolist hypothesis, and the question of whether or not AAE is a 'separate system'. In addition to that, the special extended meanings of such words tend to be described as slang; and AAE scholars frequently insist, in their characterization of AAE *that it is not slang*. The issue of slang and its place in the study of AAE is one of several usage issues taken up in the next section.

English Usage in the African American Speech Community

A considerable amount of linguistic diversity characterizes the African American speech community. Members of different age, regional and socio-economic backgrounds speak AAE, Standard AE or both natively. AAE speakers speak one sub-variety or another of AAE with varying mixtures of regional, social and ethnically marked features. Persons raised in AAE speaking communities typically speak AAE as an unmarked choice. Their speech tends to contain the kind of AAE dialect features discussed above as a result of following, unconsciously and intuitively, their internalized grammar. Those who grow up in predominantly white, middle-class communities speak the standard dialects of those communities as an unmarked choice.

African Americans raised in rural communities in the South may speak a vernacular in which southern regional dialect features constitute the normal or unmarked pronunciation; and for them it counts as a dialect feature. Other African Americans might speak a variety of AAE in which the unmarked choice is a non-southern pronunciation, but have – as part of their communicative competence (Hymes 1972) – the ability to pronounce certain words in a southern manner, reminiscent of older family members, and serve hence as identity markers.

While AAE features occur most frequently in the speech of working class persons, evidence of middle-class African Americans codeswitching indicates that some African Americans are bilingual speakers of AAE and standard AE (DeBose 1992). Such bilingualism is accounted for in part as the consequence of historical patterns of mobility of African Americans, discussed in detail below. Such patterns entail population movements from the rural South to metropolitan areas in the North and West, sometimes accompanied by upward mobility of individuals and families who assimilate linguistically standard vernaculars of AE.

The issue of the place of slang in the study of AA language is part of the more general issue, subsumed under the above-mentioned tendency for some Black English scholars to use the term Ebonics as a synonym for AAVE, in spite of the insistence of other scholars that Ebonics is not non-standard English. Typical of the view that Ebonics is not a synonym for Black English is an article by Robert L. Williams and Mary Brantley (1975) dedicated to 'Disentangling the confusion surrounding slang, non-standard English, Black English and Ebonics'. The following quote summarizes their position:

> Ebonics is unique in both its stylistic and linguistic dimensions. The stylistic dimension includes features such as rhyming, signifying, playing the dozens, jiving, capping, rapping, etc. (133, 34).

Williams and Brantley make a clear distinction between Ebonics and non-standard English, which is represented by two different types of sentences on a list presented to research subjects. Their finding that black subjects tend to identify certain sentences as 'uniquely black', for example: 'Joe lost his gig and had to give up his crib', and others as 'typically spoken by Blacks and whites', for example: 'I been trying to call you all day', support an approach to Black language and culture that treats AA structural features, slang expressions and non-verbal behaviour as parts of a seamless whole called *Ebonics*.

Smitherman (2000) addresses the issue of non-standard English versus Ebonics, insisting that 'Nonstandard American English refers to those language patterns and communication styles that are non-African in origin and which are used by the working class'. She goes on to give the following examples, 'the pronunciation of "ask" as "axe", the use of double negatives . . . and the use of "ain't." Such features of American English are often *erroneously* characterized as Ebonics. They are not' (p. 10).

Recent work in discourse analysis highlights ways in which speech community members use language in particular acts of speaking as a way of indexing their social identity. When African American language is studied from such a perspective, interest shifts from identifying speakers of AAE based on the presence of particular features in their speech to studying the speakers' *agency* in the negotiation of shared social identities.

Bucholz (2005) characterizes *indexing* as a 'process of forging and making links between social practices (including linguistic practices) and social categories' (423). The frequent need for African Americans to index their identity through language has resulted in a number of features of vocabulary, pronunciation and grammar that serve that very purpose. A conversational exchange reported by Mitchell-Kernan between Barbara, an informant; Mary, one of her friends; and the researcher is amenable to analysis from such a perspective:

> BARBARA: What are you going to do Saturday? Will you be over here?
> R: I don't know.
> BARBARA: Well, if you're not going to be doing anything, come by. I'm going to cook some chit'lins. [Rather jokingly] Or are you one of those Negroes who don't eat chit'lins?
> MARY: [Interjecting indignantly] that's all I hear lately - soul food, soul food. If you say you don't eat it you get accused of being saditty . . . (1971: 166)

Mary goes on to expound on her culinary preferences for 'prime rib and T-bone' over 'chit'lins', explaining, before she leaves, that it has nothing to do with her 'trying to be white'. Mitchell-Kernan uses the conversation to illustrate the African American practice of 'signifying', which she defines as

> a way of encoding messages or meanings in natural conversations which involves, in most cases, an element of indirection. (1971; 165)

In the present example, although Barbara seems to be directing her invitation to 'eat chitlins' to the researcher, it is taken by Mary as an (indirect) insinuation that Mary is 'one of those Negroes who don't eat chit'lins'. Mitchell-Kernan explains the cultural meaning of eating *chitterlings* – as the raw entrails of the hog are referred to in packaged form,

> Chit'lins are considered a delicacy by many black people, and eating chit'lins is often viewed as a traditional dietary habit of black people. Changes in such habits are viewed as gratuitous aping of white people . . . Thus, not eating or liking chit'lins may be indicative of assimilationist attitudes, which in turn imply a rejection of one's black brothers and sisters.

In view of the ideological content of the inter-change, it not only serves as a good example of the indirection, which is the essence of signifying; but also as an illustration of the usefulness of a perspective that pays special attention to 'speakers' agency' (Bucholz 2005: 422).

When the focus of research on AA language shifts from invoking membership in a particular social category, that is, Black working class, to their ability to use language strategically to achieve goals in spite of the constraints of cultural ideologies . . . (Bucholz 2005: 422) it is not the presence or absence of particular linguistic features in the speech of a population under study so much as the way that speakers use language to index their membership in fluid and shifting identities, for example, 'assimilationist', that is of central interest.

The virtual absence of AAE dialect features in the Mitchell-Kernan conversation just cited might lead an observer to classify the participants simply as middle-class AA females who speak Standard AE. In another conversation reported in the same article, however, Mitchell-Kernan demonstrates the ability to *codeswitch,* as she and a male interlocutor encountered in a public park engage in playful banter. He opens the interaction with the words *Mamma you sho is fine, to which the researcher replies, That ain't no way to talk to your mother. (1971: 170)*

Although the informant's pronunciation of *sure* as /šo/, and his use of <u>is</u> with a second person subject, are commonly associated with non-standard English, it is not perceived as such in African American cultural settings such as the one under discussion. As such, it illustrates how a single particular linguistic feature may serve, in various contexts, to identify a speaker as lower class, to identify a situation of use as casual, or to mark the discourse context of a particular speech event as talking Ebonics.

DeBose 1992 discusses a case of AA codeswitching in which a middle-class, college educated female, 'P', alternates between standard (SE) and markedly AAE variants of the same lexical items in a manner that supports their classification as identity markers.

> From listening to the first few minutes of the recording, one might get the impression that P. is a monolingual SE speaker, incapable of speaking BE (Black English). As the session progresses, however, she makes several notable switches to BE (DeBose 1992: 161).

DeBose takes note of an aspect of the 'first few minutes of the recording' which motivates her choice of SE.

> The beginning of the first tape contains casual conversation between P. and N., (DeBose' research partner) picked up while the latter was setting up the recording equipment, and P. did not realize the recorder was on. Her use of standard English, therefore cannot be attributed to the 'observer effect'. N.'s status as an outsider to the ethnic community is apparently the cue for P.'s choice of SE here.

P's first utterance contains the negated modal auxiliary *can't.* DeBose refers to her pronunciation of it as /kænt/, rather than the marked dialectal variant, *cain't* /keynt/ as an indication that the segment is SE.

> P. I just can't stay in bed late. I can't do it.

In a later segment, P. narrates an incident in which she 'fusses' at her daughter who is late coming home from a music rehearsal, and admits to having spent time at a local mall. As P. quotes herself speaking AAE to the daughter, she repeatedly produces the marked form *cain't*.

> Oh I fussed and cussed. I said, 'You on punishment now for six months. You cain't look at no TV. You cain't do nothin!'

P's codeswitching behaviour is consistent with what Meyers-Scotton (1993) characterizes as *codeswitching as a marked choice*, as is the classification of *cain't* as one of a set of AA forms that serve as resources for indexing various aspects of fluid and flexible identities that AA speakers might choose to highlight at one time or another.

Future Implications

Continuing the study of AA with a focus on the features characterized above as identity markers can add significantly to our present level of understanding of its structure, history and use, as well as its implications for vital and yet unresolved questions of educational and public policy (DeBose 2001a; Hollins, et. al. 2005). The historical depth of such features revealed at a macroscopic level through diachronic study of diaspora languages on both sides of the Atlantic Ocean – encompassing West African and Caribbean peoples and languages – informs studies at the microscopic level of speech acts in which speech community members with varying degrees of productive and/or receptive AAE competence draw upon the rich store of AA language and culture experienced in interaction with parents, grandparents, older siblings and friends/relatives of various regional and socio-economic backgrounds, to index one aspect or another of fluid and flexible identities. Such an approach is consistent with the official definition of Ebonics as

> [T]he linguistic and paralinguistic features which on a concentric continuum represent the communicative competence of the West African, Caribbean, and United States slave descendants of African origin. It includes the various idioms, patois, argots, ideolects, and social dialects of black people . . . (Williams ed.1975 vi).

The inclusion of identity markers along with dialect features in the discussion of AAE grammar suggests a way of highlighting the difference between AAE and Ebonics, that is, by defining AAE as a dialect, and the unmarked choice of native speakers in everyday public interaction; and striving for an adequate definition of Ebonics, based on the notion of using AA identity markers as a marked choice. Continued efforts in that direction can contribute greatly to our understanding of the linguistic diversity of the AA speech community, an adequate account of which should be informed by an accurate and up-to-date description of the language situation in the African American speech community.

Bibliography

Alleyne, M. C. (1980). *Comparative Afro-American:An Historical Comparative Study of English-Based Afro-American Dialects of the New World.* Ann Arbor: Karoma.

Bailey, B. L. (1965). Toward a new perspective in American Negro dialectology. *American Speech*, 40: 171–77.

Baugh, J. (2000). *Beyond Ebonics: Linguistic Pride and Racial Prejudice.* New York: Oxford University Press.

—. (1983). *Black Street Speech.* Austin: University of Texas Press.

Bucholz, M. (2005). Language, Gender and Sexuality. In E. Finegan and J. R. Rickford (eds), *Language in the USA: Themes for the Twenty-first Century.* Cambridge, UK: Cambridge University Press, 410–29.

Burling, R. (1973). *English in Black and White.* New York: Holt-Rinehart.

Chomsky, N. (1965). *Aspects of the Theory of Syntax.* Cambridge: MIT Press.

DeBose, C. E. (2005). *The Sociology of African American Language: A Language Planning Perspective.* Hampshire, UK: Palgrave Macmillan.

—. (2001a). The African American literacy and culture project. Presented at Parasession on Reading and Dialect. 2001 Annual Meeting of the Linguistic Society of America.

—. (2001b). The status of variety X in the African American linguistic repertoire. Presented at NWAV 30, Panel of the Sociolinguistics of Hip-Hop. Raleigh North Carolina, October, 2001.

—. (2001c). Patterns of complementation in African American predicates. Presented at Symposium on Recent Directions in the Study of African American Language. 2001 Annual Meeting of the Linguistic Society of America.

—. (1999). Factors affecting the rate of language change: the case of Samaná English. Presented at the Ninth International Colloquium on Creole Studies, Aix en Provence, France.

—. (1996a). Creole English in Samaná. In F. Ingemann (ed.), *1994 Mid America Linguistics Conference Papers.* Lawrence: The University of Kansas. Vol. II: 341–50.

—. (1996b). Question formation in Samaná English. Presented at NWAV 25 Las Vegas, Nevada.

—. (1994). A note on ain't versus didn't negation in African American vernacular. *Journal of Pidgin and Creole Languages.* 9.1: 127–30.

—. (1995). Creole features in Samaná English. Society for Pidgin and Creole Linguistics, Annual Meeting, New Orleans, January 1995.

—. (1992). Codeswitching: Black English and Standard English in the African-American Linguistics Repertoire. In C. M. Eastman (ed.) *Journal of Multilingual and Multicultural Development: Special Issue Codeswitching.* 13(1 and 2): 157–67.

—. (1988). Be in Samaná English. Society for Caribbean Linguistics, Occasional Paper No. 21, St. Augustine, Trinidad.

—. (1983). Samaná: a dialect that time forgot. *Proceedings of the Ninth Annual Meeting of the Berkeley Linguistic Society*, 47–53.

—. (1977). The status of native speaker intuitions in a polylectal grammar. *Proceedings of the Third Annual Meeting of the Berkeley Linguistic Society*, 465–74.

DeBose, C. E. and Faraclas, N. (1993). An Africanist Approach to the Linguistic Study of Black English: Getting to the Roots of the Tense-Aspect-Modality and Copula Systems in Afro-American. In S. S. Mufwene (ed.), *Africanisms in Afro-American Language Varieties*. Athens: University of Georgia Press, 364–87.

Dillard, J. L. (1972). *Black English: Its History and Usage in the United States*. New York: Vintage Books.

—. (1971). The Creolist and the Study of Negro Non-Standard Dialects in the Continental United States. In D. Hymes (ed.), *Pidginization and Creolization of Languages*. London: Cambridge University Press, 393–408.

Fasold. R. W. (1969). Tense and the Form Be in Black English. *Language*, 45: 763–76.

Fasold, R. W. and Wolfram, W. (1975). Some Linguistic Features of Negro Dialect. In P. Stoller (ed.), *Black American English: Its Background and Its Usage in the Schools and in Literature*. New York: Dell Publishing Co., 49–83.

Fishman, J. A. (1980). Bilingual education, language planning and English. *English World Wide: A Journal of Varieties of English*. 1.1: 11–24.

Green, Lisa (2002). *African American English: A Linguistic Introduction*. Cambridge University Press.

Hancock, I. F. (1970). A provisional comparison of the English-derived Atlantic Creoles. *African Language Review*. 8: 7–72.

Hannah, D. (1995). The Copula in Samaná English: Implications for research on the linguistic history of African American Vernacular English. Unpublished manuscript, Presented at NWAVE 24, University of Pennsylvania.

Hoetink, H. (1962). Americans in Samaná. *Caribbean Studies*. Vol II(1): 3–22.

Hollins, E. R., McIntyre, L. R., DeBose, C. E., Hollins K. S., and Towner A. G. (2005). Literacy Development in the Primary Grades: Promoting a Self-Sustaining Learning Community Among Teachers. In B. Hammond et al. (eds), *Teaching African American Learners to Read: Perspectives and Practices*. Newark, Delaware: International Reading Association, 233–52.

Holm, J. A. (1989). *Pidgins and Creoles. Volume 2. Reference Survey*. Cambridge: Cambridge University Press.

Hymes, D. (1972). Models in the Interaction of Language and Social Life. In J. Gumperz and D. Hymes (eds), *Directions in Socialinguistics: The Ethnography of Communication*. New York: Holt-Rinehart, 35–71.

Labov, W. (1969). Contraction, deletion, and inherent variability of the English copula. *Language*. 45: 715–62.

—. (1972). *Language in the Inner City: Studies in the Black English Vernacular*. Philadelphia: University of Pennsylvania Press.

Lockward, G. A. (1976). *El Protestanismo en Dominicana*. Santo Domingo: Editora del Caribe.

Meyers-Scotton, C. (1993). *Duelling Tongues: Grammatical Structure in Codeswitching*. Oxford: Clarendon.

Mitchell-Kernan, C. (1972). Signifying and Marking: Two Afro-American Speech Acts. In J. Gumperz and D. Hymes (eds). *Directions in Sociolinguistics: The Ethnography of Communication*. New York: Holt-Rinehart, 161–79.

Morgan, M. (2002). *Language, Discourse and Power in African American Culture*. Cambridge University Press.

Mufwene, S. S. (ed.) (1993). *Africanisms in Afro-American Language Varieties*. Athens: University of Georgia Press, 423–435.

—. (1983). *Some Observations on the Verb in Black English Vernacular*. Austin: Afro-American Studies Research Center. University of Texas.

Poplack, S. and Sankoff, D. (1987). The Philadelphia story in the Spanish Caribbean. *American Speech*, 62(4): 291–314.

Rickford, J. and Rickford, R. (2000). *Spoken Soul: The Story of Black English*. John Wiley and Sons, Inc.

Rickford, J. R. (1977). The Question of Prior Creolization in Black English. In A. Valdman (ed.), *Pidgin and Creole Linguistics*. Bloomington: Indiana University Press, 190–221.

Smith, E. (1998). What is Black English? What is Ebonics? In L. Delpit and T. Perry (eds), *The Real Ebonics Debate: Power, Language and the Education of African American Children*. Boston: Beacon Press.

Smitherman, G. (2000). *Talkin that Talk: Language, Culture and Education in African America*. New York: Routledge.

—. (1994). *Black Talk: Words and Phrases from the Hood to the Amen Corner*. New York: Houghton Mifflin.

Stewart, W. A. (1967). Sociolinguistic factors in the history of American Negro dialects. *Florida Foreign Language Reporter*, 5: 1–7.

Van Keulen, J. E., Weddington, G. T. and DeBose, C. E. (1998). *Speech, Language, Learning, and the African American Child*. Needham Heights, Massachusetts: Allyn and Bacon.

Williams, R. L. (ed.) (1975). *Ebonics: The True Language of Black Folks*. St. Louis: Williams & Associates.

Williams, R. L. and Brantley, M. (1975). Disentangling the Confusion Surrounding Slang, Nonstandard English, Black English and Ebonics. In R. L. Williams (ed.), *Ebonics: The True Language of Black Folks*. St. Louis: Williams & Associates, 133–138.

Williams, S. W. (1993). Substantive Africanisms at the End of the African Linguistic Disaspora. In S. S. Mufwene (ed.), *Africanisms in Afro-American Language Varieties*. Athens: University of Georgia Press, 406–22.

Wolfram, W. (1969). *A Sociolinguistic Description of Detroit Negro Speech*. Washington, DC: Center for Applied Linguistics.

Chapter 7

English in the American West

Lamont D. Antieau

Background of the Region

Although the American West has served as the backdrop for countless works of film and literature, the cultures of the region remain enigmatic in many ways to those hailing from outside the region. The reasons for this lack of understanding are complex and varied but include, to some extent, the region's expanse over a large geographical area comprising several unique cultural centres (Meinig 1972), mischaracterizations in the media and the differences – both obvious and subtle – that hold between it and the eastern United States. Additionally, the culture of the West, including its language use, has not been studied to the same extent as the culture of the East. This chapter aims to shed light on one aspect of Western American culture by describing the variety and varieties of American English in use in the region and comparing them to other varieties of English in the United States.

While opinions vary as to which states comprise the American West (see, for instance, Dippie, 1989: 5–6), this chapter limits the region to 11 states – Arizona, California, Colorado, Idaho, Montana, Nevada, New Mexico, Oregon, Utah, Washington and Wyoming – that have been the focus of most of the geographical studies of the American West, for example, Meinig (1972). Although this classification leaves out such states as Kansas and Texas, which are sometimes characterized as western states, it should be noted that they are often also included in discussions of regions comprising states east of the River Mississippi, for example, the Midwest and the South, respectively, while the eleven states covered in this study are rarely if ever included in such discussions. Finally, with respect to the literature on American dialects, the eleven states here are included in such discussions on Western speech as those presented by Carver (1987) and Labov et al. (1997) and are the only states to be included in their entirety in the framework of the Linguistic Atlas of the Western States (Pederson and Madsen 1989).

Several physical characteristics distinguish the American West from the eastern United States. Topographical features such as the great expanse of mountains, canyons, high plains and desert are the most apparent of these differences; the relative aridity of the greater part of the region is also an important characteristic that distinguishes it from states east of the Mississippi. Although several important rivers flow from the Continental Divide, including the Colorado and the Rio Grande, there are relatively few large bodies of natural standing water in the West, Utah's Great Salt Lake being a notable exception. As is the case for all ecosystems, the topographical and climatic characteristics of the American West have historically exerted a strong influence on all forms of life in the region and continue to do so.

The first people known to inhabit the American West were members of the Native American tribes scattered throughout the region. The cultures of the earliest western tribes reflected variations in the environments of the regions they occupied. Southwestern tribes such as the Pueblo, for instance, inhabited adobe houses or cliff dwellings, while northwestern tribes like the Salish resided primarily in longhouses made of timber and subsided on a diet rich in salmon and shellfish. As the first Europeans settled along the Atlantic coast and began expanding westward in search of inland opportunities, eastern Native American tribes migrated westward into the Great Plains and Rocky Mountain regions in order to avoid the European settlers and in search of game beyond the frontier. This proved to be an imperfect and temporary solution for eastern tribes; conflicts between the newcomers and earlier Plains and mountain tribes arose over territory, particularly hunting grounds, and later there were clashes between tribes and Anglo-American settlers pushing westward to attain their 'Manifest Destiny' in the 1800s. Eventually, many of the people of the Native American tribes would be killed in battle or by disease or would be placed in reservations established by the American government west of the Mississippi.

While the first English people to settle in the New World primarily did so along the Atlantic seaboard of what is now the United States, and concentrated their early efforts on developing that region, the Spanish and the French became the first Europeans to actively explore what is now the western United States. Moving northward from Mexico at least as early as the mid1500s, Spanish explorers searched for signs of mineral wealth, as well as souls to convert to Christianity, in the region, establishing communities and missions in modern-day New Mexico, Arizona, California and, later, Colorado. The French, meanwhile, travelled northwestward from New Orleans and southwestward from Canada and the Great Lakes region into the Rocky Mountains in the eighteenth century, mainly to trap beaver, the pelts of which were a commodity in high demand in European markets at the time. The wariness of the Spanish and French towards each other made them quick to claim significant portions of the region in the names of their respective kings, which resulted in some overlap between the two claims – and even greater tension between the two groups – a problem that would ultimately only be reconciled when the United States took possession of both claims. Elsewhere in the region, the British and the Russians – mostly trappers, traders and fisherman – occupied the Pacific Northwest region in the eighteenth century.

Nearly thirty years after declaring its independence from the British and becoming a nation, the United States acquired all of France's holdings between the Alleghany and Rocky Mountains in 1803, in a deal that became known as the Louisiana Purchase, thereby taking an important step towards attaining President Jefferson's goal of extending the nation's borders from the Atlantic to the Pacific Ocean. The acquisition of the Spanish claims in the West was a more complex process, however, as it depended on a succession of events: Mexico winning its independence from Spain (1821); the Republic of Texas seceding from Mexico (1836) and being inducted as an American state (1845); and the United States winning the Mexican War and signing the Treaty of Guadalupe Hidalgo (1848). Additionally, the United States negotiated with the British to obtain the Oregon Territory in 1846, and its agreement with Mexico that culminated in the Gadsden Purchase (1853) effectively completed its acquisition of the West, establishing the current borders of the continental United States.

Although the boundaries of the American West had been established by the mid1800s, there was little economic motivation for Americans to migrate to the region, especially considering the highly agrarian nature of the United States at the time and the well-known depiction of much of the western region as the 'Great American Desert' by the Long party. With the passing of the fur fad in Europe, as well as a decline in the beaver population in the Rockies, the western fur trade essentially ended by the 1840s, by which time many of the trappers and traders associated with the trade had already left the region or had entered other professions, some of them becoming guides for early American explorations of the West, such as those led by Lewis and Clark (1803), Zebulon Pike (1806) and Stephen Long (1820).

The first impetus for large-scale Anglo-American migration to the West was the lure of mineral wealth during a succession of gold rushes throughout the region, notably those beginning in northern California in 1849 and Colorado in 1858. The rushes were important for several reasons: 1) They brought large numbers of workers to the area; 2) they encouraged the development of communication and transportation networks, sometimes by enhancing those that had been created during the earlier fur trade; 3) they were instrumental in creating a demand for other industries that were required for support of the mining industry and also benefited long-term development, such as logging, ranching and farming; and 4) they spawned several supply towns, for example, Denver and San Francisco, that would eventually evolve into major cities of the United States. However, many of the towns created during the gold rush years followed a boom-and-bust pattern due to the depletion of minerals or because labourers – mostly men – grew discouraged and left for other opportunities or enlisted for military service during the American Civil War. While mining is still done to some extent throughout the West, sustained growth of the region depended on the development of other industries.

Although its initial growth in the region was spurred by the existence of mining communities, ranching would essentially usurp mining as the West's major industry by the last quarter of the nineteenth century by taking advantage of the advancements created to do the business of mining and modifying them for their own advantage. During the boom years in Colorado, for instance, Texas ranchers began driving a portion of their stock northwestward into the territory to supply mining camps with beef rather than to the railheads in Kansas where it had traditionally been taken for shipping to eastern markets. The extension of railroad lines westward into the Rocky Mountain region and beyond, primarily for the purposes of moving labour and supplies into and out of the region, had a great effect on the movement of cattle in the region, as well as the creation of permanent ranches in the western states. In addition to cattle ranching, sheep ranching also became an import economic activity throughout the West, attracting Mexican, Basque and Australian sheepherders to the region.

While mining and ranching were important to the development of the West, permanent settlement and large-scale growth in the region depended on the development of agriculture; however, several conditions of the West made it undesirable to American farmers who were used to different conditions east of the Mississippi river. Most importantly, the agricultural methods that had been developed in the eastern states relied on greater precipitation than that normally experienced in the arid West. Additionally, farmers feared the possibility of conflict with Native American tribes and with western ranchers, who had become accustomed to a free range system of raising cattle without the land-use restrictions required for agricultural development.

There were, however, reasons for prospective farmers to move to the West despite these challenges. First, the Homestead Act of 1862 entitled settlers to claim 160 acres of land provided they live on and develop the land, and because much of the land in the eastern third of the United States was already privately owned and could not be claimed, the act created an opportunity in the West that was not available in the East[1]. Furthermore, some efforts had been made to minimize the challenges of farming in the West. For example, experimental irrigation methods, particularly in the region's agricultural colonies, and the development of new farming equipment and drought-resistant crops also encouraged the migration of farmers from the East. Native American tribes were relocated to reservations in isolated areas far from the main settlement routes that migrants followed from the eastern United States into the Rocky Mountain region. Ongoing railroad construction and the development of railroad towns provided prospective settlers greater access to land in the region as well as additional security. Finally, the invention of barbed wire in the 1870s enabled farmers to better protect their croplands from roaming herds of livestock. With these developments, eastern Americans, as well as recent immigrants to the United States, began actively homesteading the West.

At the same time, there were social groups that looked to the West as a place to escape the persecution they had experienced in the eastern United States. Among the groups that belonged to this category was the Church of Latter-Day Saints, often referred to as the Mormon Church. After the death of founder Joseph Smith, Brigham Young took over leadership of the church and led the Mormons to the Great Basin, claiming a large portion of the West and naming the entire area the State of Deseret, before settling primarily in the area around what has become known as Salt Lake City, Utah. In addition to the concentrated population of Mormons that remain in and around Salt Lake City, there are also small, tightly knit Mormon communities throughout the West, particularly in remote areas of Nevada, Idaho, Wyoming and Colorado (Meinig 1965).

African Americans also entered the region in an effort to escape prejudices in other regions of the United States, particularly the American South. Records indicate the earliest African Americans in the West served as miners or as slaves to miners in California and Colorado. There were also some African American cowboys, among the most famous being Nate Love and Bill Pickett, and the cavalry troops who acquired the nickname 'buffalo soldiers'. The first significant African American migrations to the region followed shortly after the end of the Civil War, when African Americans established several towns west of the Mississippi river, such as Deerfield, Colorado. It was not until the 1940s that California experienced its large gains in African American migrants (Denning 1989: 152). Today, populations of African Americans in the West are largely concentrated in the region's major cities, particularly in Los Angeles and the San Francisco Bay area, as well as in the cities of Nevada and in the Pacific Northwest.

Today, the states that make up the American West are home to approximately 61.4 million people, or 21.8 per cent of the entire US population.[2] The West, however, comprises 33.2 per cent of the land mass in the United States, making the ratio of people to square mile of land in the West nearly half that of the United States as a whole (46.9 to 79.6). Nevertheless, the population density in the region differs widely. The West includes the least-populated state in the Union (Wyoming pop. 493,782), as well as numerous counties with populations of fewer than a thousand inhabitants; on the other hand, it also includes the highest-populated state in the nation (California, pop. 33,871,648), and the most populous county in the United States (Los Angeles County, pop. approximately 10 million). Other well-populated areas include the San Francisco Bay area in northern California; the area surrounding the Puget Sound in the Pacific Northwest; and the Front Range in Colorado. The relatively great distance between large populations, however, has led such scholars as Meinig (1972) to propose the American West be viewed as a set of dynamic regions, rather than as a contiguous population, such as that along the Atlantic seaboard in the eastern United States.

With respect to its racial makeup[3], the West is predominately white (88.5 per cent), exceeding the national average of 80.4 per cent. Persons of Hispanic or Latino origin comprise the region's largest minority with a percentage slightly greater than the national average (17.7 per cent of the population, compared to 14.1 per cent). The Hispanic population in the West has greatly increased in recent years, just as it has in areas throughout the United States, but it remains largest in those states where there have traditionally been large populations: Arizona, where 28 per cent of the population is of Hispanic descent, California (34.7 per cent), Colorado (19.1 per cent), Nevada (22.8 per cent) and New Mexico (43.5 per cent). On the other hand, the African American population in the West is significantly smaller than the national average (2.9 per cent compared to 12.8 per cent). The African American population in the West resides primarily in Nevada (7.5 per cent) and California (6.8 per cent), which as a state has the fifth largest African American population in the country, while African Americans make up less than 1 per cent of the populations of Idaho, Montana, Utah and Wyoming. Asians make up about 3.4 per cent of the western population, which is slightly lower than the US average of 4.2 per cent; however, the Asian population in California comprises about 12.1 per cent of the state's total population. Native Americans comprise a small population in the western states (3.0 per cent, over the national average of 1.0 per cent), but New Mexico has a relatively high percentage of Native Americans (10.1 per cent), followed by Montana (6.4 per cent) and Arizona (5.0 per cent).

Although English is the first language of the majority of western inhabitants, the sharp increase in the Hispanic population in recent years has meant a significant increase in the number of Spanish speakers (see Silva-Corvalán 2004). The use of French as a first language in the region is primarily restricted to recent immigrants and tourists, but it is used by some Asian immigrant groups as a second language (Beltramo 1981: 348). Among the indigenous languages of the West, Navajo has the greatest number of speakers by far with about 80,000. Although there have been great numbers of speakers of other languages in the West, many were either isolated on farms or were so quickly assimilated into English-speaking society that their language did not have a great impact on the English of the West. Even German, which was such a commonly spoken language in Colorado that the state's laws were printed in the language until 1890 (Fritz 1941: 249), has had little apparent effect on the variety of English spoken in the West.

The West has a diverse economy that includes agriculture, fishing, military, mining, ranching, recreation and forestry. The defence industry has played an important role in the economy since the early twentieth century, both in the number and in the size of military installations and testing grounds in the region. Tourism has become a major industry in the West, particularly because of its natural wonders. Outdoor recreation has also become an important part of the western economy.

Linguistic Background and Contacts

When speakers of American English first arrived in the West, they found a physical environment bearing little resemblance to what they had known in the East and often lacked the lexical inventory needed to represent the unfamiliar topographical features and plant, animal and human life they encountered. As one historian has put it: 'On the frontier, environment dominated inherited culture, forcing old customs to conform to new realities' (Dippie 1989: 5), and this pertains to the linguistic culture that the early pioneers brought with them as well. Consequently, early English speakers in the West resorted to the same basic linguistic strategies they had employed in other regions, including the eastern United States, to create new varieties of English: 1) They borrowed lexical items from languages that already described the physical features in question, particularly from Spanish and French in the case of the West and, to a lesser degree, from some of the Native American languages that were used in the region; 2) they created new lexical items using productive English word-formation processes, particularly compounding; and 3) they altered the meaning of English words that already existed in their linguistic inventories, typically by broadening the semantic domains of these words, to include new referents.

With respect to languages other than English, Spanish served as the greatest direct source of words (some of which the Spanish had themselves borrowed earlier from Native American tribes), and its impact on Western American English is apparent with respect to several semantic domains. For instance, English borrowed several words from Spanish for landforms that are characteristic of the West, including *arroyo*, *canyon* and *mesa*; types of plant life, including *alfalfa*, *(saguaro) cactus*, *chico (brush)*, *chaparral*, *loco (weed)* and *yucca*; and species of animals, including *armadillo* and *coyote*. Spanish influence is also apparent in foods that have been popular in the region for some time, including *enchilada*, *frijoles*, *jerk(y)*, *pinto (beans)*, *tamale*, *tequila* and *tortilla*. Other Spanish words that have traditionally been associated with the West include *adobe*, *desperado*, *fiesta*, *gringo*, *hacienda*, *hoosegow*, *patio*, *plaza*, *poncho*, *pueblo* and *sombrero*.

However, it is in the terminology of ranching, which derives in large part from the ranching culture of Mexico, that Spanish has made its greatest mark on the lexicon of the West.[4] As Americans in the West adopted ranching as a livelihood, they learnt Spanish words for things that play a significant role in what was at one time a largely Spanish activity, including *bronco*, *burro*, *cavvy*, *corral*, *chaps*, *cinch*, *dally*, *hackamore*, *lariat*, *lasso*, *latigo*, *mustang*, *palomino*, *penco*, *quirt*, *ranch*, *remuda*, *rodeo*, *stampede* and *wrangler*.

As is the case for other early languages of the region, Spanish is reflected in the place names of the region, including the state names *Colorado* and *California*. Naming in Spanish can be roughly broken down along three lines: 1) Names that denote objects that have some association with a particular area, including

Alamosa 'cottonwood', *Conejos* 'rabbits', *La Junta* 'the junction', *Huerfano* 'orphan', and *Las Mesitas* 'little tables' in Colorado; 2) the names of early Spanish explorers, including *Castilla, Escalente* and *Salina* in Utah; and 3) the names of Catholic saints, including *San Diego, San Jose* and *San Francisco* in California. Spanish influence is also apparent in the names of the mountain ranges of the West, many of them reflecting the religious orientation of the explorers who named them, including the *Sangre de Cristo* 'blood of Christ' and *San Juan* 'Saint John' ranges in the Rocky Mountains. Many of the important rivers of the region have Spanish names as well, including the *Rio Grande* 'big river', which flows out of Colorado towards the Gulf of Mexico, and the *San Juan* and *San Rafael* in Utah. Other topographical features bearing Spanish names include *Mesa Verde* 'green plateau' in southwestern Colorado and several valleys, including the *San Luis* in Colorado, the *San Joaquin* and *San Fernando* in California, and the *San Cristobal* and *Verde* in Arizona.

In comparison to Spanish, French had a relatively minor impact on the general lexicon of the western American English with its greatest contribution being what Davidson (1938) called 'old trapper talk'. Use of the term *cache* to refer to a hiding place is attributed to French and survives in the speech, as well as in several place names, of the mountains; *butte* 'flat-topped hill' and *prairie* are also attributed to the French and are still used today in speech and in place names. Several phrases used by the French were later literally translated into their English equivalents, including *herbe salee* 'salt grass', which is a type of grass that livestock refuse to eat, and *bois de vache*, the literal translation of which still survives in *buffalo chips* 'animal excrement'.

The importance of the French in the early exploration of the West, particularly in the Rocky Mountains, is represented by numerous French place names in the region, including *Bellvue, Florissant* and *Platte* in Colorado; *Boise, Bruneau, Coeur d'Alene* and *Dubois* in Idaho; *Butte, Choteau* and *Rivulet in* Montana; *Duchesne, La Sal, La Verkin* and *Provo* in Utah; and *Bonneville, Dubois, Fontenelle* and *La Barge* in Wyoming. French names for topographical features are also prevalent, often in conjunction with English words in compound nouns, as in *Cache la Poudre Creek* and *St. Vrain River* in Colorado, the *Grand Teton Mountains* in Wyoming, and *Cache Valley* and *Plateau Valley* in Utah. Some of these names have been replaced over time, including *Bayou Salade*, of which the literal translation is *Salt Marsh*, which has since been renamed *South Park*, Colorado. A literal translation from the French that has had more staying power is *rochejaune* 'yellowstone', which is not only the name of a famous national park, but also a county in Montana, a lake in Wyoming, and an inter-state river.

Although Native American languages have had the longest linguistic presence in the West, they have had relatively little direct impact on the variety of American English spoken in the West, partly due to a lack of recorded history from their early existence in the area. In addition, the diversity of tribes and languages, as well as the nomadic nature of some of these tribes, did little to promote the type of 'founder effect' (Mufwene 1996) that often impacts later language use in an area. Native American languages seem to have had the greatest lasting linguistic influence in the Pacific Northwest, contributing such terms as *chinook* 'warm wind' and *coho (salmon)* to the lexicon of the region.

The existence of few recognizable Native American words in Western American English is due also to the fact that many of the cultural artifacts – and the language denoting them – that were passed on from the Native American people to Anglo-Americans was done so via the Spanish and French. Smith (1984: 15), for instance, notes that:

> The earliest Spanish conquerors and explorers took from the Aztecs whatever they considered to be good, useful, and of lasting quality, as certain foods, herbs, medicines, and words. They passed these things on to succeeding generations, and much of what might seem to have a Spanish origin is really Indian.

Just as they assimilated the artifacts and ideas of the early indigenous people into their culture, the Spanish also absorbed language by 'borrowing words from the Nahuatl (Aztec), Zacatec, Caribe, Mayan, Taino, Arawak, and other Indian tribes' (Smith 1984: 16). Such words include *coyote* and *mesquite*, which were derived from Nahuatl *coyotl* and *mizuitl*, respectively, as well as *barbecue* from Teino *barbacoa*. The close relationship of the French to several Native American tribes is also evident in the language of the region: First, in its collaboration with the Cree to form Michif, a mixed language still in use in parts of Montana and Canada today (see Bakker 1997); furthermore, in serving as a conduit through which Native American words entered the English language, as in the case of *caribou*, which the French derived from Micmac *galipu* 'scraper or pawer (of snow)'; and finally in many of the names by which Native American tribes are known to others, including *Gros Ventre* 'great belly', *Coeur d'Alene* 'heart of awl' or 'sharp-hearted', and *Nez Percé* 'pierced nose'.

The Native American languages of the West have perhaps left their greatest linguistic legacy in the place names of the region. In addition to serving as names of states, numerous words associated with indigenous languages are used for names of counties throughout the region, including *Arapahoe* and *Kiowa* in Colorado; *Blackfoot* and *Shoshone* in Idaho; *Bannack* and *Kalispell* in Montana; *Paiute* in Utah; and *Cheyenne* and *Shawnee* in Wyoming. Native American words that are used as the place names of communities throughout the region include *Chama, Cochetopa, Cotopaxi, Niwot, Ouray, Yampa* and *Yuma* in Colorado; *Kooskia and Weippe* in Idaho; *Ekalaka, Moccasin, Nashua, Peritsa* and *Yaak* in Montana, *Kanosh* and *Ouray* in Utah, and *Oshoto* and *Washakie*, Wyoming. Furthermore, a great number of topographical features in the region are designated by Native American words and names, often blending and compounding with English words to do so, including *Arikaree River, Uncompahgre Plateau* and *Wahatoya* 'breasts of the earth' (now typically called the Spanish Peaks) in Colorado; *Coeur d'Alene Lake, Kootenai River* and *Lake Pend Oreille* in Idaho; *Flathead Lake* and *Sioux Pass* in Montana; *Ibapah Peak, Uintah Mountains, Wah Wah Mountains* and *Wahweap Creek* in Utah; and *Togwotee Pass* in Wyoming.

While many words entered English from other languages that were already in use in the West, this vocabulary was borrowed neither passively nor perfectly, especially at the micro levels of phonetics, phonology and morphology. For instance, the anglicization of many Spanish words meant minor changes in pronunciation, as in the replacement of the middle consonant of *lasso* [z] with [s], as well as more radical changes, as in the derivation of *wrangler* from *caballer-engero* and the shortening of *lariat, chaps, dally* and *hoosegow* from, respectively, *la reata, chapareras, dar vuelta* and *juzgado* (Adams 1968: xiii). A general change among some of the words that English borrowed from Spanish has been the omission of suffixes, as in the derivation of *ranch* from *rancho*. Other changes reflect the misanalysis of phrases as single words, of which *lariat*, from the Spanish noun phrase *la reata*, serves as the best example in its fusing of a definite article with a noun. On the other hand, in the derivation of the word *mosey* from *vamoos* 'go', the initial syllable was dropped and an ending added.

Many of the place names derived from earlier languages have also undergone changes in pronunciation. In Colorado, the town name *Buena Vista* (Spanish, 'beautiful view') is often pronounced [byunə vɪstə], or simply [byuni] by locals; the town name *Saguache* (Ute, 'water at the blue earth') has a variety of pronunciations; and the first word of the southern Colorado *Purgatoire River* (originally Spanish, *Rio de las Animas Perdido en Purgatorio* 'river of lost souls in purgatory') is often pronounced as *purgatory* or is referred to by its nickname *picketwire.*

Some borrowings have been semantically reanalysed by speakers of English and have fallen prey to the processes of folk etymology, as illustrated by the misinterpretation of the word *galon* 'braid' as a similar-sounding English term of measurement that has shifted the meaning of the phrase *ten-gallon hat* from 'a hat with ten braids' to 'a large hat'. Additionally, lack of familiarity with the original meaning of borrowings has resulted in some apparently redundant phrases and place names in American English, including *lariat rope, Rio Grande river* and *Table Mesa* (Antieau 2003b).

Due to the lack of written records, there has been some debate among scholars as to the correct etymology of many words that English borrowed from earlier languages used in the West. For instance, the word *buckaroo* is typically recognized as a corruption of the Spanish word *vacquero* 'cowboy' (see Marckwardt, 1958: 44), but it has also been argued that the word is actually a corruption of the Gullah word *buckra* 'white man' (Mason 1960: 51). Aside from such etymological puzzles, it is apparent that borrowings from other languages played an important part in the development of Western American English, particularly in the early years of Anglo-American settlement.

Despite the contributions of earlier languages, early American settlers used English as their greatest resource for talking about the West by manipulating known words to name new discoveries, often using productive English word formation strategies like compounding in doing so. For instance, after the Lewis and Clark expedition, Meriwether Lewis cataloged 178 plants that had not been previously described (Art 1990: 6–7), often creating common names, in addition to their Latinate names, through the use of compound nouns, such as *bitterroot, blanketflower* and *Rocky Mountain beeplant,* by which many of these plants are still known today. Additional lexical items created during the expedition, typically by compounding, include *ground squirrel, cottonwood, cutoff, bull snake* and *copperhead snake* (Marckwardt 1958: 87). Other compound nouns that have been created for western referents include *mountain lion, horned toad, camp robber* 'Canada jay' and *blue norther,* as well as *prairie dog,* a term that was attributed to the early mountain men and is related to such other terms as *prairie squirrel* and *prairie marmot.*

Eastern lexical variants were also sometimes used to denote western referents that shared similarities with eastern referents with the result being semantic broadening, or generalization. In the West, the term *park,* for instance, acquired the meaning of 'high grassy valley surrounded by mountains' (Kimmerle 1950: 162). Similarly, the word *hole* was used in some places to refer to small isolated areas in high mountains that were used for shelter by mountain men and later as hideouts for outlaws. Although *hole* had been used with the meaning of 'a secret hiding place' in England (Kimmerle 1950: 163), it was overlooked in favour of *holler* in the eastern states; it is now perhaps most familiar to Americans due to its use in place names such as *Jackson Hole.* Another example of this type of change was the use of the two variants *chipmunk* and *ground squirrel* for one type of animal in the East, but for two different animals in Colorado, so that *chipmunk* denoted the type of animal that could also be found in the eastern states, and *ground squirrel* was used for a larger animal associated with the West (Hankey 1961: 267).

Since speakers of English from each of the major dialect regions of the eastern United States migrated to the West, it is perhaps only natural that there has been competition in the region among dialectal variants denoting the same item. With respect to the lexicon, the outcome of this competition has sometimes resulted in one referent becoming the dominant term in the West at the expense of others, while in other cases usage has remained mixed, as in the distribution of *roasting ears/corn on the cob* and *husks/shucks* (Antieau 2006: 126–29). As variants have taken their place in the western lexicon, some semantic shifting has occurred to accommodate competing variants.

Western speech seems to have been greatly influenced by the early occupations of western settlers. As the most important early economic activity of the region, mining impacted the language of the West in several ways. Although they were not unique to the West but could be found in other regions where mining was an important economic activity, words and phrases like *bonanza, boom, boomtown, croppings, laggings, leavings, lode, pay dirt, placer, played out, prospect, shaft, sluice, strike, tailings* and *trace* were important components of the lexicon during the mining years. Such terms were not only integral to the everyday speech of miners but featured prominently in early descriptions of the speech in the region, including Crofutt (1881). The language of mining towns also reflected the nationalities of people who often worked in mines or mining towns, for example, *Cousin Jack* and *Cousin Jenny* to denote those of Cornish descent (Davidson 1930: 147) and *Bohunk*, which was first used to refer to an Austrian miner and, later, any foreign miner. The lexicon also included names for animals that worked in the mines, for example, *Rocky Mountain canary* 'burro' or 'jackass', due to the high-pitched sounds the animal made (Moore 1926: 38).

The historical importance of mining is reflected in the numerous communities with names relating to minerals or mining activities. In California, these include *Diamond Springs, El Dorado* and *Placerville;* in Colorado, *Basalt, Boulder, Bonanza City, Carbondale, Coalcreek, Coaldale, Cokedale, Copper Mountain, Gold Hill, Granite, Gypsum, Leadville, Marble, Silver Cliff, Silver Plume* and *Tin Cup;* in Idaho, *Cobalt, Silverton* and *Smelterville;* in Montana, *Coalwood, Goldcreek* and *Mill Iron;* in Nevada, *Eureka* and *Goldfield; Silver City* in New Mexico; *Bonanza, Carbonville, Coalville, East Carbon* and *Minersville* in Utah; and in Wyoming, *Cokeville, Diamondville, Iron Mountain, Marbleton, Nugget* and *Opal.* These names have kept the historical importance of mining alive in western towns, long after many of the mining operations they refer to have ceased.

The importance of ranching has impacted the linguistic landscape of the West in several ways. First, opportunities in ranching attracted speakers of a variety of languages and dialects to the region, including speakers of Spanish, Basque and Australian English. Perhaps the greatest number of people who worked in ranching in the western states, however, spoke Texas American English, which, like the western language of exploration and early settlement, also incorporated elements of languages besides English. As Adams (1968: xv) notes:

> When the Texan rode over the long trails north, he carried his customs and his manner of working all the way to the Canadian line. Montana, Wyoming, and other northern and central states adopted much of his Spanish-influenced language. In exchange, the northern cowman gave the Texan that which he had appropriated from the northern Indian and the French-Canadian, words strange to the man from the Rio Grande.

Thus, the language of the activity and the speech characteristics of those who spoke it were disseminated over a large area and, as Pederson (2001: 284) notes: 'Even today, such linguistic forms distinguish the West, however dominant Eastern institutions over the general development of these societies may be.'

Like mining, ranching is an activity that relies on a specialized vocabulary for communication among those who work in the industry. In addition to the Spanish words related to ranching mentioned above, the activity of ranching also contributed such words to the western lexicon as *bunkhouse, dogie* 'orphan calf', *bum* 'orphan cattle or sheep', and *trail,* as well as *feed bag* and *nose bag,* both denoting items used for feeding horses. A number of terms serve as variants of *cowboy,* including *cow poke, cow puncher* and *cowhand.* Additionally, many new terms were formed by creating compounds incorporating a Spanish borrowing and an English word, such as *ranch hand, ranch house* and *sheep corral.*

Ranching also contributed numerous expressions conveying the excitement and the dangers associated with the activity. *In spite of hell and high water,* for instance, refers to the determination that ranchers were required to possess to drive cattle through the deep waters of rivers and the scorching temperatures and aridity of the overland trails they followed. There are a number of euphemisms for dying that have been attributed to ranchers, including *crossed over the range* and *down grade with no brakes.* Ranchers have also contributed several colourful euphemisms for killing, presumably animals, including *eased them of their blood, frightened a few out of their skins* and *rubbed from the earth.* As in the case of mining speech, many ranching terms are now used metaphorically in other domains in American English, as is the case for such words as *branding, corral* and *stampede.*

Homesteading, an important part of the settlement of the West, also contributed a number of lexical items to Western life, including terms associated with the transportation of early homesteaders into the West, such as *stone boat, chuck wagon* and *covered wagon.* Once they had *staked their claim,* many new settlers constructed sod houses, or *soddies.* Because of the scarcity of wood on the western plains, as well as the large areas of land required for sustainable harvests, landowners had to find ways to mark their property and enclose animals differently than their counterparts in the eastern United States did; thus, after its invention in the 1870s, early western homesteaders relied on barbed wire. Alternatively pronounced as *barb wire* and *bob wire,* ranchers who relied on the open range system for their livelihood and Native Americans were reported to have called the innovation *the devil's rope.*

Thus, while the West has been home to a vast array of speakers of languages other than English, only a handful have had an obvious direct impact on the variety of English spoken in the region. Spanish, and to a lesser degree French, as well as such Native American languages as Ute, have contributed pronunciations, lexical items and phrases that are partly responsible for giving the speech of the West some of its flavor. The great number of Anglo-American settlers in the West who already spoke some variety of eastern American English and who manipulated their speech to account for their new environment provided western American English with its essential structure, but also with some of its subtle differences from eastern American English.

The Grammar of Western American English

As a variety of American English that stems from eastern sources, the English spoken in the western United States has more similarities than differences with eastern varieties, and it includes characteristic features of all the major varieties of eastern American English. While most dialectologists have maintained that, generally speaking, western American English is least similar to the variety of English associated with the southern United States (Carver 1987: 213; Metcalf 2000: 119), there has been some debate over the variety of eastern American English with which it most closely relates. These debates often stem from disagreements over whether there are two or three major eastern dialects and the features that should be associated with them, but some of these differences are also the result of scholars analysing different facets of linguistic structure to support their claims. Perhaps most importantly, characterizations of western American English suffer due to the lack of comparable data throughout the region (Carver 1987: 210).

The major differences between eastern and western American English are most obvious in the lexicon, particularly with respect to the distribution of Spanish words in the West. Other words, often indicating the presence or, perhaps more often, the relative frequency and importance of certain objects in the West, are also found. For instance, the aspen is a tree that can be found throughout most of the United States, but it takes on a greater importance in the mountainous western region, where the beauty of the tree serves as a significant tourist draw. The popularity of the tree is marked by a number of variant terms for it, many of which apparently refer to the shimmering quality of its leaves, including *quakies, quakers, quaking aspen, quivering aspen* and *quivering asp* (Pederson 2001: 285; Antieau 2006: 167–68); the name of the tree even serves as the name of one of Colorado's most popular ski destinations.

While the lexicon displays some obvious differences between eastern and western varieties of English, there are also differences in the pronunciations of some lexical items used in both regions. These include *coyote* [kaiot], as opposed to the typical eastern pronunciation [kaioti] (Metcalf 2000: 121), as well as the realization of /æ/ in the second and third syllables, respectively, of *Nevada* and *Colorado* and the pronunciation of *Oregon* with a weakly stressed final syllable (Pederson 2001: 285).

Although earlier dialectological surveys, particularly those focusing on lexical variation in the region, noted that the scattered distribution and the leap-frogging nature of settlements provided obstacles to dialect formation in the West in general (Carver 1987: 220), and the Rocky Mountain region specifically (Kimmerle et al. 1951: 254), more recent research focusing on the phonology of the region suggests that western American English has become more cohesive in recent years. Based on data collected in western cities for the Phonological Atlas of North America, Labov et al. (1997: 2) state that:

The picture of the West that emerges is that it has developed a characteristic but not unique phonology. It is closest to the South Midland as a dialect in which the merger of /o/ and /oh/ is firmly coupled with /uw/. Though there are many speakers in the South Midland who show this pattern, it is still only a third of those we have interviewed, as opposed to four fifths of Westerners.

Thus, according to Labov et al. (1997: 2), the phonology of the region does not reveal 'the diffuse or unmarked character that was predicted for the West. Instead, we find that in the phonological system, a fair degree of homogeneity is emerging, with specific features that differentiate the West from other dialect areas'.

Although Labov et al. (1997) use the presence of the merger of /ɑ/ and /ɔ/ as the low back vowel /ɑ/ as one of the major points of evidence for a cohesive dialect in the West, they also point out that is not exclusive to the West. Rather, the merger seems to be part of change that has been ongoing in several varieties of English. Kurath & McDavid (1961) noted its presence in earlier Atlas records in western Pennsylvania and eastern New England, and Gordon notes that it is a widespread feature of American English (Gordon 2006).

Evidence suggests that the merger is a recent development in the West (Metcalf 1972; Di Paolo 1992; Labov et al.). Pederson (2001) reports that 'the coalescence of /ɑ/ and /ɔ/ in all contexts among younger speakers points toward the loss of the /ɔ/ phoneme in the northern Rockies' (285); Antieau (2006) provides evidence that among older, rural speakers in Colorado, women generally participate in the merger while men do not. The urban data of Labov et al. (1997) also provides evidence of the fronting of the high-back vowel /uw/ (as in the word *boot)* to be common in the West, and several studies throughout the West have suggested there is a tendency for back-vowel fronting throughout the region (Di Paolo and Faber 1990; Conn 2000; Conn 2005; Eckert and Mendoza-Denton 2005; Hall-Lew 2005).

Although perhaps not to the same degree as other eastern American dialects, there is some evidence that southern American English has exerted some influence over western pronunciation and that this influence was even greater in the Wild West days, as suggested by the r-less pronunciation of such words as *hoss, cuss* and *podnuh* for *horse, curse* and *partner,* respectively, among older generations of westerners (Metcalf 2000: 120). Although they find that western pronunciation generally aligns with that of the Midland region, and more specifically the South Midland region, Labov et al. (1997) note some apparent southern influence on Western American English in the pronunciation of the vowel in *on,* as well as in the occurrence of inglides with short vowels. Perhaps due to the influence of the Texas cattle culture on the West, several other characteristics typically associated with the pronunciation of Southern American English can also be found, notably the monophthongization of vowels in the words *tire* and *fire*, particularly in the pronunciation of *wire* in rural Colorado (Antieau 2006: 206–09).

Research on the syntax of Western American English and that of eastern varieties of American English has revealed no qualitative differences; rather, such research has typically focused on the use of syntactic constructions that are also associated with eastern varieties of English. Of these, some are relatively widespread and apparently well accepted in the region, for example, positive *anymore* (Murray 2004); while others have a more limited distribution in both regions. For instance, Antieau (2003a: 397–98, 2006) provides evidence of use among older speakers of English in rural Colorado of a-prefixing, a morphosyntactic process exemplified by a sentence like 'I'm a-going home now', which is often associated with Southern American English (see Wolfram and Christian 1976)[5]. Graham and Launspach (2004) have presented evidence of the use of personal dative constructions, as in, for example, 'I just bought *me* a new truck', a linguistic construction also typically associated with Southern American English (Wolfram and Schilling-Estes 1998: 284). Finally, Di Paolo (1989) and Antieau (2003a: 398) present evidence in Utah and Colorado, respectively, on the use of double modal constructions, as in 'I *might could* do that', despite such constructions being generally associated with Southern American English (Wolfram and Schilling-Estes 1998: 44–5). Such evidence suggests that Southern American English may have had a greater influence on the speech of the West than previously assumed or that more work needs to be done characterizing features along various dimensions in American English.

With respect to the semantics of Western American English, the preceding section explained how new objects and experiences in the West occasionally resulted in the manipulation of existing vocabulary items to provide coverage for the new range of experience. That is, speakers would sometimes apply words that already existed in their lexicon to new things, based on some relationship or similarity between the new, unfamiliar referent and the familiar referent and thus broaden the referent. On the other hand, western migrants also narrowed the meaning of words in verbally accounting for their new environment. One example of such a phenomenon is *irrigation ditch*. Because irrigation was required rather than simply desired in western agriculture, and as such was a likely topic of discussion, many early westerners apparently shortened the term for a channel dug into the earth as a conduit for water from *irrigation ditch* to simply *ditch*. Thus, for other types of ditches, such as those along the side of an upgraded road used for run-off, westerners adopted a variety of alternate terms, including *bar pit, borrow pit, borrow bit, bar ditch, borrow ditch, barrow ditch, grader ditch* and *gutter* (Kimmerle 1950: 164–5).

Although little work has been done on discourse structures peculiar to western speech, numerous colourful idioms have been associated with the West; as Davidson (1942: 72) noted: 'Much of the spirit of the West is embodied in the picturesque phrases and proverbs that one finds scattered through early-day newspapers and the diaries of pioneers.' Many of these phrases have been attributed to mountain men, such as *the horse has stopped* 'tired' and *water scrape* 'a trip in which water is scarce'. The famous mountain man Jim Bridger was reported to have used the expression 'A bird can't fly over thar without takin' a supply of grub along' to refer to the desert. Even common homesteaders had interesting ways of expressing mundane events, as in the use of *drive stakes* 'to settle down'. Davidson (1942: 72) noted, however, that the difference between the use of western and eastern expressions had begun diminishing by the turn of the twentieth century. In his writings on American English during the first half of the twentieth century, Mencken (1986: 464) reported that sayings attributed to the western cattlemen such as *fall guy, to get in bad, locoed, to hit the hay* and *to mooch* had been popularized to such an extent through film, television and pulp fiction that they no longer struck the average American as anything other than mainstream English.

English Usage within the Region

Although lacking in the comprehensive manner that such research has been done in the eastern states, systematic research on language variation in the American West has been conducted since the late 1940s and has resulted in numerous dissertations and scholarly articles contributing to a greater knowledge of western speech and variation in American English in general. While there are differences in some of the conditions that underlie language variation in the eastern and western United States, the same principles generally apply: Namely, such variation is never the result of one factor; rather, a variety of social factors exert an influence over dialectal variation, including settlement patterns, cultural centres and physical geography (McDavid, 1958: 483–85).

As is the case in the eastern states, settlement patterns were one of the most important factors in shaping western varieties of American English. During the early 1800s, the movements of explorers were restricted by the border with Spain to the south and by the availability of fresh water, which meant travelling near the few waterways that flowed throughout the region. Upon completion of the western acquisition and after the gold rushes, western settlement was often due westward so that '[f]rom Montana and Idaho through Wyoming, Utah, and upper Colorado, Western dialects preserve an essentially Northern pattern' (Pederson 2001: 284), while south of central Colorado through New Mexico and Arizona, regional speech is largely an extension of the Midland region and a southern influence that diminishes as one goes west (Pederson 2001: 285).

Despite some evidence of the extension of eastern dialectal divisions, research has also shown a great deal of dialect mixture in the West, which has been attributed to both the leap-frogging nature of western settlement and to the dialect mixture spoken in the original communities of many early western settlers, particularly those from the Great Lakes region (Kimmerle et al. 1951; Jackson 1956). Other scholars have noted the importance of the Mississippi Valley as a stage in the development of western speech, as it was there that 'regional speech extended and reformed the three primary eastern patterns' and served as a source of western dialects (Pederson 2001: 280–81). With respect to the distribution of lexical items in the Rocky Mountains, several scholars have noted the existence of Yankee speech islands (Kimmerle et al. 1951; Hankey 1960; Pederson 2001).

Some scholars have argued that while westward settlement was having an effect on speech patterns in the West, the southern part of the region was also having a great effect on speech differences in the region. Adams (1968: xiv-xv) reports that after the conflict with Mexico that resulted in the fall of the Alamo, Texans attempted to create an identity distinct from their Mexican past, which resulted not only in a deviation from the Spanish style of ranching but from the language used to discuss ranching. However, because of the state's lengthy history with the Spanish, the language could not be abandoned so readily and much Spanish vocabulary was instead corrupted. On the other hand, Californians lacked the animosity towards the Spanish that Texans had and therefore retained the Spanish traditions and the language intact. These different perspectives on the Spanish language would then be projected onto the language of the region as a whole as the cultural and linguistic influence of southern California eventually spread northward to Oregon and Central Washington and eastward into Western Idaho, and the speech patterns of Texas spread through the Great Plain and Rocky Mountain states (Wolfram and Schilling-Estes 1998: 112).

Despite the difficulties in making strong generalizations about language variation in the West, one of the most obvious differences in the region is the relatively large number of Spanish loanwords in the Southwest (Mencken 1986: 465; Carver 1987; Wolfram and Schilling-Estes 1998; Pederson 2001). Using Atlas records from the 1950s, Kimmerle (1952) pointed out that the Spanish variant *penco* 'orphan lamb' was limited in its areal distribution to southern Colorado, while the variants *bum* and *poddy* were used elsewhere. Antieau (2006: 164–65) found that *penco* was still in use among rural speakers at the turn of the twenty-first century and had approximately the same areal distribution as Kimmerle had observed half a century earlier. Furthermore, Antieau (2003b) found Spanish folk terms to be more common in southern Colorado than elsewhere throughout the state, suggesting that older settlement patterns still play a role in the distribution of folk variants. Carver (1987: 221-2) also noted isoglosses for several Spanish terms from the colonial period, including *arroyo* and *frijoles*, following roughly along a Hispanic borderland that include the southern regions of Arizona and Colorado, as well as New Mexico and Texas.

Just as many of the lexical differences between eastern and western varieties of American English are the result of physical differences between the two regions, physical differences also result in lexical differences among the western regions. For instance, environmental differences between the plains region and the mountains region have created some differences in lexical distribution between the inhabitants of the two areas. Hankey (1960: 82), for instance, found evidence supporting several isoglosses along the Front Range of Colorado, including the eastern limits of *park* 'prairie meadow' and the western limits of *prairie (dog) owl*. Antieau (2006: 128, 146) found significant statistical differences in the use of the terms *(corn) shucks* and *fishworms* based on whether informants lived in eastern Colorado or elsewhere in the state. The Pacific Northwest, which is considered one of the most coherent dialect regions of the West (Wolfram and Schilling-Estes 1998: 112), has several lexical features associated with it, including *chinook*, and *coho* and *sockeye (salmon)*, as well as *geoduck*, the name of a local shellfish that is typically pronounced [guidək] (Metcalf 2000: 131).

Metcalf (2000) provides evidence of each of the western states possessing lexical singularities, due to either the cultural or linguistic histories of the state's settlers or to physical characteristics either unique to a state or having a stronger association with one state than with others. For instance, in Colorado, the term *fourteener* is often used to refer to any of the state's 50-odd mountains measuring over 14,000-feet high, and the *pika*, or *cony*, are small mountainous mammals that are indigenous to the area (Metcalf 2000: 125). Other examples of variation associated with a single state include the use of the term *lucerne* 'alfalfa' and the phrase *cube of butter* rather than *stick of butter* in Idaho (Metcalf 2000: 126). In southern California, speakers often refer to a highway by its number preceded by the definite article, as in *the 80* or *the 15*, a phenomenon that can often be heard in films and on television programmes that are broadcast from the area.

Because of the geographical and social isolation of Mormon communities, Utah is a state with a relatively strong linguistic identity. A number of phonological characteristics have been noted in the state, chief among these being the merger of the sounds /ɥ/ and /o/ before /r/, a linguistic phenomenon sometimes referred to as the *card/cord* merger (Bowie 2003).[6] There is also the tendency for speakers to pronounce the tense high back vowel sound in words like *pool* and *fool* with the lax counterpart such that the realizations sound more similar to *pull* and *full* (Bowie and Morkel 2005). The religious orientation of the Mormons and their strong influence in the area have also shaped the language more directly, as many Utah place names are named after places and people in the Book of Mormon, such as *Nephi, Lehi, Moroni, Manti* and *Bountiful* (Van Cott 1990: xviii).

While some variation in western speech seems to be based on region, scholars have noted that other social factors seem to have a greater bearing on linguistic variation in the West (Metcalf 2000: 121). Mencken (1986: 464) noted that differences in western speech tend to be based less on regional differences than on occupation. In Arizona, Hall-Lew (2005) notes some linguistic differences based on whether speakers live in, or identify with, either rural or urban communities.

Research on speech in the West has suggested little in the way of regionally-marked discourse features. There has been some evidence suggesting that in California, quotatives incorporating *be like* are being replaced by *be all*, as in 'So she *is all* "What are you looking at?"' Research in other places, such as New York City, has provided little evidence of the construction (Eckert and Mendoza-Denton 2005: 141).

Media Use of Language

Although linguists typically downplay the linguistic effect that the media has on the language of its audience on the grounds that the speech situation is not interactive (Kurath 1949: 9; Chambers 1993), some have suggested that the lexicon may be susceptible to change from the media, albeit in terms of supplement rather than replacement (Johnson 1996: 91). Because of its status as the centre of the American motion picture industry, Hollywood, California, has been important in this regard, contributing a seemingly never-ending stream of (typically, transient) phrases and words to American English. Television programmes that have been popular among the young, such as Buffy the Vampire Slayer, The Fresh Prince of Bellaire and others, have had a similar effect. It may of course be the case that some of these effects are cyclical in that the media does not so much create linguistic variants as it absorbs them and then broadcasts them to a wider audience.

Several social and linguistic stereotypes of westerners have also been presented by the media since at least the early twentieth century. These stereotypes follow along several lines. One of the oldest is the portrayal of cowboys in the old westerns. Although the heyday of the Hollywood western has long since past, a relatively recent movie that includes a cowboy stereotype is *The Big Lebowski* (1998), in which the narrator of the piece, played by Sam Elliot, incorporates many of these features: he uses colourful expressions often associated with the western cowboy, such as 'Catch you further on down the trail', has a distaste for the word *dude*, and uses some linguistic features associated with southern speech that have also been attributed to western cowboys, such as perfective *done*.

There have also been several stereotypes focusing on California English, especially as used by the young, including depiction of surfers, stoners and valley girls (or Vals). Perhaps the best-known stereotype of valley speech is that depicted in Frank and Moon-Unit Zappa's 1982 song 'Valley Girl' with its use of such linguistic markers as *fer sure, totally, awesome* and *grody*, as well as the ubiquitous *like* (Metcalf 2000: 138). Depictions of southern California youth speech can be found in such movies as *Fast Times at Ridgemont High* (1982), *Valley Girl*

(1983) and *Clueless* (1995) and several television shows, including *Buffy the Vampire Slayer* (1997–2003). While many of these depictions might be interpreted to suggest that youth are the only Californians obsessed with image, several movies also depict older generations similarly obsessed, most notably the 1991 movie *L.A. Story* starring Steve Martin, although the latter primarily focuses on how this is articulated via discourse features rather than the lexicon or pronunciation.

Many films focusing on the lives of African Americans have included the use of African American English, including *Waiting to Exhale* (1995) and *How Stella Got Her Groove Back* (1998). Several films that include African American English in southern California have centred on life among gang members in Los Angeles, including *Colors* (1988), *Boyz n the Hood* (1991) and *Training Day* (2001). Some of the popular music of the region also makes use of African American English, particularly in the language of West Coast rap used by such artists as Dr. Dre, Ice Cube and Snoop Doggy Dog.

Current Trends

There are several noteworthy trends in Western American English. With respect to the western lexicon, one would expect that the folk vocabulary of farmers and ranchers will be lost as fewer and fewer people adopt that way of life and instead adopt the vocabulary of the industries that now form the bedrock of the western economy, such as the heavy concentrations of those working in the computer industry in Silicon Valley and in Seattle. Nevertheless, several scholars (see Kretzschmar and Tamasi (2001), Burkette (2001), and Johnson (1996)) point to evidence that lexical items are not necessarily lost when replaced by newer lexical items but are often retained as low-frequency variants in language varieties. Using evidence from Colorado Atlas records, Antieau (2006) contends that the presence of a low-frequency variant in the dialect of a region retains the possibility for its resurgence in the speech of later generations, either as a competing variant for the original object or as a designation for a new object.

Social, political and economic impact of English within the region

As is the case elsewhere in the United States, the argument that English should be recognized as an official national language is a topic of heated debate in the West, particularly in the Southwest. Several states in the West have enacted legislation recognizing English as the official language of the state, including Arizona, California, Colorado, Montana, Utah and Wyoming. Several western states, however, acknowledge the importance of Spanish in various ways, including posting signs that are written in both English and Spanish. The state laws of

New Mexico are printed in both English and Spanish, and California has traditionally offered government services in a variety of languages, including Spanish. Time will tell how legislation designed to limit a state's responsibility in providing services in other languages will impact offices faced with the problem of providing aid to large numbers of speakers of other languages.

In addition to those issues pertaining to the use of languages besides English in the West, particularly Spanish, there are also some social issues regarding dialectal varieties of English in the West. The issue of African American English was officially dealt with in the Ebonics debate in Oakland, California, in 1996, and led to heated arguments in a public forum about the variety's origins, as well as its value, in an attempt to determine how schools should best address the issue. The use of Spanglish, particularly in areas of the United States with high concentrations of Hispanic-Americans, has also been the topic of debate in schools and in communities in southern California, Arizona and New Mexico.

Future Implications of English in the Region

In his essay on American dialects, Pederson (2001: 288) states that:

> . . . Western dialects suggest the immediate future of the national language more reliably than any other regional pattern. As products of American social history since the Civil War, local speech of the West incorporates features from eastern sources and reforms them across the plains, mountains and coastal subdivisions of the Western states.

Such a characterization suggests that Western American English is an interesting and worthwhile study not only in and of itself, but for the insight it may provide on all dialects of American English. This study should not only aim to provide overall coverage of the region but should also examine the influence this variety might have on other varieties, especially through the means of mass media, given the status of southern California in this regard.

While it is to be expected that Western American English will endure as the primary means of communication in the West, it will be interesting to see how the variety is affected by its close and relatively long-standing relation to Spanish. Many studies have been conducted on the effect of Spanish on American English, but it would also be instructive to see more research on the impact that English has on Spanish (Lozano 1976: 202), as well as on other immigrant languages. Johnson and Boyle (2006: 244) speak of the mutual effect that English and Spanish speakers have on each other in reference to their contact in north Georgia. Such contact issues are obviously as important in the western United States as in other regions of the country.

Finally, it will be interesting to see how Western American English changes as the West itself changes: From its place in the American psyche as a symbol for rugged individualism to a more mainstream part of the American experience with its own history and its own pressing concerns: A dialect that reflects its past and proclaims its place in the present and the future.

Notes

[1] Later, the Enlarged Homestead Act of 1909 made marginal western lands more appealing as it expanded the area that could be claimed by homesteaders to 320 acres.

[2] All general population numbers are from the 2000 U.S. Census Bureau State and County Quick Facts.

[3] All numbers on race are from the 2004 U.S. Census Bureau State and County Quick Facts and count only persons self-reporting one race.

[4] For more on Spanish borrowings in American English, see Marckwardt, (1958), Atwood (1962), and Bright (1971). Dillard (1973) provides evidence of several languages contributing to the ranching vocabulary of the southwest and proposes the existence of a lingua franca in the region based on this data.

[5] However, Antieau (2001: 146) discusses the occurrence of the form in Atlas records of all the eastern regions, and Wolfram and Schilling-Estes (1998: 30) characterize a-prefixing as a rural rather than southern phenomenon.

[6] See Bowie (2003) for a review on the literature of this phenomenon.

Bibliography

Adams, R. F. (1968). *Westernisms: A Dictionary of the American West*. Norman: University of Oklahoma Press.

Antieau, L. (2001). '"I'm a-goin' to see what's going on here": a-prefixing in The Adventures of Huckleberry Finn', *Language and Literature*, 10: 145–157.

—. (2003a). 'Plains English in Colorado', *American Speech*, 78: 385–403.

—. (2003b). 'Spanish contributions to Colorado English', *Linguistic Association of the Southwest XXXII*, Edinburg, Texas.

—. (2006). A Distributional Analysis of Rural Colorado English. PhD dissertation, University of Georgia.

Art, H. W. (1990). *The Wildflower Gardener's Guide: Pacific Northwest, Rocky Mountain, and Western Canada Edition*. Pownal, Vermont: Storey Communications.

Atwood, E. B. (1962). *The Regional Vocabulary of Texas*. Austin: University of Texas Press.

Bakker, P. (1997). *A Language of Our Own: The Genesis of Michif, the Mixed Cree-French Language of the Canadian Metis*. New York: Oxford University Press.

Beltramo, A. (1981). 'Profile of a state: Montana', in C. Ferguson and S. Heath (eds), *Language in the U.S.A.* Cambridge: Cambridge University Press, 339–80.

Bowie, D. (2003). 'Early development of the card-cord merger in Utah', *American Speech*, 78: 31–51.

Bowie, D. and Merkel, W. (2005). 'Desert dialect', in W. Wolfram and B. Ward (eds), *American Voices: How Dialects Differ from Coast to Coast*. Malden, Massachusetts: Blackwell, 144–48.

Bright, E. (1971). *A Word Geography of California and Nevada*. Berkeley, California: University of California Press.

Bright, W. (2004). *Native American Placenames of the United States*. Norman, Oklahoma: University of Oklahoma Press.

Burkette, A. (2001). 'The story of chester drawers', *American Speech*, 76: 139–57.

Carver, C. (1987). *American Regional Dialects: A Word Geography*. Ann Arbor: University of Michigan Press.

Cassidy, F. G., et al. (eds). (1985). *Dictionary of American Regional English*. Cambridge: Harvard University Press.

Chambers, J. K. (1993). 'Sociolinguistic Dialectology', in D. R. Preston (ed.) *American Dialect Research*. Amsterdam: John Benjamins.

Congressional Record. (2006a). 109th Congress, 2nd session. 18 May. pp. S4735–739, 52–57, 61–70.

—. (2006b). 109th Congress, 2nd session. 18 May. pp. S4757–761, 70.

Conn, J. 2000. The Story of /æ/ in Portland. M.A. thesis, Portland State University.

—. (2005). 'Dialects in the Mist (Portland, OR)', in W. Wolfram and B. Ward (eds), *American Voices: How Dialects Differ from Coast to Coast*. Malden, Massachusetts: Blackwell, 149–55.

Crofutt, G. A. (1881). *Crofutt's Grip-Sack Guide of Colorado*. Omaha: Overland.

Davidson, L. J. (1930). 'Mining expressions in Colorado', *American Speech*, 5: 144–47.

—. (1938). 'Old trapper talk', *American Speech*, 13: 83–92.

—. (1942). 'Westernisms', *American Speech*, 17: 71–73.

Denning, K. (1989). 'Convergence with divergence: a sound change in vernacular black English', *Language Variation and Change*, 1: 145–67.

Di Paolo, M. (1989). 'Double modals as single lexical items', *American Speech*, 64: 195–224.

—. (1992). 'Hypercorrection in response to the apparent merger of (ʉ) and (ɑ) in Utah English.' *Language and Communication*, 12: 267–92.

—. (1993). 'Propredicate *do* in the English of the intermountain west', *American Speech*, 68: 339–56.

Di Paolo, M. and Faber, A. (1990). 'Phonation differences and the phonetic content of the tense-lax contrast in Utah English', *Language Variation and Change*, 2: 155–204.

Dillard, J. L. (1973). 'The lingua franca in the American Southwest', *Revista/Review Interamericana*, 3: 278–89.

Dippie, B. W. (1989). 'American wests: Historiographical perspectives', *American Studies International*, 27(2): 3–25.

Eckert, P. and Mendoza-Denton, N. (2005). 'Getting Real in the Golden State', in W. Wolfram and B. Ward (eds), *American Voices: How Dialects Differ from Coast to Coast*, Malden, Massachusetts: Blackwell, 139–43.

Fritz, P. (1941). *Colorado: The Centennial State*. New York: Prentice Hall.

Gordon, M. J. (2006). 'Tracking the Low Back Vowel Merger in Missouri', in T. E. Murray and B. L. Simon (eds), *Language Variation and Change in the American Midland*, Amsterdam: John Benjamins, 57–68.

Graham, J. and Launspach, S. (2004). '"Go west, and get you another homestead": the expatriate personal dative in Idaho', 58th Annual Rocky Mountain Modern Language Association Convention, Boulder, Colorado.

Hall-Lew, L. (2005). 'One Shift, Two Groups: When Fronting Alone Is not Enough', in M. Baranowski and U. Horesh (eds), *Penn Working Papers in Linguistics 10.2: Papers from NWAVE 32*, 105–16.

Hankey, C. (1960). A Colorado Word Geography. PhD dissertation, University of Michigan.

—. (1961). 'Semantic features and eastern relics in Colorado dialect. *American Speech*, 36: 266–70.

Hansen, H. (ed.) (1970). *Colorado: A Guide to the Highest State*. New York: Hastings House.

Jackson, E. H. (1956). An Analysis of Certain Colorado Atlas Field Records with Regards to Settlement History and Other Factors. PhD dissertation, University of Colorado.

Johnson, E. (1996). *Lexical Change and Variation in the Southeastern United States, 1930–1990*. Tuscaloosa: University of Alabama Press.

Johnson, E. and Boyle, D. (2006). 'Learning Spanish in the North Georgia Mountains', in T. E. Murray, and B. L. Simon (eds), *Language Variation and Change in the American Midland: A New Look at 'Heartland' English*. Amsterdam: John Benjamins, 235–44.

Kimmerle, M. (1950). 'The influence of locale and human activity on some words in Colorado', *American Speech*, 25: 161–67.

—. (1952). 'Bum, poddy or penco', Colorado Quarterly, 1: 87–97.

Kimmerle, M., McDavid, R., Jr., and McDavid, V. M. (1951). 'Problems of linguistic geography in the Rocky Mountain area', *Western Humanities Review*, 5: 249–64.

Kretzschmar, W. A., Jr. and Tamasi, S. (2001). 'Distributional foundations for a theory of language change', *New Ways of Analyzing Variation 30*, Raleigh, North Carolina.

Kurath, H. (1949). *Word Geography of the Eastern United States*. Ann Arbor: University of Michigan Press.

Kurath, H. and McDavid, R. I. (1961). *The Pronunciation of English in the Atlantic States*. Ann Arbor: The University of Michigan Press.

Labov, W., Ash, S., and Boberg, C. (1997). *A National Map of the Regional Dialects of American English*. July 15, 1997. http://www.ling.upenn.edu/phono_atlas/NationalMap/NationalMap.html

—. (2006). *Atlas of North American English: Phonetics, Phonology and Sound*. Berlin: Mouton de Gruyter.

Leap, W. L. (1993). *American Indian English*. Salt Lake City: University of Utah Press.

Lozano, A. G. (1976). 'The Spanish Language of the San Luis Valley', in J. de Onis (ed.), *The Spanish Contribution to the State of Colorado*. Boulder, Colorado: Westview Press, 191–207.

Marckwardt, A. H. (1958). *American English*. Oxford: Oxford University Press.

Mason, J. (1960). 'The etymology of buckaroo', *American Speech*, 35: 51–5.

McDavid, R. I., Jr. (1958). 'American English Dialects', in W. N. Francis (ed.), *The Structure of American English*. New York: The Ronald Press Co.

Meinig, D. W. (1965). 'The Mormon culture region: strategies and patterns in the geography of the American west, 1847–1964', Annals of the Association of American Geographers, 55: 191–220.

—. (1972). 'American wests: preface to a geographical interpretation', Annals of the Association of American Geographers, 62: 159–84.

Mencken, H. L. (1986). *The American Language: An Inquiry into the Development of English in the United States*. R. I. McDavid (ed.). New York: Alfred A. Knopf.

Metcalf, A. (2000). *How We Talk: American Regional English Today*. Boston: Houghton Mifflin Company.

—. (1972). 'Directions of change in Southern California English.' *Journal of English Linguistics*, 6: 28–34.

Moore, H. L. (1926). 'The lingo of the mining camp', *American Speech*, 2: 86–88.

Mufwene, S. S. (1996). The founder principle in creole genesis. *Diachronica*, 13: 83–134.

Murray, T. (2004). 'Positive anymore in the west', 58th Annual Rocky Mountain Modern Language Association Convention, Boulder, Colorado.

Pederson, L. (2001). 'Dialects', in J. Algeo (ed.), *The Cambridge History of the English Language Volume VI: English in North America*. Cambridge: Cambridge University Press, 253–90.

Pederson, L., and Madsen, M. (1989). 'Linguistic geography in Wyoming', *Journal of English Linguistics*, 22: 17–24.

Silva-Corvalán, C. (2004). 'Spanish in the Southwest', in E. Finegan and J. Rickford (eds), *Language in the U.S.A.* Cambridge: Cambridge University Press, 205–29.

Smith, C. C., Jr. (1984). *A Southwestern Vocabulary: The Words They Used*. Glendale, California: Arthur H. Clark.

Van Cott, J. W. (1990). *Utah Place Names: A Comprehensive Guide to the Origins of Geographic Names: A Compilation*. Salt Lake City: University of Utah.

Wolfram, W. and Christian, D. (1976). *Appalachian English*. Arlington, Virginia: Center for Applied Linguistics.

Wolfram, W. and Schilling-Estes, N. (1998). *American English: Dialects and Variation*. Malden, Massachusetts: Blackwell.

Indigenous Peoples and Languages of Alaska

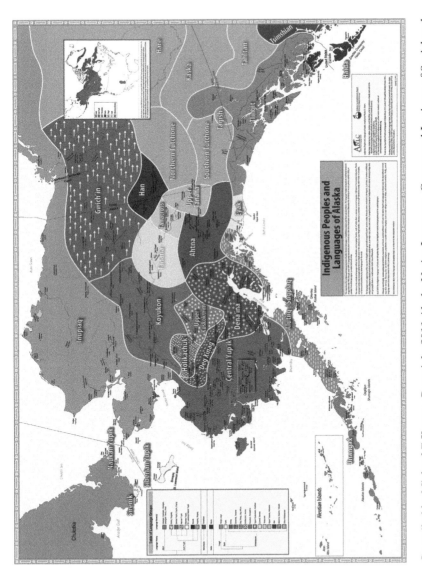

Compiled by Michael E. Krauss. Copyright 2011 Alaska Native Language Center and Institute of Social and Economic Research. Used with permission.

Indigenous Peoples and Languages of Alaska

Chapter 8

Alaskan Englishes

Patricia Kwachka

Introduction

Alaska, the largest and most northern of the states in the United States, is predominantly English speaking. Bordered to the west by Canada, an English-dominant country (although officially bilingual with French), Alaska is not affected by immigrations of non-English speakers as are, for example, Texas and California. However, the presence of 18 indigenous languages has produced a wide spectrum of English varieties as these populations have shifted, sometimes slowly and sometimes relatively abruptly, from their Native languages to their own unique representations of English. These English varieties have not for the most part been described.

Prehistorically, Alaska provided the stepping stone and later the home for many indigenous language speakers. Today, some Local English (LE) speakers constitute only the fifth generation to use this language as their first and only tongue.

Collectively, these English varieties are referred to as *Village* or *Bush* English, and considered by both speakers and non-speakers alike to be 'broken' or pidgin English (Vandergriff 1982; Pulu 1978; Loon 1991). These LEs have not been systematically documented, nor has recent research examined their development from 'learner' English to a fully flourishing, systematic means of communication. The conclusion of the more recent investigations supports the position that these LEs are as rule-governed and as completely functional as any variety of American English.

The purpose of this chapter is to present the findings of the small number of studies which have examined some of these LEs. Discussion will focus on their grammatical characteristics and phonological differences from Standard English (SE) that contribute to their recognition as a non-standard dialect but, by all accounts, rarely impede communicative efficacy. It will be later argued that difference in discourse patterns has a much greater effect on successful intercultural and inter-dialectal communicative efficacy.[1]

Background of the Region

Alaska has experienced two major waves of immigration, yet compared with its physical size, its population is extremely sparse. The first immigration was that of the indigenous peoples who scattered throughout the Americas. Much later, non-Native people arrived, largely attracted by the state's rich resources both animal and mineral. The following discussion briefly summarizes these immigrations.

The first Alaskan immigrants

According to archaeological and linguistic evidence, some 10,000–20,000 years ago, the first immigrants crossed a then-existing land bridge (Beringia) from eastern Asia/Russia to what is now North, Central and South America (Campbell 1997:97; Oswalt 2006:10–17). Based on the current geographical density of their constitutive languages, the two major Alaskan language families, Aleut-Eskimo and Athabaskan, are thought to have been the last to arrive. Today, there exist 11 Athabaskan languages in the state and five Aleut-Eskimo languages (Krauss 1979). In addition, two other unrelated Native American Indian groups, the Tsimshian and the Haida, reside in the southeastern portion of the state. Despite the number of languages and relative recency of both migration and of contact with non-Natives, very few of these languages support a threshold level of speakers sufficient to guarantee their continued existence.[2]

Approximately 16 percent of the state's population is Alaska Native, the Eskimo and Aleut (c. 36,000 people) inhabiting the coastal areas, and the Athabaskans (c. 15,130) the interior (Krauss 1974). Almost half of that population has moved from remote villages to urban areas where they continue to participate, to the extent possible, in their cultural traditions and maintain their self-identification as Natives (Sprott 1994).

Except in the few areas where they border one another, the two macro families have little in common, culturally or linguistically. On the basis of a lack of shared vocabulary, that is, evidence of borrowing, they have never maintained a prolonged coexistence even in proto-language periods (Krauss 1979:805). Both inter- and intra-group variation is considerable and serves as identity markers among tribal members. For example, among Athabaskans, the differences between the Gwich'in and the Ahtna or, among Aleut-Eskimos, between the Yup'ik and the Iñupiaq, are matters of social importance[3].

Before focusing on Alaskan LEs, a few general comments on culture and worldview will situate these dialects in their social contexts. (For a more detailed discussion, see Helm 1981 and Damas 1984.) Athabaskans have been described as supremely flexible in their interactions with their environment, capable of dealing with unforeseen circumstances and adept at adapting existing knowledge to changing natural and social conditions (Van Stone 1974). For example, with reference to language, it was they who, in trading or other intercultural circumstances, became bilingual (Kwachka 1985:68). Given the formidable nature of their environment, this trait has certainly contributed to their successful survival. In general terms, Athabaskans view their world as cyclical, spiritual, sentient and in delicate balance. Emphasis is on autonomy and the independence of individuals in establishing the nature of their relationship with the world (Nelson 1973, 1983; Honigmann 1981; Scollon 1979; Hagey 1990:16). Their location in the geographic interior of the state, an area consisting of taiga intersected by rivers, affords them access to both land and riverine food resources (principally bear, caribou, moose, water fowl, salmon and beaver, as well as edible vegetation, primarily several species of berries).

Eskimos have been characterized as consensus-oriented, cautious, indirect (in terms of emotions and discourse), with an emphasis on being prepared to accept any eventuality, and of thinking positively in order to effect positive outcomes in the world. In addition, and as a corollary to being prepared, 'staying busy' is considered a positive attribute (Hutchinson 2003). Briggs noted (1970) that, while it is difficult to generalize from one Eskimo group to another, research with Eskimo and Inuit groups across the Arctic broadly supports these attributes as pan-Inuit (Fienup-Riordan 1986; Morrow 1990; Briggs 1998; Jolles 2002). In Alaska, their coastal, riverine and tundra environments support the hunting of sea mammals (seal, otter and whales), various types of fish (herring, salmon, halibut and cod), migrating birds, and the gathering of eggs, berries and miscellaneous edible vegetation.

Ethnic identity based on language heritage is strong as are the associated cultures, despite the fact that they have altered with and adjusted to changing circumstances. Regardless of language loss and changed economies, Native cultures in the state contrast definitively with those of non-Native groups, not only because of their isolated geographical locations but because of a strong, grassroots interest in the maintenance of Alaska Native identity and their strong voice in the state's political discourse.[4]

Later immigrants

In comparison with other states, Alaska's non-Native population arrived recently. Russians were the first, arriving in the mid-1700s, but their influence, while considerable, diminished with the near decimation of the fur animals and of the Aleuts they conscripted to exploit these mammals. In the very late 1800s, the gold rushers arrived, but again, with the disappearance of accessible gold, they largely returned to their original homes. In the 1930s, would-be farmers settled the Matanuska-Susitna river valleys in response to a federal effort to promote agriculture, in order to achieve a sustainable resource for the territory.

Descendants of these two latter groups are referred to as '*pioneers*'. A third influx arrived in the 1970s with the building of the trans-Alaska oil pipeline. A final, smaller group of immigrants consists of ex-military personnel who, after having been stationed at one of the state's several military installations, have chosen to retire there.

Alaskans are proudly ethnocentric, considering themselves to be a unique, hardy and independent group of individuals. The state's nickname, *The Last Frontier,* entails a number of connotations associated with archetypical American values which Ruesch termed 'puritan' and 'pioneer mortality': self-sufficiency, freedom and personal liberty, autonomy, independence, opportunity, 'wilderness' to be 'conquered' (1951:97) and a quality not mentioned by Ruesch, a tacit approval of occasional, individual recklessness.

Alaska does exhibit a number of unique characteristics: it is the only state bounded by international borders; it was the next to the last state to be added to the union (1959); and it is by far the largest state (16 per cent of the US land mass). Known for its physiographic extremes, Alaska has the highest mountain in North America, the fiercest climatological conditions and the largest percentage of state land reserved for national and state parks, preserves and monuments (67 per cent). Although the state is extraordinarily rich in resources, these are difficult and expensive to extract and bring to market.

At the other statistical extreme, its population consists of only some 664,000 individuals, a number fewer than that of many cities in other states. The population density averages approximately 1.2 people per square mile, but this figure misrepresents the actual experience of most individuals. The vast majority of inhabitants (66 per cent) are gathered around fewer than six urban or regional centres. The largest, Anchorage, contains slightly more than a third of the state's population (c. 273,000). The two other major cities, Fairbanks, in the interior, and Juneau, the capitol, in the southeastern panhandle, together contain c. 61,553 inhabitants.

Besides the state's Alaska Native population, a small percentage of other minorities is present: 4.1 per cent is Hispanic; 4 per cent is of Asian background, and 3.5 per cent is African-American (Wright 2005). Age demographics for the state overall indicate it has a much younger population than others: 7.6 per cent are under five years of age (vs. 6.8 per cent for the United States as a whole); 28.7 per cent (vs. 25 per cent) are under 18; and only 6.5 per cent (vs. 12.4 per cent) are 65 years or older (http://quickfacts.census.gove/qfd/states/02000.html).

Language in Alaska

Terminologically, *Alaska(n) Native* refers inclusively to both Eskimo and American Indian groups, paralleling the Canadian term *First Nations*. Within the state and with reference to self as well, *Alaskan Native* appears in formal or public contexts. The most widely used label is the unmodified (and non-pejorative) *Native*, as in 'I am a *Native*' or 'Most of them are *Natives*'. This term extends to include any Native language, as in 'I was speaking *Native* to my mother and English to my daughter'.[5]

Alaskan Native residents additionally distinguish themselves specifically from all other aboriginal groups. The state's American Indian population refers to non-Alaskan Native Americans as *Outside Indians*. Even though the Athabaskan population is linguistically related to the Navaho and Apache (and many smaller groups in the Pacific Northwest), there is a general lack of interaction with these or other Native American communities.[6] Eskimos, whose languages spread from southwestern Alaska across Canada and into Greenland, distinguish themselves by retaining the designation *Eskimo* instead of adopting the label *Inuit*. They interact with outside groups in two specific, international contexts: The Inuit Circumpolar Conference, held every four years, and the annual meetings of the International Whaling Commission.

Both groups of Alaskan Natives refer to immigrants as *non-Natives*, less frequently as *Whites*, and in the abstract as *The White Man*. Most common, however, is the label *gussuk* (derived from Russian *kazak/cossack;* Tabbert 1991:51) which, depending on the region, ranges in connotation from mere appellation, to pejorative, to epithet. For the Yup'ik, it is no more than a label, originally glossed as 'white person' but gradually extended to other non-Natives (including African-Americans), especially in regional centres where mixed populations coexist. In the interior of the state, however, where the dominant population is Athabaskan, the term is derogatory, avoided in conversations with people so designated.

Alaskans, both indigenous and immigrant, refer to the other states as *Outside*, *The Lower Forty-eight States* or even *America* and to non-Alaskans as *Outsiders*. Within the state, non-urban areas (i.e. most of the state) are referred to as the *Bush*.

With regard to a recognizable non-Native Alaskan English dialect, there is none. Immigrants come from every region of the United States as well as abroad and, while some individuals choose to maintain their original regional dialect, in general there exists a 'leveling' of geographically based dialects and non-standard usages with the exception that most Alaskans have adopted the general northwestern plural second person, *you guys*. There do survive, however, a small number of lexical items originating with early traders and gold-rushers.

The more widespread of these terms among non-Natives are *cheechako* (newcomers, a label derived from the Chinook jargon, implying ignorance at life-threatening levels), and *sourdough* (long-time residents, descendants of gold-miners, pioneers or those who arrived either before the 1964 earthquake or the 1967 flood).[7] These are noted because length of residence serves as a badge of identity among the non-Native population, more important than financials status, position in the community or any of the other more common components of social prestige. For example, in introductions, the first information after one's name is: ' . . . and I have lived in Alaska since . . . .'

Two other general lexical items include *siwash* (not in good shape, e.g. an emergency camp while hunting), and *skookum* (good, excellent). In urban settings, use of these terms appears to be increasingly the province of older generations and unrecognized by younger Alaskans.[8]

In LEs, several gold rush lexical items persist, perhaps sustained through later interaction among various tribal groups at boarding schools. Three of the most common are: *grub* (food taken for travelling and hunting trips); *to pack* ('to carry', frequently referring to water from a source, but can apply to most objects); and *bum* (not good, as in 'bum weather', or 'I feel bum'). These items appear in the casual speech of all generations and in both Athabaskan and Eskimo areas.

A Brief Summary of the Contact History

When compared with Native American populations in the contiguous United States, two important differences emerge. First, direct contact between Alaska Natives and non-Natives was relatively recent, dating from the mid-1700s, whereas contact in the contiguous United States began in earnest in the 1500s. Secondly, the results of contact were not uniform, some areas experiencing intensive abrupt interaction and others a more diffused but sustained relationship with outsiders. Factors such as location, geographical features, resources and sociocultural conventions regarding 'out groups' (Native or non-Native) affected the nature and the consequences of the contact.

It should be noted that even before non-Natives arrived in Alaska, contact dynamics were already in play. From the east, the fur-hunting trade of the Hudson Bay and the Northwest companies affected Athabaskan populations in Canada and Alaska from the1700s on, not only introducing, through indirect, diffusional chains, non-local material items and goods, but creating shifts in traditional seasonal subsistence cycles to satisfy the increased demand for furs. Then, in the late 1800s, gold rushes resulted in cultural chaos primarily in the interior, Athabaskan areas, but extended to the northwest coast Inupiaq as well. The dislocations were so extensive that, in some areas, documentation of cultural patterns prior to that time remains problematic.

Even before the Russians' direct presence was felt in the Aleutians and Kodiak Island, interior Athabaskans participated in established, institutionalized trading relationships with Eskimos along the Kobuk River to the north who had, in turn, established trade 'fairs' with Siberians, promoting the exchange of non-local goods (Vanstone 1974:90–104). While the northern Inupiaq were also involved in these prehistoric diffusional networks, direct contact with whalers, who began plying their coasts in the mid 1800s, occasionally over-wintering, had the most powerful impact (Chance 1990; Langdon 1981).

As mentioned above, direct contact from the west first occurred when the Russians invaded the Aleutians in search of furs in the mid 1700s. The resulting collapse of sea mammals precipitated Russian migrations inland and up the Kuskokwim and Yukon rivers where they set up trading posts and inveigled Yup'ik and Athabaskan populations to supply furs and subsistence goods.

In the wake of every exploration and invasion (and sometimes in advance, disseminated by the nomadic, seasonal movements of many Alaska Native groups), disease decimated the Native populations (see Fortuine 1992). Following resource exploitation, the final[9] invasion was that of the missionaries, determined to capture a more ephemeral prize, the Christianization of 'pagan souls'. Missionaries established both religious centres and schools, the latter intended to support and extend the former. While their religious goals were variably achieved (today Russian Orthodoxy has a firm hold on Kodiak Island, whereas Catholicism exists harmoniously and syncretistically with indigenous belief systems in the Interior) a cumulative consequence was the shift from nomadism to sedentism. Life ways in every area were permanently altered, along with accompanying economies and social institutions. Populations stabilized and localized, with consequent shifts in social structure, economies and of relevance to this discussion, language.

Prior Research on American Indian Englishes

Given the prevalence of American Indian Englishes, especially in the contiguous United States where American Indian languages have all but disappeared to be replaced by some variety of English, it is surprising that relatively little attention has been paid to either their synchronic description or their diachronic development. A glance at the relevant literature (most completely presented in Leap 1993) demonstrates that the majority of accessible studies began to appear in the 1970s and continued through the early 1990s when the attention of linguistics teachers, and Native American communities alike turned to the pressing and complex issues of language revitalization.

The first bloom of research was undoubtedly nurtured by the passages in 1968 and 1974 of the Bilingual Education Acts which guaranteed that students with limited English receive educational opportunities equal to those of native speakers. Prior to the 1970s, Leechman and Hall's report (1955) on the English developed by Native American children sent to boarding schools was the first recognition or documentation of Native American Englishes. These schools, funded by federal or missionary support, first opened in the late 1800s, promoting rigorous assimilatory policies including the suppression of the children's Native languages. Despite their negative impact on students' languages and cultures, still bitterly remembered by older generations of Alaska Natives, the schools inadvertently contributed to the development of regional pan-Indian solidarity, later forming the bases for grass-roots political activism, for example, the passage of the Indian Self-Determination Act (PL 93–638), and other unified Native American political movements.

In the 1990s, a shift in attention to Native American language revitalization was fuelled not only by the pan-Indian focus on language loss, but also by the passage in 1990 of the Native American Languages Act (PL 101–477), although funding was not immediate and was initially limited to $2m per year, administered by the Administration for Native Americans under the Department of Health and Human Services.

However, given the passage of the 'No Child Left Behind' educational act by the Bush administration, requiring regular testing for even young children in the English language, it is doubtful that the Native American Languages Act will counter the overwhelming emphasis on English as the only acceptable language in the United States. The future of the Native American Languages Act is unclear, but it is likely that educational organizations will be reluctant to support bilingual education if they believe it will threaten children's test scores in English.

Alaska Native Englishes

Research on Alaskan Local Englishes (LE) has not been voluminous. Several studies were published in the 1970s and early 1980s, some in response to school district and State Department of Education needs and others undertaken by concerned, independent researchers involved with Alaska Native (AN) students in classrooms. Information about the nature of the various dialects of that time can also be drawn from less direct investigations, for example, handbooks for teachers.

In the past and still today, the Englishes spoken by most ANs are considered not only non-standard but 'sub-standard' both by the general public and the speakers themselves. As mentioned in the Introduction the dialects are monolithically referred to as *Village English*, typified as 'broken English' or pidgin. AN speakers consider their language to be inadequate and, especially in academic, written contexts express concern regarding its 'correctness'; yet conversely, speakers consciously use the Local Englishes to transmit and support ethnic identity. As Hanna Loon, an Inupiat resident of Kotzebue, remarked (1991): 'Village English is truly a spoken language. It is a form of communication used by the Inupiat people of this region, young and old. The Inupiat enjoy the humorous side of life, so they speak village English with a sense of humor. Pidgin English is infectious once you've spent time in the village.'

Depending on geographical area, some speakers have used the LE dialect for three or more generations; in other areas, particularly the Yup'ik (southwestern Alaska) and some Interior Athabaskan areas, English has been used only sporadically by some speakers for two generations. In almost all regions where the Native language has not entirely expired, there still remain a few fluent speakers in the older generations. However, their numbers, relative to the small populations of most communities, are dwindling and their impact on Native language retention negligible. In this generation, Eyak, a Cook Inlet coastal and once powerful Athabaskan group, has become extinct. No Athabaskan language has a significant, threshold number of children speaking the language.

The fate of the Eskimo languages is similar, although their demise not so immediately imminent. Perhaps as a result of larger populations, Central Yup'ik still remains vibrant in many communities, despite decreasing numbers of child speakers. Until this decade, Siberian Yupik, spoken on St. Lawrence Island, isolated by the waters of the Bering Sea between the United States and Russia, seemed secure, but children today are increasingly speaking English. Inupiaq (Inuit), located on the northern coast of the state, is spoken fluently by older adults but not by children.

Review of early research on LEs

English, in many flourishing varieties, has become the default language of Alaska Native communities. Monolingual Native language speakers are increasingly rare, fluent bilinguals (Native language and English) becoming less common, and English-only speakers the norm. The terms 'Village' or 'Bush' English suggests a shared spectrum of distinguishing, diagnostic characteristics, whereas in reality these Englishes are as various as the regions and villages in which they are spoken. Early descriptive research efforts are summarized below.

The Lake and Peninsula School District

Pulu (1978) examined the students' English of the Lake and Peninsula School District (an area in southeastern coastal Alaska which includes both Eskimo and Athabaskan languages), concluding that low test scores resulted from the fact that students had few opportunities to use Standard English beyond the school environment, thus inhibiting literacy. Her data were drawn from students reading out loud and writing samples from some 210 students, grades 1–12, and are compared with very formal forms of spoken Standard English. She observed that many of the 'errors' in the speech and writing of the school children are 'fossilizations' that, without increased interaction with SE, will remain in the students' dialects.

The Pribiloff Islands

A study of the English spoken by school-aged children in the Pribiloff Islands was conducted by Taff in 1978. At that time, most of the older generation spoke Aleut. Taff, a teacher in the local school, tape recorded children after school, engaging them in conversations about topics of their interest. Her goal was to ensure that 'Attempts to provide students with a Standard English must not simultaneously quash Pribilof English Aleut. A respect for this dialect and its roots could stop the linguistic harassment with which American educators have beleaguered Pribilobians since the 1860's . . . .' (1978:4) She observed that phonological differences did not impede interlingual understanding (1978:19), but that grammatically the differences between Pribiloff Island English and Standard English were extensive, resulting in a language that might be characterized by an outsider as 'vague', but one that speakers can 'get away with' because, according to the author, in such a small community, everyone knows everything about everyone else as well as recognizing the subtle, intricate manifestations of natural cycles (cf. Bernstein 1966 on 'restricted codes').[10] Thus, context obviates a need for extensive vocabulary or complex syntax. Among her findings were the 'standard nonstandards', for example, *got* for *have*, *seen* for *saw*, *brang* for *brought* as well as the re-categorization of mass nouns and collectives as count nouns (*stuffs, furnitures, homeworks, peoples*), a process which appears, from my own observations, to be spreading throughout the state's populations.

She attributes other features, especially at the syntactic level, to substrate influences, for example, a topicalizing appositive structure, for example, '*My brother, he* goes to school' is described as a derivative of Aleut syntax.[11] She also notes the use of a sentence-final question marker, {-haeh}, for yes/no questions phrased otherwise as declaratives (a direct transfer from Aleut). Yes/no questions may also appear as declaratives, interrogation marked by rising intonation. Several non-standard negative forms occur, some the standard non-standards, for example, double negatives, but others she believes to have been influenced by Aleut. She specifically mentions the use of 'never' to express the Aleut habitual aspect, for example, *I'm never good at it* (vs. *I'm not good at it*), and the use of *always* in positive, habitual statements: . . . *when you always put your hands over your eyes . . . .* for . . . *when you put your hands over your eyes . . . .*

The Alaskan interior

A third study appearing during that period considered the Athabaskan Englishes of students in the Alaskan interior (Higgins 1978). Also a teacher, Higgins' philosophy was similar to Taff's. She states that ' . . . it is a central premise of this report that one of the major impediments to the Native child's school experience is *precisely* the view that Nonstandard English is substandard, a language to be remediated, a communication disorder, a language which has no value in school, a language which impedes the child's potential for learning and which may have dire consequences in all the child's education' 1978:vii). She furthermore agrees with Taff with respect to comprehension: ' . . . this author does not believe that children who speak Nonstandard English do not understand Standard English' (p. ix). Her data were derived from a standardized test as well as recorded readings, recorded answers to teacher questions, interviews with pairs of students and writing samples.

She found, contrary to expectations, little gender 'confusion'[12], or double negatives. The syntactic patterns she noted were: the omission of tense on verbs (although examples indicate that tense was established, in narratives, on the first sentence of a sequence and subsequently by adverbs); and the omission of preposition and article. As did Taff, she thought phonological differences to be of trivial importance in cross-dialect comprehension. She concluded that students, both Native and non-Native, were very aware of dialect variations and these differences did not account for the fact that Native students did not score as well on standardized tests as non-Natives.

These studies, conducted almost thirty years ago, beg for contemporary, diachronic, comparative research to determine the dialects' chronological maturation. Because of their geo-cultural isolation, LE development has been relatively *sui generis* thus allowing us to address extremely interesting questions: which features have remained 'frozen'? have some features been dropped or changed? have some features come to more closely resemble SE? what new elements have been introduced? These questions, and many others, provide a fruitful approach for understanding fundamental processes of language evolution.

Alaska Native Language Center Booklets for teachers

In the early 1980s the Alaska Native Language Center published three booklets intended to assist teachers working with AN students (Jacobson 1984; Kaplan 1984; Thompson 1984). Although the data are largely anecdotal, their credibility rests on the deep familiarity of the researchers with the speakers' Native languages and their varieties of English. With regard to Eskimo Englishes, both Jacobson and Kaplan note the ambiguous status of 'let' in English, whose Eskimo roots can be [+ causative] so that, *I let him cry* can mean, when translated to SE, *I made him cry* [13]. As Kaplan and McNabb previously noted (1981:7), the relevant Eskimo morpheme can be variously interpreted as causation, permission or obligation.

Other features of Eskimo English include the omission of the third person singular {-s} (s*he eat* vs s*he eats*), interrogatives formed by intonation rather than auxiliary insertion[14], third person pronoun gender inconsistency, and, as Taff noted, plurals for singulars or collectives. Verb tenses are frequently transmuted to aspectual adverbials (*he eat already* for *he ate*) and the positive habitual similarly indicated (*he always eat dinner early* for *he eats dinner early*).

Both Kaplan and Jacobson address non-verbal communication patterns and discourse styles which, in their opinion, exacerbate difficulties teachers experience in communicating with their students. For example, the Eskimo equivalent of a 'yes' head-nod, is an eye-brow flash, frequently unnoticed by non-Natives. In addition, the culture considers it both polite and necessary to carefully deliberate replies to interlocutors, resulting in pause lengths longer than most teachers are accustomed to. The unhappy result of these differing practices and expectations is that the children are deemed non-communicative and blame is mistakenly placed on their non-standard variety of English.

Thompson, in addressing Athabaskan Englishes, also notes differing discourse conventions and non-verbal communication, eye-widening being the Athabaskan equivalent of the Eskimo eye-brow flash. Particularly problematic for western-style education is the belief that you should not put your best foot forward (1984:41, that others should discover your virtues for themselves; as a corollary, 'showing off' or 'boasting' are frowned on. A final convention, again one which might cause difficulties in intercultural settings, is a societal injunction against speaking too specifically of the future; not only is that 'presumptuous' but may cause unfortunate consequences.

Although Thompson does not provide a great deal of linguistic detail about Athabaskan Englishes he does indicate areas where differences in language typologies may be expected to affect the LE, for example, Athabaskan verbs are highly inflected and obligated to note completion (perfective/imperfective) but not time (tense); pronouns are not gendered; few nouns form plurals; and, rather than articles, the languages have complex paradigms of locative-demonstratives. Finally, he notes that while these differences may affect LEs, no systematic linguistic description of any of Alaska's LEs had at that time been undertaken. His concern was more educational than linguistic; curricula should incorporate an understanding of potential dilemmas such that students should not be made ashamed of their LE and should also be capable of switching to SE when occasion requires.

Koyukon Athabaskan English

In the late 1980s, travelling by river boat some 400 miles down the Middle Yukon river, I began a systematic study of the English spoken by bilingual Koyukon adults, visiting and interviewing in seven villages in the Central Koyukon Athabaskan dialect area. The data base consisted of 2,000 clauses extracted from interviews with 22 elders in their homes. The interviews were ethnographically 'casual', focusing on changes the interviewees had observed in their lifetimes[15]. Five types of features were examined and compared with a corpus of SE (Cartarette and Jones 1974)[16]. Because the study was intended to provide base-line data and because, in some venues, numbers and statistics carry more scientific probity than other approaches, I undertook a quantitative analysis. Methodologically, every occurrence of an item was included; with regard to determinable options, for example, contraction, occurrence versus non-occurrence was computed as well.

Lexical features

The first groups of features examined involve the lexicon, where a number of assumptions exist regarding non-standard dialects and SE: for example, mono- versus multi-syllabicity; noun/verb ratios (Givon 1979); and degree of contrac-tion. For each of these features, the LE and the SE were sufficiently similar that no statistically significant difference was evidenced.

Non-standard and 'learner' English features

The second group of features is those considered indexical for other types of non-standard Englishes: negative construction, subject/verb agreement and verb tense consistency. Article usage, a common issue for 'learner' English, was also considered. With regard to negatives, fully 43 per cent of those used by the LE speakers were standard; only 4 per cent were the 'standard non-standard', the double negative. (Unfortunately, the number of negatives in the SE sample was too limited to provide a comparison, i.e. 14 occurrences of negatives in the SE data and 100 in the LE). A double (and, in this case, triple) negative is illus-trated by the following example:

"*Not* everybody *don't* have *no* inboard motor." (NS:85)[17]

A surprising number of LE negatives, in fact the second most commonly appear-ing form in that sample (27 per cent), was a variety which would be considered extremely formal in SE. I have labelled these 'liturgical' negatives, guessing at their provenance. For example:

"They had *no* guns." (107TE)
　"Lot of them had *no* last name them days, because they never see white people." (73–74HB)
　　"Some winters there was *no* snow." (133TE)
　　"There was really *no* school." (RCH:40)

The second feature examined in this section was subject/verb concord in the third person singular. The [-s] did not occur in 25 per cent of the LE sample, but was always present in the SE data, a significant difference. Although Koyukon Athabaskan does not mark subject number in the verb stem, a more likely interpretation of these findings is analogic levelling, a process common to many non-standard Englishes.

The third feature, consistency of verb tenses, proved more difficult to analyse from a quantitative perspective. The determination of appropriate tense is problematic, complicated by factors ranging from the merely phonological to quotative practices and other discourse conventions. Even after eliminating ambiguous instances from the LE data, the difference between the LE and the SE is significant, 11 per cent unequivocally inappropriate in the LE and only 1 per cent so in the SE. Wolfram (1984) has examined this phenomenon in two southwestern varieties of Native American English, concluding that non-standard tense formation represents an attempt to express habitual aspect, a feature found in many Native American languages. While aspect constitutes an important attribute of Athabaskan verb systems, my data suggest that, as with the English 'narrative present', event-time may be established in the narrative introduction, then moved into a more momentaneously involving mode, for example, 'They *went* to dinner, and she *says* . . . .and he *says* . . . .'. An example from the LE data is the following:

"Pretty soon X. *came.* 'I think Daddy'*s getting* worse,' she said ." (48–9TD)

Because the listener's understanding of quotation depends on pause and intonation phenomena, the process of transcription requires careful attention to these indicators. In an analysis of high school students' writing from this area, many apparent instances of inappropriate tense shift may simply indicate a lack of sophistication regarding written rhetorical conventions. McGary (1983:61) noted the example below as an inappropriate tense shift, whereas the clause in question may equally well be interpreted as a quotative:

"People were saying *there's races at 2 p.m.*"

The issue of tense formation and practice deserves further investigation in view of its widespread mention by investigators of both Alaskan LEs and other non-standard dialects.

Finally in this group of features, article use was considered, a widespread issue for English L2 learners, but not a classic feature of non-standard, regional dialects. Again the Cartarette and Jones' sample was insufficient for valid statistical comparison, but the LE data yielded 515 potential and obligatory sites for article insertion; 30 per cent of the articles were omitted at these sites. The indefinite *a* was omitted much more frequently (75 per cent of all cases) than the definite *the* (25 per cent), a fact which may be due to the low acoustic prominence of *a*. Nonetheless, considering that Koyukon does not employ a similar definiteness distinction, there may exist a tendency for LE speakers to mark only those nouns which they deem to require notice of their singularity. From the lack of pattern in either article appearance or choice of definiteness, 'singularity' may be idiolectally determined. The following example illustrates the variability (parentheses denote omission at an obligatory site):

"Gee he, I heard her father-in-law was, uh, was *a* magician, ( ) medicine man, you know." (63–4KN)

Other cases appear to be 'frozen' expressions, since the NPs never appear with articles either in these data or in data collected from younger speakers during other field work sessions in this area:

"My dad, uh, he snowshoed ahead of my uncle with () dog team." (13KME)
   "Probably she made ( ) bow and arrow for herself." (229TJ)

Because of the variability of article appearance, omission cannot at this time be regarded as a systematic feature of the LE. A future project with second and third generation monolingual LE speakers will contribute to a better understanding of this feature.

Tense and discourse

Two other sets of features were examined, the first, those considered to be characteristic of a fully established English dialect (irregular past tense and complex verb phrases), and the second, discourse features, including types of clauses and the syntactic devices deployed to relate them.

Irregular past tense forms appeared appropriately in 72 per cent of opportunities in the LE sample and 81 per cent in the SE, a significant difference, but not a great one. Similarly, complex verb phrases were used 23 per cent of the time in the LE, and 33 per cent in the SE sample. Examples of irregular past tense formations in the LE include:

"They *knew* it was war, you know, this one Russian *went* out, and they *came*, well and, you know they *shot* him with bow and arrow." (140–142KN)

Below is one of the few examples of an overgeneralized past tense:

" . . . and even right here I *teached* three or four days up here." (88KS)

As indicated above, complex verb phrases were relatively rare in both corpora, not surprising since such forms are more characteristic of formal registers than of casual conversation. Nonetheless, their differential usage achieves statistical significance. Examples from the LE are:

"I *have to stay* away from home." (73GP)
"The, uh, manager asked what I *had planned on doing.*" (101–2GO)

Incidence of the irregular past tense (e.g. *caught* vs. **catched*) suggests speakers have not only adopted the regular past tense rule, but have also incorporated the large number of exceptions to that rule, adjusting their LE to SE usage, an indication that the second language has become thoroughly incorporated. Complex verb phrases, similarly, indicate a mastery of the second language to the extent that the LE is functional in a wider range of pragmatic contexts[18]. In other words, these features indicate that the LE is not 'learner' English, but English which is fully operational for both in- and out- group communicative interactions.

Clausal constructions, including coordination and embedding, were considered, in order to examine potential differences in discourse style. SE practices rapid turn taking and brief contributions, especially in the experimental pseudo-circumstance (a cocktail party) in which the Cartarette and Jones' data were collected. (Refer to End Note 16 for further discussion of the difficulties in the comparability of data sets). On the other hand, a great deal of Koyukon conversation depends on narrative, individual speakers 'holding the floor' until the completion of their contribution. Extended feedback or commentary by the addressee in mid-narrative is not expected; in fact, when such events do occur, they are considered interruptions and the narrators do not respond but pick up exactly at the point where the sequential break occurred (Kwachka 1992).

The first feature examined was the percentage of completed clauses, defined as a predicate with obligatorily accompanying arguments (compared with the total number of predicates). Perhaps despite or because of Cartarette and Jones' practice of omitting false starts, the two dialects are not significantly different; 85 per cent of sentences attempted were completed in the LE and 90 per cent in the SE data. Given linguists' varied judgements about the coherence of everyday speech, these data suggest that these two dialects are, in terms of broad sentence syntax, highly grammatical at the sentential level.

The degree to which sentences are joined by either subordination or coordination has been thought to indicate differential tendencies between formal and informal English, the first characterizing formal and the second informal styles. On this parameter, significant differences between the two dialects were found. The SE group used substantially more subordinators (31 per cent) than the LE speakers (20 per cent); however, an unexpected finding was that the SE group coordinated clauses at an even higher rate (60 per cent) than did the LE speakers (39 per cent). From these percentages, a rather striking fact emerges – almost half (49 per cent) of LE sentences are 'bare', whereas only 28 per cent of SE clauses are not joined via a connective device.

Reported features not found

Finally, two features frequently noted by SE speakers as prominent in all Alaskan LEs were investigated. These are inconsistency of third person singular pronoun gender and the conversion of mass nouns to count nouns. Contrary to expectation, gender was not randomly assigned, but consistent with the gender of the person referred to and only 9 per cent of 'mass' nouns were reclassified as 'count' nouns, for example, *furnitures, stuffs, homeworks.*

Eskimo English

A second variety of an Alaskan LE observed in the Eskimo areas was investigated with a set of data drawn from the initial essays of freshman students in university-level introductory English courses[19]. Because of the Eskimo students' limited experience with writing and minimal exposure to SE, it could be credibly argued that their initial writing parallels their oral language more than does that of other freshmen whose educational backgrounds incorporated a great deal more written expression throughout their schooling. Basham and I (1989, 1990) suggest that several of the features characteristics of this LE (as compared with Athabaskan LE) derive from a restructuring of the L2 which allows traditional Eskimo cultural values, specifically circumspection with regard to bald assertion, to be maintained in the replacement language, even by second and third generation monolingual speakers of the LE.

For example, one of the characteristics we identified as distinguishing Eskimo student texts from those of the general college freshman population was a series of features we termed 'qualification'. These included: 1) adverbial and adjectival qualification; 2) "doubles" (explained below); and 3) non-standard uses of modal auxiliaries. Below, each of these features is briefly illustrated.

Adverbial and Adjectival Qualification

'I could see the phone booth from this angle and there are *about* three people talking . . . .'

'The difference between a religion and a cult is *probably* how they act and carry out a duty.'

'When the village men go out to hunt, they would be on a look out for the Break-up which *usually* happens during the spring.'

The last example is particularly compelling since if Break-up (the melting of the ice in the oceans and rivers) were a 'usual' rather than an annual event, Alaska would resemble Antarctica.

Doubles

This feature is one of repetition and occurs with qualifiers, with nouns, and with verbs; occasionally, even entire clauses are duplicated in paraphrase.

'They *all or most of them* are eating.'
'Stress can happen in all different *patterns or ways.*'
'Some have *to realize or think* what they really came for.'

Modals

These were the most pervasive, non-standard feature of the Eskimo student texts. From an analytical point of view, given the complexity of their semantics, they are an extremely slippery item. Furthermore, their unique usage is particularly difficult to appreciate out of context. Although we identified three types, for present purposes I will simply illustrate the variety of their appearances:

'I actually hated my own sister. That *would* be too mean and I was not about to cause any trouble.'
'The experienced sewers which usually is the older ladies, *would* all meet [SE: meet] in the captain's house usually around 8:00 a.m.'
'There [sic] songs were all different . . . . Like they *would* have more meanings . . . .'

Unless these appear the random variation of the inexperienced writer, close examination of their contexts indicates they are not only non-standard but systematically so. (No similar constructions appear in the general freshman texts.) Two analytical perspectives can be brought to bear on these features: the first linguistic and the second cultural. From the linguistic point of view, Eskimo languages are replete with the morphological means to achieve indefiniteness and define degrees of evidentiality (Hensel et al. 1983; Jacobson 1984). Thus, there exist ample bases for substrate influence, but because of the typological differences between Eskimo and English, we argue that this influence becomes diffused through a wide variety of English grammatical devices, such as the those identified above.

From the cultural perspective, circumspection, caution and the opportunity for consensus are maintained. Direct assertion, implying the abstract veracity of the speaker's point of view, is generally avoided. We conclude that these features demonstrate the continuity of a cultural value so central that its expression has survived language shift.

English Usage within the Region

With the exception of very limited loci, English is the dominant tongue throughout the state. Alaska was one of 24 states to pass an English-Only law (1998), a conservative political campaign waged state by state throughout the nation. That the exceptions to English dominance can be readily identified illustrate that language's pervasive influence. Three locales are reliably predictable. The first involves a non-Native language, Tagalog. In Kodiak, an island fishing community whose population brings in thousands of tons of fish annually from the Gulf of Alaska and the Bering Sea, the island's original inhabitants spoke a dialect of Suqpiaq Eskimo. After Russian colonization, much of the indigenous population became bilingual. Today, however Tagalog is the most common non-English language and can be heard in many public and industrial settings. Attracted by a familiar occupation, fishing, and plentiful job opportunities, Philippine immigrants have contributed steadily to that island's population for the past two decades. In the largest village, Kodiak itself, the staff of the local general store shift from English with customers to Tagalog among themselves. This is also the case among workers in the island's many fish processing plants.

Alaska Native languages appear, briefly, on ceremonial occasions such as potlatches, where elders may give speeches in their own language, and songs and dances are performed in the local Native language. The exception is the Yup'k Eskimo area where almost all adults and many young people still use that language as frequently as they do English. Currently, young parents, even though they may be bilingual, speak to their children almost exclusively in English. In both Eskimo and Athabaskan communities, when elders visit each other (a daily activity in most communities), they usually communicate in their native language.

The final exception is that of Bush airline waiting rooms.[20] Even where only small pockets of Native language speakers remain, such as the Gwich'in Athabaskan region, one can hear more Gwich'in in such a waiting room in Fairbanks than in a Gwich'in village itself. Obviously speaker demographics and spatial compression contribute to this phenomenon. Adults (who are most likely to be speakers of the Native language) fly in greater numbers than children (who are more likely to be non-speakers) and the physical context encourages conversation.

Media Use of English and Current Trends

With few exceptions, daily newspapers, weekly regional newspapers in predominantly Native areas, and television and radio programming (broadcast
by 'repeater' mechanisms to even the most remote villages) are in English.
One exception exists, again in the Yup'ik area, where the local radio station
sponsors a Yup'ik call-in programme weekly. Given the extent to which linguists, Native advocates and local communities are committed to indigenous
language revitalization, it is rather surprising that the media have not been
engaged as a means to extend their efforts. Among Native Americans in the
contiguous states, for example, tribal newspapers frequently carry reports,
crossword puzzles, etc. in the Native language to encourage literacy and
maintenance.

With regard to current trends, the internet certainly represents the most
important of these but its effect on the English language use of non-native or
bilingual speakers appears minimal. Several factors account for this lack of
impact. First, in most Alaska Native villages, only older adults still speak the
Native language (with varying commands of English), and it is this segment of
any population which is least likely to be computer-savvy. Also, because of
geography and limited financial resources, remote villages usually have only a
single internet connection installed in the local school. This connection is
available for general use (if at all) only after school hours and only during the
nine-month school year. It is therefore likely that the internet will only rein-
force and extend SE dominance in those areas of the state where it is already
widely spoken.

Social, Political and Economic Impact of English within the Region and the Future of the English Language

As the contact history demonstrates, the arrival of the English language in
Alaska precipitated massive cultural shifts. These shifts resonate today, with
many of the state's indigenous populations still suffering adverse social,
health and educational effects. Although the majority is English-speaking,
these indigenous minorities constitute marginalized populations whose
rights and institutional relationships are constantly called into question in
various political and social arenas. While we can predict that their future
language will be that of the dominant population, English, we cannot predict
that the societal opportunities of that population will be shared as freely as
the language.

Conclusion

Alaska dialects of English spoken by the state's indigenous people deserve a great deal more attention than they have received. From a theoretical standpoint, comparing those dialects' morphology, syntax and the cultural implications of their semantics with those of the substrate Native language can help us understand what aspects of the Native language persist through manipulations of the second language's structural and semantic opportunities. The maintenance, for example, of narrative as discourse (Athabaskan) or verbal discretion (Eskimo) suggests that core practices of those cultures have endured through the cataclysms of language shift and culture change. This is not to argue that nothing is changed or lost, but to draw attention to the possibility that language shift does not necessarily or totally obliterate salient cultural features. Both anthropologists and linguists have long subscribed to the axiom that 'if you lose your language you lose your culture', but this quasi-ideological position flies in the face of the continuing and current existence of self-identifying cultural groups (no matter what language they speak) who differentiate themselves from others on non-linguistic bases, for example, food, clothing, beliefs, discourse habits and many other ethnically iconic indices.

A second point of theoretical interest lies in issues surrounding the question of 'universal' grammar. Do these dialects contain those properties we assume to be fundamental to language *qua* language? This review of research to date supports the position that even after two generations of speaking English only, the LE is adequate both to the needs of its speakers and to their interlocutors. Speakers do not exhibit the traits of 'semi-lingualism' (Skutnabb–Kangas 1979).[21]

An even more interesting question is the nature of the LE's diachronic evolution. Since the studies of the 1970s and 1980s, what features remain static? Which have accreted and what is the source of these additions? Are they an analogic reaction to existing features of the dialect's structural patterns? Are they acrolectal? Are they fossilized fads which have disappeared in other dialects? Attention to these questions will provide pertinent information on processes of language change. This opportunity is unique in that we can determine, to a reasonable degree of certainty, the social, historical and ethnographic factors which have affected the dialects' developments since their inception.

The ultimate puzzle is that, state-wide, dialects are a topic of vigorous consideration, reflecting and projecting ethnic alliance, derided and enjoyed, blamed or dismissed as factors in educational achievement. Alaskans are very aware and sensitive about their dialects whether LEs or SE. While recognition of difference certainly begins at the phonological level, these differences do not obscure communication – they simply serve as overt dialect identifiers. The deep sense of difference expressed by speakers of different dialects must be rooted in discourse conventions and evidentiality concerns which disrupt, at a very covert and unconscious level, expectations of both groups of speakers.

Acknowledgements

I am grateful to Gary Holton, Alaska Native Language Center, for the use of the newly revised map of the Indigenous Peoples and Languages of Alaska.

Notes

[1] Regarding the potential for phonological factors affecting communication, as Wolfram and Shilling-Estes note ' . . . we find that dialects having no apparent contact with one another share features. For example — the dropping of final consonants in words like *test* and *desk* are common in Latino English vernacular varieties in California, Native American English vernacular varieties and many European American English vernacular varieties throughout the US' (1998:45).

    Nonetheless, among older indigenous adults, misunderstandings can occur, especially in the context of medical interviews, a notorious site for miscommunications, for example, *fibroids of the uterus* became transmogrified to *fireballs of the eucharist*, as reported by an itinerant physician's assistant.

[2] Most villages, of which there are approximately 150, usually with fewer than 300 inhabitants, are accessible only by air or river. As a consequence, transportation and living expenses (e.g. electricity, fuel, store food, etc.) are very costly. Villages depend primarily on a cash economy but on subsistence practices (e.g. hunting, fishing and gathering) and state/federal grants.

[3] Recognition of these distinctions is practically non-existent among the non-Native population who tend to lump all Natives as either Eskimo or Indian and are generally unable to differentiate between the two groups.

[4] Much of this discourse is bound up in the code word 'subsistence' which superficially refers to the right and ability to 'live off the land', but since access to resources (fish, game) is highly regulated and Alaskan Natives have a slight privilege, public discussions covertly refer to fundamental ethnic divisions. See Hensel (1996) for in-depth discussion.

[5] The comparable term in the Lower 48 is *Indian*, as in 'I was speaking *Indian* to my grandmother.'

[6] The geographic position of Alaska, and the consequent expense of travel, only partially explain the detachment of Alaska Natives from other indigenous groups in the contiguous United States. Another factor may have to do with the fact that, politically, Alaskan Natives are organized as corporate entities rather than sovereign nations (one result of the Alaska Native Claims Settlement Act, 1971), established to settle potential disputes over commercial land use rights for the

building of the trans-Alaska oil pipeline. Thus, their interests are more state-centred and market-economy oriented than are those of other Native American groups. In addition, Alaskan Natives, as do all Alaskans, consider themselves unique, especially with regard to the maintenance of a subsistence lifestyle where a family can still make a living, at least partially, off the land. Pan-Native American emblems, such as *pow-wows* and *smudging*, appear only occasionally, usually in the context of urban, ceremonial gatherings.

⁷ See Tabbert 1991 for thorough presentation of these and many other lexical items specific to Alaskan usage, but not necessarily related to Chinook Jargon or gold rush vocabulary as are these.

⁸ I have not conducted systematic field work on this question but have informally polled my university classes and both my older and contemporary colleagues and friends on their understanding of several of the more common of these items, for example, *cheechako* ('a greenhorn'). This rather widely used term was recognized by only a few of my university students (many of whom were born and raised in Alaska).

⁹ The Aleuts, Suqpiaq and Yup'ik are an exception to this chronology. The Russians established churches and schools very early in their occupation, with the exceptional foresight of using the Native languages (and thus contributing to their maintenance) as a means of persuasion and transition. As recently as the 1970s some Pribiloff Islanders were bilingual in Aleut and Russian, with only minimal English (Taff 1978).

¹⁰ These findings resonate with those of Bernstein (1966), suggesting the use of a 'restricted' code. Familiarity of context and highly predictable circumstances and consequences promote elliptical reference and as a result, discourse which might be more accurately characterized as 'casual' or 'informal' rather than 'restricted'.

¹¹ As Taff notes, Wolfram and Fasold (1974:171) have found this form in Black English Vernacular, labelling it 'left dislocation' and proposing a syntactic motivation. In Athabaskan Englishes, the form emphasizes the limits of the speaker's responsibility for the truth content of the statement so that a generalization cannot be inferred, for example, it is a type of evidential. This form also appears in Cajun, although in the latter case, the pronoun usually occurs in sentence final position. As for the Cajun form, my data derive as much from a passing familiarity with the area as they do from extensive reading of the novels of James Lee Burke.

¹² Neither Eskimo nor Athabaskan languages mark gender on pronouns.

¹³ Jacobson (1984:26) posits a sociocultural explanation: ' . . . Eskimo culture is not nearly as compulsive as Euro-American culture; people are not often forced to do things they do not want to do'. Thus, context differentiates the interpretation of the morpheme in Eskimo languages.

¹⁴ This appears to be a feature of all casual registers in all dialects of English, suggesting its origins are not independently motivated in every instance.

¹⁵ Interviews frequently lasted one to two hours. In order to introduce a semblance of objectivity and to organize the tremendous amount of data into a manageable corpus, I analysed the first continuous 20–30 minute monologic segment of each interview. The elders were gracious with their time and their memories, and I thank them again.

[16] The following LE data have appeared in various forms in Kwachka 1988, 1996a, 1996b. I should note that at the time of this research, corpus linguistics was in relative infancy; finding an adequate sample of SE was a challenge. That selected, Cartarette and Jones' work was based on recordings of college psychology students engaged in pseudo-cocktail party conversation. The data were 'cleaned up' by eliminating interrupted or incomprehensible phrases in order ' . . . to preserve the continuous and sequentially dependent structure of speech' (1974:26). This assertion positions their theoretical stance at the still contentious question, in both discourse and language acquisition research, regarding the actual coherence of everyday conversation, and the relative importance of mutual contextualized understandings. Certainly, the approach resulted in the under representation of clauses attempted (vs. clauses completed) in their analysis.

[17] Codes refer to the author's data base, randomized for anonymity. Also note that these negatives are not rooted in Athabaskan morphology.

[18] For purposes of this study, complex verb phrases were defined as any that were not simple past, present or progressive.

[19] Initial 'placement' essays of Eskimo and 'general' (non-Native) students enrolled in freshman writing courses at an Alaskan state university over a four-year period formed the data base. The discussion here is an abbreviated version of data originally and more extensively presented in Basham and Kwachka 1989, and Kwachka and Basham 1990.

[20] Alaska has few roads. Travel between villages within c. 100 miles of each other is usually by river, via boats in the summer and snow machines in the winter when the rivers become frozen highways. Travel of greater distance is accomplished of necessity by air, supported by numerous small airlines operating light aircraft on regular mail, freight and passenger routes. Only larger regional Native centers, for example, Bethel in the Yup'ik area, can accommodate jet planes.

[21] This conclusion must be temporized by two observations. Speakers with little exposure to SE appear to have only two registers available: formal and informal. Alaska Native college freshmen, returning home to their Bush communities at Christmas holidays (after only four months at the university), are derided by their friends for their manner of speaking. Secondly, fluent bilingual speakers appear to have a much greater range of registers in English than do individuals whose only language is LE. These observations merit further research.

Bibliography

http//www.alaska.st.us; accessed July 15, 2006.

http://quickfacts.census.gov/qfd/states/02000.html), accessed July 26, 2006.

Basham, C. and Kwachka, P. (1989). 'Variation in Modal Use by Eskimo Student Writers'. In S. Gass, C. Madden, D. Preston, and L. Selinker (eds), *Variation in Second Language Acquisition Volume 1: Discourse and Pragmatics*. Clevedon: Multilingual Matters Ltd, pp. 129–143.

Bernstein, B. (1966). 'Elaborated and Restricted Codes'. In S. Lieberman (ed.), *Explorations in Sociolinguistics*. The Hague: Mouton, pp. 126–133.

Briggs, J. (1970). *Never in Anger, Portrait of an Eskimo Family*. Cambridge: Harvard University Press.

—. (1998). *Inuit Morality Play, The Emotional Education of a Three-Year-Old*. New Haven: Yale University Press.

Campbell, L. (1997). *American Indian Languages, The Historical Linguistics of Native America*. New York: Oxford University Press.

Cartarette, E. and Jones M. H. (1974). *Informal Speech, Alphabetic and Phonemic texts with Statistical Analyses and Tables*. Berkeley: University of California Press.

Chance, N. A. (1990). *The Inupiat and Arctic Alaska, An Ethnography of Development*. Chicago: Holt, Rinehart and Winston.

Damas, D. (1984). 'Arctic'. W. C. Sturtevant (gen. ed.), *Handbook of North American Indians*. Vol. 5. Washington, DC: Smithsonian University Press.

Fienup-Rierdon, A. (1986). 'The real people: the concept of personhood among the Yup'ik Eskimos of Western Alaska.' *Inuit Studies*, 10 (1–2), pp. 261–270.

Fortuine, R. (1992). *Chills and Fever, Health and Disease in the Early History of Alaska*. Fairbanks: University of Alaska Press.

Givon, T. (1979). 'From Discourse to Syntax: Grammar as a Processing Strategy'. *Syntax and Semantics. Discourse and Syntax*. In T. Givon (ed.), New York: Academic Press, 12, pp. 81–112.

Hagey, R. (1990). 'The Native diabetes program: rhetorical process and praxis'. *Medical Anthropology*, 12, pp. 2–33.

Helm, J. (1981). 'Subarctic'. W. C. Sturtevant, gen. (ed.), *Handbook of North American Indians*. Vol. 6. Washington, DC: Smithsonian Institution.

Hensel, C. (1996). *Telling Our Selves, Ethnicity and Discourse in Southwestern Alaska*. New York: Oxford University Press.

Hensel, C., Blancett, M., Alexie, I., and Morrow, P. (1983). *Qaneryaurci Yup'igtun*. Bethel: Yup'ik Language Center, Kuskokwim Community College.

Higgins, N. (1978). *Nonstandard English–A First Look*. Boulder, Colorado: Western Interstate Commission for Higher Education.

Honigman, J. J. (1981). 'Expressive aspects of subarctic Indian culture'. In J. Helm (vol. ed.) and W. C. Sturtevant (gen. ed.), *Handbook of North American Indians, Subarctic*, 6, pp. 718–738.

Hutchinson, S. H. (2003). Women, Health, and Aging in Yup'ik/Cup'ik Culture. M.A. Thesis. Department of Anthropology, University of Alaska, Fairbanks.

Jacobson, S. (1984). *Central Yup'ik and the Schools, A Handbook for Teachers*. Juneau: Bilingual/Bicultural Education Programs.

Jolles, C. Z. (2002). *Faith, Food, and Family in a Yupik Whaling Community*. Seattle: University of Washington Press.

Kaplan, L. (1984). *Inupiaq and the Schools, A Handbook for Teachers*. Juneau: Bilingual/Bicultural Education Program.

Kaplan, L. and McNabb, S. (1981). 'Village English in Northwest Alaska.' Paper delivered to the Society for Applied Anthropology, Denver.

Krauss, M. (1974) (revised 1982). *Native Peoples and Languages of Alaska*. Map. University of Alaska, Fairbanks: Alaska Native Language Center.

—. (1979). 'Na-Dene and Eskimo-Aleut'. In L. Campbell and M. Mithun (eds), *The Languages of Native America*, Austin: University of Texas Press, pp. 803–901.

Kwachka, P. (1985). 'Perspectives on the viability of Native languages in Alaska'. *Laurentian University Review*, 18, pp. 105–115.

—. (1988). 'Oral and Written Discourse of the Koyukon Athabaskan Area'. APEL Research Report, IV. Nenana: Yukon-Koyukuk School District.

—. (1992). 'Discourse structures, cultural continuity, and language shift'. *International Journal of the Sociology of Language*, 93, pp. 67–73.

—. (1996a). 'Substance and Salience: Native Englishes in Alaska.' In R. Hammond and M. G. McDonald (eds), *Linguistic Studies in Honor of Bohdan Saciuk*. West Lafayette: Learning Systems, Inc, pp. 285–302.

—. (1996b). 'Who's Talking to Who/m? The Last Frontier of Discourse'. Invited presentation to symposium Language Communities, States, and Global Culture: The Discourse of Identity in the Americas. Laura Graham, convener. Iowa City: The University of Iowa.

Kwachka, P. and Basham, C. (1990). 'Literacy acts and cultural artifacts: on extensions of English modals'. *Journal of Pragmatics*, 14, pp. 413–429.

Langdon, S. J. (1981). *The Native People of Alaska*. Anchorage: Greatland Graphics.

Leap, W. (1993). *American Indian English*. Salt Lake City: University of Utah Press.

Leechman, D. and Hall R. A. 1955. 'American Indian Pidgin English: attestations and grammatical peculiarities'. *American Speech*, 30, pp. 163–71.

Loon, H. (1991). 'Pidgin English Still Alive'. Sun Star Student Newspaper. Fairbanks: University of Alaska.

McGary, J. (1983). *An Analysis of Student Writing Samples from the Yukon-Koyukuk School District*. Nenana: Yukon-Koyukuk School District.

Morrow, P. (1990). 'Symbolic actions, indirect expressions: limits to interpretations of Yupik society'. *Inuit Studies*, 14 (1–2), pp. 141–158.

Nelson, R. (1973). *Hunters of the northern forest, designs for survival among the Alaska Kutchin*. Chicago: University of Chicago Press.

—. (1983). *Make Prayers to the Raven*. Chicago: University of Chicago Press.

Oswalt, W. H. (2006). *This Land Was Theirs, A Study of Native North Americans*. New York: Oxford University Press.

Pulu, T. (1978). *A Preliminary Study of Village Student English Language Ability in the Lake and Peninsula School District with Recommendations for Language Instruction*. Anchorage: Bilingual Bicultural Materials Development Center.*

Ruesch, J. (1951). 'Communication and American Values: A Psychological Approach'. In J. Ruesch and G. Bateson (eds), *Communication, The Social Matrix of Psychology*. New York: Norton, pp. 94–134.

Scollon, R. (1979). 'The context of the informant narrative performance: from sociolinguistics to ethnolinguistics at Fort Chipwyan, Alberta'. National Museum of Man Mercury Series, Canadian Ethnology Service Paper no. 52.

Skutnabb–kangas, T. (1979). 'Language in the process of cultural assimilation and structural incorporation of linguistic minorities'. National Clearing House for Bilingual Education: Rosslyn, Virginia.

Sprott, J. E. (1994). 'Symbolic ethnicity' and Alaska Natives of mixed ancestry living in Anchorage: enduring group or a sign of impending assimilation? *Human Organization*, 53(4), pp. 311–322.

Tabbert, R. (1991). *Dictionary of Alaskan English*. Juneau: The Denali Press.

Taff, A. (1978). *Some Features of Pribiloff English*. Ms. http://www.languagearchives.org/archives/anla.uaf.edu

Thompson, C. (1984). *Athabaskan Languages and the Schools, a Handbook for Teachers*. Juneau: Bilingual/Bicultural Education Programs.

Vandergriff, J. (1982). 'Kotzebue English: Some Notes on Inupiaq English'. In G. Bartelt, S. P. Jasper, and B. Hoffer (eds), *Essays in Native American English*. San Antonio: Trinity University Press, pp. 121–156.

Vanstone, J. W. (1974). *Athapaskan Adaptations, Hunters and Fishermen of the Subarctic Forests*. Arlington Heights: Harlan Davidson, Inc.

Wolfram, W. (1984). 'Unmarked tense in American Indian English'. *American Speech*. 59(1), pp. 31–50.

Wolfram, W. and Fasold, R. (1974). *The Study of Social Dialects in American English*. Englewood Cliffs: Prentice Hall.

Wolfram, W. and Shilling-Estes, N. (1998). *American English, Dialects and Variation*. Oxford: Blackwell.

Wright, J. W. (ed.) (2005–2006). *The New York Times Almanac*. New York: Penguin.

Index